the cinema of TOM DiCILLO

DIRECTORS' CUTS

Other selected titles in the Directors' Cuts series:

the cinema of WES ANDERSON: *bringing nostalgia to life*
WHITNEY CROTHERS DILLEY

the cinema of ROBERT ALTMAN: *hollywood maverick*
ROBERT NIEMI

the cinema of HAL HARTLEY: *flirting with formalism*
STEVEN RYBIN (ed.)

the cinema of SEAN PENN: *in and out of place*
DEANE WILLIAMS

the cinema of CHRISTOPHER NOLAN: *imagining the impossible*
JACQUELINE FURBY & STUART JOY (eds)

the cinema of THE COEN BROTHERS: *hardboiled entertainments*
JEFFREY ADAMS

the cinema of CLINT EASTWOOD: *chronicles of america*
DAVID STERRITT

the cinema of ISTVÁN SZABÓ: *visions of europe*
JOHN CUNNINGHAM

the cinema of AGNÈS VARDA: *resistance and eclecticism*
DELPHINE BÉNÉZET

the cinema of ALEXANDER SOKUROV: *figures of paradox*
JEREMI SZANIAWSKI

the cinema of MICHAEL WINTERBOTTOM: *borders, intimacy, terror*
BRUCE BENNETT

the cinema of RAÚL RUIZ: *impossible cartographies*
MICHAEL GODDARD

the cinema of AKI KAURISMÄKI: *authorship, bohemia, nostalgia, nation*
ANDREW NESTINGEN

the cinema of RICHARD LINKLATER: *walk, don't run*
ROB STONE

the cinema of BÉLA TARR: *the circle closes*
ANDRÁS BÁLINT KOVÁCS

the cinema of STEVEN SODERBERGH: *indie sex, corporate lies, and digital videotape*
ANDREW DE WAARD & R. COLIN TATE

the cinema of TERRY GILLIAM: *it's a mad world*
JEFF BIRKENSTEIN, ANNA FROULA & KAREN RANDELL (eds)

the cinema of TAKESHI KITANO: *flowering blood*
SEAN REDMOND

the cinema of THE DARDENNE BROTHERS: *responsible realism*
PHILIP MOSLEY

the cinema of MICHAEL HANEKE: *europe utopia*
BEN McCANN & DAVID SORFA (eds)

the cinema of JAN SVANKMAJER: *dark alchemy*
PETER HAMES (ed.)

the cinema of LARS VON TRIER: *authenticity and artifice*
CAROLINE BAINBRIDGE

the cinema of WERNER HERZOG: *aesthetic ecstasy and truth*
BRAD PRAGER

the cinema of TERRENCE MALICK: *poetic visions of america (second edition)*
HANNAH PATTERSON (ed.)

the cinema of ANG LEE: *the other side of the screen (second edition)*
WHITNEY CROTHERS DILLEY

the cinema of TODD HAYNES: *all that heaven allows*
JAMES MORRISON (ed.)

the cinema of DAVID LYNCH: *american dreams, nightmare visions*
ERICA SHEEN & ANNETTE DAVISON (eds)

the cinema of GEORGE A. ROMERO: *knight of the living dead (second edition)*
TONY WILLIAMS

the cinema of KATHRYN BIGELOW: *hollywood transgressor*
DEBORAH JERMYN & SEAN REDMOND (eds)

the cinema of
TOM DiCILLO

include me out

wayne byrne

WALLFLOWER PRESS LONDON & NEW YORK

A Wallflower Press Book
Published by
Columbia University Press
Publishers Since 1893
New York • Chichester, West Sussex
cup.columbia.edu

Copyright © 2017 Columbia University Press
All rights reserved

Wallflower Press® is a registered trademark of Columbia University Press

A complete CIP record is available from the Library of Congress

ISBN 978-0-231-18534-9 (cloth : alk. paper)
ISBN 978-0-231-18535-6 (pbk. : alk. paper)
ISBN 978-0-231-85120-6 (e-book)

Columbia University Press books are printed on permanent
and durable acid-free paper.
Printed in the United States of America

Series design by Rob Bowden Design
Cover image of Tom DiCillo courtesy of www.tomdicillo.com

CONTENTS

Acknowledgments vii
Foreword ix
Introduction 1

1 The Language of Dream: Deciphering DiCillo   7
2 *Johnny Suede* (1991)   20
3 *Living in Oblivion* (1995)   44
4 *Box of Moonlight* (1996)   69
5 *The Real Blonde* (1997)   92
6 *Double Whammy* (2001)   112
7 *Delirious* (2006)   133
8 *When You're Strange: A Film About The Doors* (2009)   163
9 *Down in Shadowland* (2014)   189

Notes   199
Filmography   200
Bibliography   201
Index   203

This book is dedicated to the memory of Jane Gil

ACKNOWLEDGEMENTS

First and foremost, my sincerest thanks to Tom DiCillo, for several years' worth of discussions and sharing of ideas. Throughout it all you have helped me identify with clarity what it is that makes me passionate about your work in the first place and encouraged me to write about it straight from my heart. These few words barely cover the gratitude I feel is due. Most of all, thank you for the films.

Very special thanks to Steve Buscemi for providing this book with a wonderful foreword and for offering an intimate, personal insight into your work and friendship with Tom.

I am greatly indebted to the following people for their memories, candour and generous assistance in putting this project together: Kevin Corrigan, Maxwell Caulfield, Melonie Diaz, John Densmore, Peter Dinklage, Gina Gershon, Catherine Keener, Robby Krieger, Alison Lohman, Matthew Modine, Chris Noth, Sam Rockwell and John Turturro. This book wouldn't be what it is without your invaluable help and moral support.

My immense gratitude to Jim Southwick and David Dutkowski for your help in opening Doors; to Kenny Nemes at Jampol Artist Management; to Jennifer Levine and Elise Konialian at Untitled Entertainment, to Jenny Rawlings at Principato-Young Entertainment, and to Adam Rackoff for the administrative assistance.

I wish to express special appreciation to Kildare County Council Library & Arts Services for an Arts Grant, the support of which enabled me to travel and conduct initial research for this book. To the wonderful people at Wallflower Press and Columbia University Press, especially Yoram Allon, Commissioning Editor and Editorial Director at Wallflower Press, for believing in this project and for the constant help and guidance. I would also like to acknowledge the kind technical support, computer wizardry and general I.T. assistance of Brian McCarthy and Ronan Cruise.

Finally, heartfelt thanks to my wife Jen and my parents Angela and Patrick for their love and support, and to my friends and family for the continual encouragement and shared enjoyment of DiCillo's films on many an evening.

Much obliged to all.

FOREWORD

"Is anyone okay, is everyone hurt?"
– Wanda, 1st AD, *Living in Oblivion*

In any film that ever gets made, there are certain compromises made along the way. It's the nature of the beast, be it with casting, locations, script or catering. But it's where you draw the line that matters. There are many directors who give away too much in order to have the opportunity just to make their film. Then there are the rare filmmakers who fight like hell to tell their stories the only way they know how. Believe me, that is definitely the road less travelled.

For me, Tom DiCillo is an American classic. His work is truly his own, the embodiment of what Independent Film aspires to be; the unique and artistically pure expression of the filmmaker. There's an emotional truthfulness that runs throughout Tom's work, no matter how surreal or comedic the characters or stories may be.

I first noticed Tom's work as a brilliant cinematographer, most notably of Jim Jarmusch's *Stranger Than Paradise*. Those stark black & white images and the beautifully long master takes affected me deeply. I wanted to live inside the film. And I wanted to know and work with everyone involved in making it.

In the East Village of the 1980s where I was living at the time, there was a strong community of like-minded artists; actors, writers, musicians, dancers, performance artists and young filmmakers. Almost any night of the week there was an opening, a performance, or a new band to see. Tom and I would often run into each other at various events and venues like Rocket Redglare's Taxi Cabaret, Theater for the New City, or the Collective for Living Cinema. He and his girlfriend Jane Gil came to many of the theatre pieces I was doing at the time with Mark Boone Jr at La Mama, 8BC, or the Limbo Lounge.

It was inspiring to hear Tom's thoughts and ideas about everything that was happening. And it always gave me a boost of confidence when he complimented or critiqued my work. Back then, talking about the work was just as important as doing it. We were all still figuring it out. Honestly, that process never stops, nor should it. But I do miss the easy access we all had to each other.

Tom was absolutely instrumental in my own pursuit of wanting to write and direct. We would show each other the screenplays we were developing; *Johnny Suede*, which became his brilliant first feature, and *Trees Lounge*, which I did a few years later. Little did I know that before I would realise my own dream of being a director, I would play one in Tom's second feature, the wildly entertaining and heartbreaking *Living in Oblivion*. It's one of my all time favorites and I'm still getting compliments about it from random fans twenty-five or so years later. It amazes me that almost every time I'm on a movie set, there will inevitably come that moment when an annoying beeping sound from somewhere temporarily disrupts the filming. I often joke that it's the curse of Oblivion that follows me around, but in truth I'm always happy to be reminded of Tom and that first film we did together. I feel extremely lucky to be in a few of Tom's films over the years.

One of the things I love about him is how adaptable and tenacious he can be. He initially offered me one role in *Double Whammy* that I thought I was too old for. So he switched gears and presented the idea of me playing Denis Leary's sexually confused police partner. We had great fun with that one. I turned him down so many times for the role of Les in *Delirious* that I thought he would never speak to me again. Instead he kept plugging away, making the role right for me without giving up one iota of Les's character traits that I initially found difficult to wrap my head around. I'm grateful he didn't give up.

It's not uncommon that many good films get less than they deserve distribution-wise, for whatever reason. You work your ass off and put all you've got into something you believe in, only to be disappointed when you feel it's not reaching an audience. You start to wonder if anybody out there is paying attention.

Well, I'm happy to report that not only has Wayne Byrne been paying close attention, he is doing his absolute best in spreading the word. As the author of this insightful and entertaining book, he delves in deep and comes up with the goods. Through his conversations with Tom we see the thought process and strategies on each of his films, his hopes and frustrations, and everything in between. One thing about Tom, he doesn't hold back. We also hear from many of Tom's collaborators, and he has worked with some of the best in this business.

In short, this wonderful book details the ultimate triumphant journey of one of independent cinema's smartest, funniest and fiercest warriors.

Enjoy.

Steve Buscemi
September 2017

INTRODUCTION

"I'm sorry, there's nothing here on Tom DiCillo."

More than any other statement, the one above reverberated most frequently in the many years spent browsing book stores and libraries in search of written consideration of the man who gifted the world *Living in Oblivion*. Yet, while that search has illuminated a dearth of analytical prose on DiCillo and his work, it also reiterated the surfeit of tomes on filmmakers of far lesser esteem and critical regard. To list the many awards and accolades DiCillo has won and has been nominated for would render this piece to be of formal *curriculum vitae* standard, but suffice to say his filmmaking has been recognised and rewarded from Sundance to Venice, Locarno to Deauville, and with a Grammy Award thrown in for good measure. As cinematographer, DiCillo captured some of the most recognisable images of post-New Hollywood American Cinema; as writer-director, he has produced distinctive and imperative works which kick-started the careers of some of the most powerful and profitable marquee names in contemporary cinema and television. He has worked with legendary rock group The Doors in making what is considered by the band themselves to be the definitive visual record of their already exhaustively chronicled career. Still, there has been no book-length academic or journalistic account of DiCillo's career; until now.

DiCillo and his films have indeed been referenced and discussed in notable books on independent cinema and filmmaking, in works such as *Cinema of Outsiders: The Rise of Independent Cinema* (Levy 2001), *Contemporary North American Film Directors: A Wallflower Critical Guide* (Allon et al. 2000), *Personal Visions: Conversations with Independent Filmmakers* (Falsetto 1999) and *Alex Cox's Introduction to Film: A Director's Perspective* (Cox 2016). But in the first full-length discourse on DiCillo, this book offers more than a cursory glance at the director's career. Here, with chronological in-depth analyses and discussion of each of DiCillo's eight films, we get to examine the production, the artistry and the personal and professional battles that were waged in bringing not only his touchstone works (*Johnny Suede*, 1991; *Living in Oblivion*, 1995) to the screen, but as much time and consideration is afforded the creation and release of less-acknowledged films such as *The Real Blonde* and *Double Whammy*.

The opening chapters set out the *modus operandi* of the book: to chart the writing, production and release of the films while also putting into sharp focus the recurring themes that permeate the DiCillo oeuvre, those that are both on the surface and subtextual. Of course, when endeavouring to highlight themes that run the course of a filmmaker's career, one runs the risk of what John Caughie (1981) would refer to as trying to 'crack the code' by mining for themes at the expense of attention to the formal values inherent throughout the work. The thematic, nay, *auteurist*, approach taken here isn't a case of critical shorthand or reductiveness, but a valid attempt to put the films in a greater perspective than has previously been afforded them; nor is an analysis of mise-en-scène, editing, cinematography, scripting and performance abandoned in pursuit of said themes. On the contrary; much time is spent on the aesthetic formalism and technical mechanics of the films as that of meanings (apparent or otherwise) and allegorical readings.

The first third of this book, beginning with a Q&A between DiCillo and myself, and continuing with the respective chapters on *Johnny Suede* and *Living in Oblivion*, charts both the director's early years and his collaborations in the alternative, underground art scene of 1970s New York City. The so-called No Wave movement was a post-punk milieu that birthed a small but significant number of prominent filmmakers, musicians, actors, writers and artists. During this period DiCillo worked as a cinematographer for notable independent filmmakers such as Howard Brookner (*Burroughs: The Movie*, 1983; *Robert Wilson and the Civil Wars*, 1987), Bette Gordon (*Variety*, 1983), Jim Jarmusch (*Permanent Vacation*, 1980; *Stranger Than Paradise*, 1984), and Eric Mitchell (*Underground U.S.A.*, 1980). The succeeding analysis and discussion of DiCillo's directorial debut *Johnny Suede* and his lauded follow-up, *Living in Oblivion*, films of marked invention and independent resolve, brings us into a changing industrial landscape of US cinema in the early- to mid-1990s. The book notes the development of DiCillo's erstwhile stage persona of Johnny Suede into the film's titular protagonist, the honing of the script at the Sundance lab, his discovery of a then-unknown Brad Pitt, and the film's post-production and subsequent release by Miramax. The chapter on *Living in Oblivion* offers an insight into the despair that encouraged DiCillo to craft the deftly metatextual neo-verité world of his most acclaimed and beloved work, and examines how this defiantly independent production became a festival and critical favourite, and became the director's signature film.

Moving on to the latter-half of the 1990s and the turn of the millennium with respective chapters on *Box of Moonlight* (1996), *The Real Blonde* (1997) and *Double Whammy* (2001), things get a little more political, in the industrial sense that is. In the aftermath of *Living in Oblivion*, DiCillo soon found himself much sought-after, which inevitably led to working with higher budgets and corporate hierarchies. These three chapters reveal the expectations heaped upon a lauded filmmaker coming off fresh critical and festival success, the struggles of on-location shooting, as well as illuminating the practicalities of trying to maintain authorship of one's art in the face of boardroom bureaucracy. An examination of these films is particularly interesting from an industrial and historical perspective, coming later in the career trajectory of a filmmaker who came to the fore at a time when American Independent Cinema was gaining traction as perhaps the most vital and most welcome moment in American cinema since the countercultural New Hollywood era. These later films were released as the independent film landscape was morphing into what some refer to – whether pejoratively or approbatory – as 'Indiewood' (see King 2005; Newman 2011). Thus, the respective chapters on these films present a subjective account, from DiCillo and the actors from the films, of a moment in recent US film history where auteur sensibilities clashed with the more ministerial practices of corporate studio mandate. Despite positive reviews in some quarters of the media (see LaSalle 1998; Siskel 1998) and high regard in academic press (see Falsetto 1999; Soter 2002), *The Real Blonde* and *Double Whammy* retrospectively seem further unfortunate incidents of interesting, thought-provoking, and yet approachable work directed by a singular talent of erstwhile independent credibility and renown, having a film distributed by a major studio who ultimately didn't seem to know which constituency of cinema to canvass for turnout; see also: Hal Hartley's *No Such Thing* (2001), Kevin Smith's *Mallrats* (1995) and Stacy Title's *The Last Supper* (1995).

The final three chapters – *Delirious* (2006), *When You're Strange* (2009) and a coda on *Down in Shadowland* (2014) – interprets DiCillo's later work as some of the most vital and interesting releases of his career. There's a solid argument to be made for *Delirious* being his best film, if perhaps not his most iconic; it is *Living in Oblivion* after all which graces the covers and pages of books on cinema (see Holmlund 2004; Turan 2004; Berardinelli 2005). DiCillo assumes a direct and eloquent approach in these later works that manages to both recall the stirring qualities of the earlier films while projecting an evolved, dynamic display of cinematic style, as well as a more devastating handling of his key themes. *Delirious* proved to be a striking comeback after the commercial and critical misfire of *Double Whammy*. The chapter here examines a director in the midst of career nadir and saddled with the weight of having a film gone straight to video, but returning triumphant with perhaps his most playful, compassionate, and emotionally-charged film to date, featuring a searing lead performance by Steve Buscemi at his finest and funniest. And while this film saw DiCillo recharged and in fighting form, as well as accoladed with numerous film festival awards, it also suffered a torturous release and a non-existent marketing campaign; however, some critics rallied to its defence (for example, Ebert 2007) as a film deserving a much wider release and recognition. In examining the preceding films as we do here, *When You're Strange* and *Down in Shadowland* take on an added poignancy and depth that a greener viewer may not take away from such films at first glance. Not to mention those latter two films being a complete departure for DiCillo in terms of form and content, both non-fiction pieces of varying documentary styles. *When You're Strange* is a kinetic feature music documentary, one of DiCillo's most coruscating pieces of pure cinema, while *Down in Shadowland* is a hypnotising tone poem, at once refined and explosive, featuring some of the director's most dazzling displays of editing and use of music, while also providing a platform for the most politically-charged rhetoric of his career.

This book was born out of a keen, passionate interest to understand more about a filmmaker whose worked spellbound me enough to consider the study of cinema my life's endeavour and in doing so it became much more revelatory than initially intended. As a teacher of Film Studies with a journalist background, my instinct at the early stage was to objectively chart the production of the films and note their laudable aesthetics, as if that would be enough. But with DiCillo lending uncountable hours and affording me unlimited access to his opinions, memories and insights, as well as the swift and willing participation of many of the actors who have appeared in his films, this book became something bigger and, conversely, more personal. Even though the book eschews traditional academic formatting in favour of a more narrative-based journalistic approach which sometimes evokes a biographical tone, it also functions as an auteur study which should serve aesthetic, industrial and historical contexts of a Film Studies curricula. The periods of US Independent Cinema (the late 1970s to present day) covered here have been already widely considered in academia, but perhaps less so from the first-hand perspectives of many of those who were actively involved in that movement, whose voices are present in this book.

As is the wont of many an auteurist writer, an armchair-psychological profiling of the artist in question is inevitable, although in this case, completely unintended. The result of examining the subtextual layers of the films here has led to a deeply personal and revealing journey for DiCillo, and in taking such a frank approach to film analyses this book affords the reader to make thematic connections that may otherwise be arcane and speculative on my part, were it not for DiCillo's candid discussions of how the personal and the professional sides of his artist's life intertwine. To wit, discussions of themes such as masculinity, identity and family allow the reader to connect fictional constructs like DiCillo's eponymous hero Johnny Suede with non-fiction public figures, such as Jim Morrison. Those aforementioned three themes are a central discourse throughout the book and are relevant to each of DiCillo's films. The revelatory Q&A segments between DiCillo and I which succeed each chapter contextualise my thematic analysis of those films. Coming into this book I would never have considered that a documentary film about one of the great rock bands of the counterculture movement would fit so easily in the canon of a filmmaker who, on the surface, trades in satirical assassinations of venerated industries and institutions, as well as semi-autobiographical personal projects. There is certainly room to analyse DiCillo the iconoclast, as films such as *Living in Oblivion*, *The Real Blonde* and *Delirious* are without doubt mocking and sardonic in context, but this book is primarily concerned with the more human ideas and themes lurking beneath the surface. Fractured families and the resultant emotional fallout of the sons and daughters of such are a recurring motif throughout the DiCillo oeuvre.

In taking this methodology, a reader or viewer may now see beyond the immediate storylines, contexts and generic conventions of the films and see a different text. Not that DiCillo's films are waiting the harvesting of meanings and interpretations to be appreciated; one of the most perplexing things about DiCillo's lack of mainstream recognition is that his films are extremely approachable, rather than obfuscating and avant-garde. Even when reviews have been somewhat tepid, or glowing in praise, there is an acknowledgement of the simple, engaging pleasures and human quality that DiCillo's work fulfils (see Maslin 1997; Ebert 1998; Westbrook 1998). As such, DiCillo's films can be enjoyed by simply hitting their generic registers on target; they can work on a level of pure comedy or pure drama, all the while playing on a cerebral level in their confrontational yet empathic examinations of life, work, relationships and art. The question that a writer of any auteur study seeks to answer is that of the legitimacy and autobiography of an artist within their art. Which leads one to ask: how much of DiCillo is present in these films? Contesting demons past and present, DiCillo offers a rare, deeply personal frankness in detailing the psychological malaise that motivates and cripples his characters.

Sympathetic without being mawkish; intellectual without being pretentious; and stylish without flamboyant excess, DiCillo's films offer compassionate discourse on their subjects. If there were any doubts to these qualities in the films, or if some see DiCillo's satirical eye and complexity of themes substituting a lack of dramatic substance (see Levy 1999: 202–5; Welch 2001: 138–9), then the objective of this portrait of an artist is to offer another view, an alternative narrative to his career that has, to date, been under-investigated. Perhaps the problem with previous assessments of DiCillo is that they do not consider the qualities that inhabit the films released postscript: *The Real Blonde, Double Whammy, Delirious, When You're Strange, Down in Shadowland*, films which arguably contain DiCillo's most well-drawn, complex characterisations and most searing pathos. The further analyses undertaken within this book could be viewed as a response to the limited scope of erstwhile academic criticism that is published on DiCillo's work, those writings which invariably fail to recognise and connect certain subtextual thematic underpinnings of his oeuvre, and dictated as they are by their year of publication, meaning that often only DiCillo's earliest films are discussed. As DiCillo's already assured sense of film style has since evolved further in establishing a distinctive aesthetic, and with his representations of various recurrent themes having developed a stronger voice in his later work, this volume is thus a crucial text in order to reference these films and to finally understand and acknowledge DiCillo as a brilliant (but overlooked) filmmaker with the depth, breadth and scope that is long overdue.

This book therefore makes a case for DiCillo as a singular, auteur voice within contemporary American cinema. It encourages a reflection of films we might take for granted as having one primary, surface objective according to their immediate plot and associated genre conventions – *Johnny Suede*: surrealist comedy; *Living in Oblivion*: satire; *Box of Moonlight*: escapist fantasy; *The Real Blonde*: romantic comedy; *Double Whammy*: buddy-cop thriller; *Delirious*: dramatic comedy; *When You're Strange*: historical documentary; *Down in Shadowland*: observational documentary – and reframes them as densely layered, often devastatingly honest considerations of the breakdown of the family and of the human implications of one's lack of self-value and ill-defined sense of identity.

For both the student of cinema and the casual film enthusiast, this book offers firsthand accounts of life and work in both the Independent and Hollywood trenches, as told by DiCillo and industry veterans such as Steve Buscemi, Catherine Keener, Chris Noth, Matthew Modine, John Turturro and many others. It affords the budding filmmaker a look behind the lens at a precarious industry, where despair and delight often go hand-in-hand and can alternate within an instant. More than my own words, or the words one could quote from other authors in the field, those of DiCillo himself are the spine and the heart of this book. Cine-literate, fiercely intelligent, caustically witty and, according to almost every actor I interviewed for this book, dashingly handsome and debonair, DiCillo could easily make for an engrossing, solitary subject of a feature film interview à *la* the eponymous auteur of Noah Baumbach and Jake Paltrow's *De Palma* (2015), despite being only one-third as prolific. What makes DiCillo such an anomaly and so refreshing an interview subject is his willingness to talk about his work so openly, and to comment so candidly on the nature of the film business, both good and bad. There is a workmanlike approach to DiCillo's process that belies the artistic temperament that can result in difficult interviews with more demure subjects. For the numerable reasons outlined above, this book works not only as a reference on a particular moment in American cinema and as an inside look at the industrial practices of both Hollywood and Indie studio systems, but as a narrative on a life in film.

CHAPTER ONE

The Language of Dream: Deciphering DiCillo

At the age of twelve I discovered *Johnny Suede*, completely by accident. Up to that point I was an avowed action movie buff, worshipping at the altar of Steven Seagal, no less. One day in the video store I noticed an iridescently colored VHS case for a film with a striking picture of Brad Pitt sporting a huge pompadour. Something prompted me to rent the film.

I cannot underestimate the influence *Johnny Suede* had on me on that first viewing; it was a culture shock. It opened up to me the doors of cinema and all its varieties and possibilities. Films didn't just have to be about violence and spectacle; they could be about you and me, or those people just over there. The raw human emotions of the film felt real and immediate, yet its surrealist aesthetic, absurd humour and haunting music gave it a sense of the peculiar and the exotic. The effect it had on me was hypnotic.

I immediately declared my unabashed belief of *Johnny Suede* to be the greatest film I had ever seen to anybody that would listen. I longed to experience more of this director Tom DiCillo's work; his was an idiosyncratic vision that was completely and distinctively his. It felt like *Johnny Suede* was this little gem only I was privy to and I wanted to keep it, literally. Upon returning the video I proposed an offer to the clerk which would have resulted in the most expensive purchase in my life up to that point had he accepted: "I'll give you thirty pounds for it!" Deep down I knew my proposition was going nowhere; the kid was a mere employee with no ability to make such executive decisions as turning a rental cassette into a retail one; nor did I actually have thirty pounds to give him should he accept my offer. It was more of a desperate, knowingly futile attempt by me to cling tangibly to this videocassette that reached into my soul and dared to show me an alternative world of cinema beyond the only one I knew.

What I love and what fascinates me about the cinema of Tom DiCillo is that his themes and narratives speak directly to the heart and to the soul, but not without a distinctly unique cinematic aesthetic and an erudite scrutiny of what it is to be essentially human. DiCillo's films are entirely approachable, that's part of their innate charm. There are dual elements at play: the autobiographical exploration and confrontation of his personal history, and the humanist worldview that frames and underscores his narratives. Grand themes explored in a profoundly intimate manner, all staged in a very public arena. These are the works of an artist laying bare and tackling inner demons and questioning it all. Even his non-fiction film about one of the most famous and revered rock bands of the twentieth century feels like a journey into its director's soul.

Some of the greatest political battles in DiCillo's films are fought in the family living room. It is psychological warfare with real emotional bloodshed. Unless one is born and raised in complete isolation, removed and sheltered from the stresses and strains that come with being a member of the exclusive club that is family, it is hard to imagine a viewer who could not find something to relate to in a DiCillo film. His work contains an inherent and completely natural empathy for people at their most basic level. One of the things I wanted to explore in this book was DiCillo's recurrent subtext and continued discourse on family and the trauma that comes from the fractured relationships passed down and shared among fathers and sons, mothers and daughters. In tracking DiCillo's career from film to film, one is offered a continuity of ideas, themes and motifs; some placed with subtlety, some immediately present.

When I met DiCillo for the first of many discussions for this book, I didn't know what to expect. With any artist we admire there comes an expectation of them to be representative of the qualities that seduce us with their work. Meeting DiCillo for this book reiterated to me that the humanity in his films was no fluke, nor was I misreading the texts; there really is something deeply relatable in these films beyond their immediate contexts of humour and satire. I spied objects and props from his films throughout his apartment. It was like a museum of my cinematic memories: the guitar from *Johnny Suede*; the golden apple from *Living in Oblivion*; the all-seeing eyeball of *Double Whammy*! Not being familiar with the intense heat of a New York summer and sweating profusely, I perhaps made DiCillo question who he had let into his home when I asked him for ice cold beer at midday, rather than coffee or water, and duly guzzled it down in record time.

On the last night of my visit, at an Upper West Side eatery, DiCillo gifted me a package containing some rare items of his work. I opened it and the rush of emotion I experienced was intense. All of a sudden this whole venture became real. I was sitting there over food and wine with Tom DiCillo, talking life, art and movies. This project was coming to life before my eyes, and now, several years later, I am very happy to present this book which has been inspired by my immense admiration for DiCillo's distinct, singular, provocative and, ultimately, joyful work.

DiCillo presents difficult themes and encourages us to contemplate uncomfortable questions about society, ourselves and those closest to us; he just so happens to achieve this within his charmingly absurdist comedic sensibility. A DiCillo film craftily invites us into his whimsical though sharp-edged playground where we are thrilled to peek behind the veil of the most revered entertainment and media industries: film, television, music and fashion. But once past the red carpet, and when the lights go down, we witness a host of neuroses, anxieties, insecurities and utter foolishness. DiCillo's genius is to make his protagonists – from pop stars to backwoods loners, from supermodels to paparazzi – all densely layered human beings with the same flaws and eccentricities that we all share.

Wayne Byrne: *What and when was your introduction to film as a serious medium, as an art form?*

Tom DiCillo: My father was in the Marine Corps. We moved every two years, mainly to small towns across America. I didn't spend a lot of time in big cities. Perhaps if I'd had I might have been more aware of different kinds of film. My early experiences with cinema were actually pretty basic.

More mainstream?

Pretty much. But I remember being very affected by *Rebel Without a Cause* when I was around thirteen and it stood out for me as a very different film.

What was it about a film like Rebel Without a Cause?

I related to it strongly because it was about this young guy who went to a new school and felt like he didn't fit in. By that time I'd been to about five different schools. But I didn't really encounter my first art film until I went to college and saw Fellini's *La Strada*. To this moment I can still feel my mind being blown by seeing that movie.

To go back a little bit, at that point my aim was to be a writer. I was into Joyce, Thomas Mann, Kafka ... Mark Twain. At the same time I was taking a lot of photographs and printing them in my own darkroom. Then suddenly I encountered this art form that combined it *all*. Fellini's film is a monumental achievement in terms of the story, the acting, the human emotion; the philosophical intent. This brute of a man, Zampano, meets a woman, Gelsomina, and she's the only person in the world who loves him, despite his flaws. Yet he abandons her. That moment at the end of the film where he's on the beach at night and he looks up at the stars and suddenly realises he is completely alone in the universe is one of the most powerful moments I've seen on film.

Then I saw *Shoot the Piano Player, The 400 Blows, Breathless, Weekend, The Seven Samurai, Rashomon, Viridiana, The Seventh Seal*; all these amazing films which imprinted on me and, for better or worse, formed the base of my cinematic aesthetic. But, it was *La Strada* that made me say, 'I'd like to try this.'

I experienced a very similar feeling with Johnny Suede. *That's the film that got me into thinking of cinema as an art form, rather than disposable entertainment. I see some striking parallels between* Johnny Suede *and* La Strada.

Well, I would say *La Strada* and *Midnight Cowboy* had the most direct influence on my films. *Johnny Suede* contains many elements of both.

If you look at the three main characters from those three films: Johnny, Gelsomina and Joe Buck; their respective personalities leave them open to being taken advantage of. They all share this kind of wide-eyed naiveté about the world.

They do. But, Johnny has some of Zampano in him too; that intense self-interest to the degree he can't see he's hurting someone who loves him. You can't survive only on innocence. That struggle fascinates me; you have to be open in life, you have to be willing and trusting; but at the same time what do you do when somebody willfully sets out to crush you? Or you experience a disappointment so severe it cripples you, like Ratso Rizzo?

Growing up in various small towns throughout America at that time, I imagine there weren't many avenues for you to discover films like La Strada *prior to college.*

Very few. There was another thing that influenced my passion for film. My father had many rules, like sweeping the crumbs from under the dining room table every night or making us get skinhead haircuts as punishment for bad grades; but the one rule I most hated him for was not allowing us to have a television in the house.

So did your father's outlawing of this visual medium in turn influence your immersion into the world of literature?

Yes. I would for just sit for days reading, I loved it. I actually think it fostered my ability to think visually. When you read a book it interacts with your mind in such a way that you're envisioning a private film in a form that is so personal and so strong that no actual filmed representation of it will ever be equal. But even though I loved reading I still was pissed off that I couldn't watch TV. It affected my interaction with kids at school because they knew all the shows and talked about them all the time. So when my father would be stationed in Japan or Vietnam for thirteen months, the day he walked out of the house my mother would go down to the local electronic store and rent a little black-and-white television.

The illicit thrill of TV?

Yes! It was almost pornographic. We would go on these binges. I swear to God, one time I watched TV for forty-eight hours straight! I had a massive headache, I was cross-eyed. But I was fascinated by everything, even the commercials. And so from a very early age there was an almost erotic, illicit *thrill* and I still feel that – not that it's forbidden, but that the pleasure is very intense. It instilled in me an almost mythical respect for the power of cinema, and I think it set a bar for me; something I aspire to in my films.

How did your father react to your budding filmmaking career?

It's hard to say. Listen, he entered the Marine Corps which meant that he chose a *system*. This meant he always had a job and always had a paycheck. I think he respects the idea of what I'm trying to do but I don't think he's comfortable with how much of it is so nebulous and unpredictable.

How did you end up in New York City?

It was a practical choice. I graduated from a small college in Virginia and applied to two film schools. I went to the school library and looked them up. I don't even know how I got the idea; this was around the mid-1970s.

At that time the idea of attending film school wasn't yet a widely acknowledged pursuit…

It barely existed. Scorsese had gone to NYU but the only independent filmmaker I knew at that time was really John Waters. I remember him coming to my college and showing *Pink Flamingos* on a bed sheet in the parking lot. There was no independent movement, no *Filmmaker Magazine*, no Sundance Channel. Everything was wide open and formless. But, still I knew filmmaking was something I wanted to do. So I applied to two schools: NYU and this college out in Los Angeles. I had nothing; no money, no film experience and I was amazed that both schools accepted me. NYU took me because they said they liked the photographs I submitted and some short stories that I had written. Since my brother was moving to New York to start a career as a painter I thought, 'Well, do I want to go all the way out to California by myself? Maybe I'll go to New York with my brother and go to NYU.' That's how I ended up here.

Tom DiCillo (left) and Jim Jarmusch (right) during production of *Burroughs: The Movie*, 1983

What did film school teach you? Do you feel it was necessary?

For me it was necessary because I knew nothing about filmmaking. But what troubled me the most about the school was their idea of what makes a good film and what makes a bad film. I went there thinking, 'It's a school, they'll let you try things; they won't force you into a rigid or conventional way of thinking.' But I was always coming up against this and asking, 'Wait a second! Why is this not a movie? ... Why is that a movie and this isn't a movie?' One day they showed Godard's *Two or Three Things I Know About Her* and I remember Jim Jarmusch and I – he was in my class – we were the only two who liked the film. I said, 'This is a very interesting way to tell a story.' And the rest of the class was incensed. Everyone was yelling, 'I hate this movie, I hate it; this isn't a movie!'

Was the resistance so great that you found it a challenge academically?

I did well in my first, second and part of my third year. I won a scholarship grant and a paid position as a teacher's assistant. But I stumbled with my thesis film. My original idea was intense and very personal but the consensus among the faculty was, 'No, don't do this!' They were so insistent upon it that I started questioning myself. Two weeks before I was to start shooting I wrote another script, still something that interested me but not the film I'd wanted to make.

What was it about that personal film the faculty didn't want you to pursue?

They just didn't get it. But the real point is I doubted myself and ended up making a film which did not work. The head of the faculty was this Czech director named Laszlo Benedek whose main claim to fame was that he'd directed *The Wild One* starring Marlon Brando, and then *Namu, the Killer Whale*. He brought some of that old school dictatorship to NYU. A student showed up five minutes late at the beginning of class and for the next three hours Benedek ranted about how crucial punctuality is to a filmmaking career.

After I finished my thesis film he called me into his office. He said, 'I don't know what happened to you, we had such high hopes for you; your first film and second film, so good! Brilliant! Then you make this film ... I don't know what to say about it. It's not an A, it's not a C; I give it the worst grade I can, which is a B.' And I said to myself, 'There's something really wrong here. I'd tried something. Maybe it wasn't the most successful effort but is it really necessary to make me feel like shit about it?' And that's exactly what happened; I left film school feeling that I'd failed.

Do you feel film schools are relevant?

They can be. But I know now that this concept of tearing someone down is incredibly destructive. It is something that is engrained in our culture. People take great pleasure in ripping something apart. That's why I always try to acknowledge what the intent was, to say to somebody that no matter how badly they stumble that this is where the beauty is; the stumble is where the grace is, and if you can't allow yourself to stumble without the fear of being ridiculed then you will never feel free to try anything truly personal or original.

This is extremely helpful in working with actors and members of your crew. When I'm dealing with actors I never say a negative thing to them. It's not that I baby them or lie to them; it's just that I always approach the issue solely from a positive and constructive point of view. For example, I will never berate an actor, or a crew member, on the set. Even if part of me feels the actor is being intentionally resistant I give support, I give trust, and I give them encouragement to be completely open and creative. I have seen the results a thousand times. It always works. It always results in a better scene.

What did you learn from film school?

To do the opposite of what they taught at film school.

How did you progress to shooting Eric Mitchell's Underground U.S.A. *and Jim Jarmusch's* Stranger Than Paradise?

I got into cinematography completely by accident. One day at NYU a professor set up a film exercise. He assigned Jim to write a five-minute film, me to shoot it and someone else to edit it; all completely at random. I'd never shot anything before. But I think because I didn't have preconceived notions about lighting and technical things, Jim and I worked together very well. I approached it like a kind of second director. Of course, Jim was the director, but I'm just saying the way I conceived the shots was more like a director than a cinematographer: 'What's the best way to shoot this; what's the best way to have the camera help this story?' But, more than that, I think Jim and I were both excited about each other's ideas. We liked each other and we discovered we had elements of the same sensibility.

Did your interest in still photography inform your cinematic aesthetic?

Yes. It's always been exciting for me to design a shot or a camera move that hasn't been done before or that embellishes the script in a subtle but crucial way. But deep inside I knew cinematography wasn't something I wanted to make a career out of. I wanted to pursue my goal of becoming a director. But as a result of my last experience at NYU, the head of the school telling me, 'Your film is a lousy B!' I had lost a little faith in my ability.

So you kept shooting?

Right. Eric Mitchell had seen Jim's first movie *Permanent Vacation*, which I had shot, and then Eric asked me to shoot *Underground U.S.A.*, which I did; for nothing, literally, I shot it for free. But it actually was a great learning experience, as were all of the films I shot. That was really my film school. The problems and solutions were all in the real world, not in a classroom.

I watched Eric work with his actors. One night Jackie Curtis, a well-known drag queen doing a small part in the film, forgot all her lines. It was about four in the morning. We were all completely exhausted. Eric tried writing all of Jackie's lines on enormous cue cards but she still couldn't do the scene. She said she could really use some speed. So Eric, without a complaint, went out into Union Square Park and graciously scored her some speed. About dawn we eventually got the scene. That was a lesson I could never have learned in film school. Another great learning experience was watching Jim discover the scenes with his actors in rehearsal. That was new for me, the idea that everything didn't need to be strictly planned out in advance. Also, there were never any producers around. It was this amazing, completely free set where the only thing that mattered was what the director wanted to do. The only problems were artistic really, or whether we all really wanted to eat pizza again after sixteen days in a row.

But this was the New York independent film scene in the late 1970s and early 1980s. It was exhilarating. The only goal was to make a film outside the Hollywood system. In fact, no one wanted anything to do with Hollywood. We all wanted to get as far away from it as possible. On one film I shot I saw a director get so frustrated with an actor that he began screaming obscenities at her in front of the entire crew and cast. I've never heard such vile and demeaning words said to another person. He felt he wasn't getting what he wanted and didn't know how to get it. To her credit the woman just nodded and said, 'OK, I'm here to work. Let's try it again.' That moment, and many others, showed me that the most destructive conflicts on the set are about communication and misunderstanding, particularly between directors and actors. In that case I learned what I would never do.

So shooting was never really professional?

No. I would shoot a few films to help me feel I was still involved in filmmaking, but most were for first-time directors and I'd end up designing the entire visual world of the film which ultimately kept making me ask myself, 'Why aren't you doing this for your own films?'

Since I couldn't really answer that question I'd finish other people's films and go back to painting apartments. One day I was in a tiny bathroom using some newspaper to cover a medicine cabinet and I noticed it was a page from the Arts section of the *New York Times* and there was an article that read, '*Stranger Than Paradise* wins the Camera D'Or at Cannes.' I've got to be honest with you, it was a heavy moment.

For your classmate to receive such an honor, you must have been thinking, 'That should be me' or 'I should be doing that'…

Jim's film was a great accomplishment on many levels and I think it was massively influential to the independent film movement, and to me. What seeing that article did was force me to look at myself and ask, 'Why are you standing here with paint dripping from your elbow?'

And that was the moment that snapped me out of it. I realised right then that it was time for me to get back to what I started out doing: directing. I had already written the screenplay for *Johnny Suede* and it was sitting in a drawer. I said, 'It's time for you to get it out of the drawer, Tom. It's really now ... or never.'

A lot of the films of that era could be somewhat avant-garde and esoteric; but your films come with a more accessible pop sensibility, albeit aligned with the left-field aesthetics of the independent scene. Do you always intend your films to have this approachability?

I like a certain kind of anarchy; in fact I think it is a crucial ingredient to any kind of art. But at the same time I like the sense of structure and cohesion because it's telling you that someone is directing it, guiding it, and they're shaping it. My sensibility, I think, tries to combine the two.

One of the strangest places I ever lived was outside a military base in North Carolina in 1967. North Carolina is *south* and it felt like I was back in the Dark Ages; the high school was something out of Dickens. Every morning the bus would let me off in front of the school where everyone was waiting to get in. There were only two distinct groups; the hip, juvenile delinquent kids and the nerdy kids that actually studied.

And every morning I got off the bus wondering, 'Which group do I belong to?' I never really knew. For a month I'd hang out with the cool kids who were intrigued, I think, by the fact that I was a little different. But their violence and stupidity quickly became tedious and depressing. Then I'd go and stand with the nerdy kids for a month and who quickly became just as tedious. They weren't violent but they all had slide rules in leather sheaths attached to their belts. Of course, all the delinquent kids would laugh and say, 'Look at that fuckin' jerk hanging out with the nerds!' And it always bothered me to have to make that choice, that distinction. I think very early on my sensibility lay somewhere in-between. And my films are the same way.

There's a quote from François Truffaut's Day for Night, *a film about the fragility and lunacy of making movies, in which he comments on the nature of filmmaking. He says, 'Shooting a movie is like a stagecoach ride in the Old West: first you hope for a nice ride; soon you just hope to reach your destination." Is that an astute summary of working on a film?*

Well, I would say from my experience even the stagecoach is a luxury; you've got a coach, you've got horses pulling you and you have a driver. Making an independent film is much more precarious. It's like you're pulling this long, freight train up a hill in the rain. You say to yourself, 'OK, this is hard but at least I've got my crew and my actors pushing with me.' Then, just at your point of absolute exhaustion, thinking you can't take another step you turn around and you see all your cast and crew are just sitting in the cars, smoking and drinking tequila while you pull. That to me is a more accurate picture of what making a film can feel like.

In Living in Oblivion *there's a scene where Nicole and Chad Palomino both stop a take for different reasons – Nicole to take a minute to reflect on her character, and Chad who has an idea for alternative blocking for the scene. It is interesting how Nick is malleable to Nicole yet impatient with Chad, even though both are prolonging the take. Is this kind of tension, dictated by an air of preference, where a director has to react differently to the various personalities, a recurring feature of filmmaking?*

Yes, but it doesn't start out that way. When I start a film I try to establish a positive environment where everybody is happy to be there, and willing to work hard under difficult circumstances. But, as you go through the film you recognise the actors that approach each take with excitement and willingness and then you see the ones that disrespect and piss on it. And if those people continue pissing on it after several days of me trying to be positive and encouraging them, I make a conscious decision not to waste too much energy on them. But the dilemma is that no matter how much you hate doing it you still have to be supportive and encouraging because ultimately a bad performance is going to affect your film.

Billy Wilder once said, 'The director himself must play twenty different parts. You have to be a sycophant; you have to be a sadist; you have to be a nurse; you have to be a cook; you have to be a philosopher; you have to demean yourself; you have to be a screamer; but you've got to do it because the picture has to get finished.'

This is why you come home exhausted at the end of the day, because you're not just playing one role; it's a different role for each actor because they all have very specific needs. But it's interesting to me that Wilder used the word *demeaning*. It's true; it is demeaning doing some of the things you need to do to keep the film alive. That's why I put that scene in *Oblivion* where Nick is behind the set talking to Chad Palomino and he's agreeing with every awful thing Chad is saying about Nicole behind her back. He even says, 'You're right, she's not that good of an actress.' He's doing whatever he can to get this idiot to calm down so he can *finish the film*. The fact that Nicole hears every word of it presents another hornet's nest. I've been there. I've had to do that, it's a reality.

So you've had to assume those different roles on set, as Billy Wilder mentions?

On every set, with almost every actor. In fact, now that I think about it the only two actors I worked with repeatedly that I did not have to do this with were Steve Buscemi and Catherine Keener. I had a deep bond with both of them, especially Catherine.

You haven't worked with Catherine since The Real Blonde; *did you ever consider a fifth collaboration?*

We were very close and had a very intense working relationship for four films, but by *Double Whammy* it had become clear to me that time and events were kind of pulling us apart. It pained me because I felt we'd stumbled forward together. Real friends and allies are rare in this business. But she went off very successfully to do many other things with many other directors.

Did the lack of success of The Real Blonde *factor into it; did it taint the relationship?*

I've struggled with the answer to that question for many years. But I've come to see that it really has nothing to do with me. This is a very primal business. There is a relentless and completely understandable instinct to be aware of where you are at with people, and whether they will continue to provide you with the opportunity to move forward. It's all about moving forward. No one looks back in this business.

Working with Catherine was exhilarating. Just like working with Steve is exhilarating. But, with Catherine the connection had a different intensity. I loved writing for her. We inspired each other; we made each other laugh. Part of me really connected with her as a woman. There was never anything overtly romantic or sexual between us, but the intimacy of our collaboration had at times the real charge of something erotic. I'm married, and she was married, but that intellectual and creative bond was like a kind of union.

But the reality is that she is a very talented actor and there are a lot of people who want to work with her. We did some great work together but this feeling that what we had was exceptionally personal, that we were bound together in a way … I think she might have felt it restricting and may have come to resent it.

She didn't want to be seen as someone's muse?

A journalist asked her that very question at a press conference at Sundance for *The Real Blonde*. She said, 'I'm not Tom's muse. But I am amusing.' Which I thought was pretty funny even though it kind of hurt my feelings.

You mentioned earlier you were in an acting class as well as working as an actor; was it acting or directing that was your primary goal?

At that time it was really a struggle between the two. One thing that became very clear to me at film school was that I had no idea what acting was. I had no idea how to talk to actors. Sometimes in the middle of a scene I would go up to talk to an actor and literally the words would not come to me. It wasn't because I didn't know what I wanted; I knew what I wanted…

You just couldn't articulate it?

I didn't know the language to speak and it bothered me so much I knew I had to address it. A friend of mine brought me into an acting class, just to observe. Then one day Chris Noth, who was at that time an unknown actor in the class, grabbed me and said, 'Let's do a scene together.' And a week later I was up in front of the class, acting for the first time in my life.

The response was really encouraging. The teacher kept giving me more scenes to do and I ended up studying with him for eight years. It was a really crazy detour, that and shooting films. But both really helped me; especially the acting.

Can you say how, specifically?

The moment I stepped out in front of that audience and realised that I had to convince them that what I was going through was real ended up affecting the way I talk to actors forever. It is an intensely vulnerable and unpredictable place to be. And if something real and personal in you comes to life onstage then it is almost a miracle. I learned to respect that miracle and to find the most constructive ways to help bring it to life.

And did this encourage you to pursue an acting career?

It did. It was something which was exciting and at times pretty embarrassing. I did a few small independent films and some Off-Off-Off Broadway plays. Jim actually gave me a small part in *Stranger Than Paradise*, which actually freaked out all the other actors; seeing their cinematographer in front of the camera.

Your films cover several genres, though generally under the umbrella of comedy, I mean you have romantic films, crime films, music films, etc. Is this something you intentionally strive for; to weave through various genres?

I'm in awe of directors who can do it, people like John Huston and Akira Kurosawa. *Rashomon* is a lurid crime story but it has some incredibly funny things in it. Many of Kurosawa's early films combined the two; even *The Seven Samurai* had moments of both gentle and bombastic humour. But when you look at *Ran* you see a film relentlessly intense with no humour whatsoever. I'm drawn to filmmakers whose sense of the world is more open and embracing of all things. In that way I feel that Fellini is rich inspiration for any film director. His essential interest seems to be in human nature. Even in his most despairing films like *Casanova* he never gives up on the protagonist, he never says, 'This person is worthless.'

How do you feel about the nature of how we consume film these days – streaming on TV, phones, tablets? Are the ease of access and consumption on the myriad media devices numbing the sense of the excitement that we used to get from seeing a film on a cinema screen?

It's hard to say. Since we're in the middle of it right now, or even the beginning of it, it's hard to define what's actually going on. But I can only think of it in comparison to what originally motivated people to create the method of watching film that they did: on the big screen. I mean if you look at some of those early movie palaces, the screens were enormous. It was more of an *event* back then, especially before television. Look at Elizabeth Taylor in *A Place in the Sun*. When her close-up appears on that big screen it's like being under Niagara Falls, it blows you away. It's not that she's doing anything gigantic, in fact she's hardly doing anything, but the way it's shot, with her beauty and the sparkling intensity of the life in her eyes, it is so phenomenal that it literally hits your body and transports you. That is why I make films. That is what I look for when I go see films.

Your career as a director has seen you experience some extreme highs and lows. After eight films and thirty years in the film business, what does cinema mean to you?

It still means what it used to mean: something elusive, incredibly pleasurable and cloaked in mystery and magic. That's what I get out of it. In the purest sense, that's how it makes me feel.

That's also what keeps me going. On the most basic level I still get an immense thrill simply at the moment of cutting two shots together. You never know how the cut is going to work, but when it does something unborn crackles into life. That moment is for me the essence of cinema. There is some lightning bolt of energy and creation that springs to life at the instant of joining. The two pieces of film become one. There is no other art that does this. Literally, something is brought to life in that $1/24^{th}$ of a second. And a film is composed of hundreds of thousands of those cuts, and most of the time no one notices them. The audience sits there and allows this rushing flow to envelop them.

There is an incredible trust that is implicit here; in the best case it is a mutual respect and appreciation between the director and the audience. It is impossible to say that my love of cinema has nothing to do with the great pleasure I feel in gaining an audience's trust. Yes, I love working with actors and discovering pure, spontaneous behaviour. I love composing sinuous and mesmerising shots, or writing scenes that ricochet with surprise. But some of my greatest pleasures in this business have come from sitting anonymously in the back row as one of my films screened. Just watching the audience and feeling the waves of connection rippling through them is beyond description.

And to hear them laugh, I mean really laugh at something that originated somewhere in your brain? That is truly miraculous. In fact, I see cinema as a more realistic and truly inspirational kind of religion; at least a religion that doesn't insist upon pain or self-loathing from its participants. Which may be why sitting through a bad film is like being in church for me.

Cinema is as essentially human as you can get. Every single one of us writes, directs, edits, shoots and stars in a movie every night in our dreams. Film is the language of dream. When a group gathers in the darkness and experiences that one flickering dream in unison, to me that is the purest form of communion, holy or otherwise. It carries the potential for the greatest human connection. The best films show us ourselves, all aspects of ourselves, without judgement or condemnation.

CHAPTER TWO

Johnny Suede

'Suede is a funny thing. It's rough, but soft. It's strong, but quiet. It doesn't wrinkle and it doesn't crack. And it doesn't stand out so much in a crowd of leather and vinyl. You don't notice it at first, but once you do you can't take your eyes off of it and you wonder how in the hell you overlooked it in the first place.'

– Johnny Suede

To understand the art, one must understand the artist. The journey of *Johnny Suede* begins in the early 1970s, with a young Tom DiCillo's decision to move to New York City to attend NYU's Graduate Film Program. Having been struck by the emotional power of Federico Fellini's *La Strada* and fuelled by a passion for still photography and literature, DiCillo was eager to study the great consummate marriage of images and storytelling: cinema.

His intense fascination with the seminal European masters – Fellini, Godard, Bergman and Buñuel – cultivated an aesthetic in DiCillo which would merge well with the searing influence of the burgeoning New Hollywood movement of the 1960s and 1970s. Films such as John Schlesinger's *Midnight Cowboy* and Martin Scorsese's *Taxi Driver* presented a New York that might have sent a more intimidated newcomer running back to the green, green grass of home. But DiCillo had been a military brat used to moving from state to state and to even farther-flung corners of the globe; a peripatetic upbringing that somewhat prepared him for the culture shock of New York City. What DiCillo found was that the cast of freaks, punks and starving bohemians became a source of influence, one which would inform his debut feature film, *Johnny Suede*.

DiCillo recalls the formative impact of life in the city that would greatly influence the filmic world of *Johnny Suede*: 'When I first moved to New York the Lower East Side looked like a bombed-out wasteland with crumbling, abandoned buildings, drug addicts and homeless people. It was where the punk scene originated and where a lot of New York actors, filmmakers and artists lived. As dangerous and depressing as it was, there was something attractive and powerful about it. No rich people lived there; none wanted to. It was about as low as you could go and there was an incredible freedom there. I liked it because it was the opposite of the image of New York shown in most Woody Allen films, and it was even different from Scorsese's New York, which despite its brutality was still presented as somewhat romantic.'

DiCillo graduated from NYU with a master's degree in Directing and several award-winning short student films to his name, but he felt something was lacking. Sensing it was vital for him to understand the art and craft of acting, DiCillo enrolled in an acting class, a pursuit he would engage in for almost a decade.

Following a year of performing scenes and monologues from such standards as Shakespeare, Tennessee Williams and Eugene O'Neill, DiCillo had the impulse one day to break from tradition and bring in a monologue of his own. The piece was based somewhat autobiographically on a character he'd been gently nurturing, named Johnny Suede. What piqued DiCillo's fascination with this character was that on the surface Johnny looked like a guy who had it all together and that nothing could stop him in his dreamy quest for love and stardom as a musician, yet the reality being that on the inside Johnny was a wreck; a messy tangle of fear, ego and insecurity.

Tom DiCillo in character as Johnny Suede.
New York City, 1989

Having introduced and refined the character in the class, DiCillo gathered these sketches into a one-man stage show. He found sponsorship at an Off-Broadway theatre which provided him with a venue to perform the character in public for the first time. In the theatrical production of *Johnny Suede* DiCillo offered a rare glimpse into the confused and conflicted world of the male persona. 'People responded strongly,' DiCillo acknowledges. 'Women had the most interesting reactions. They seemed to really appreciate seeing this intimate, revealing aspect of a man's psyche. That's what encouraged me to write the screenplay.' Inspired by this enthusiasm the actor-writer-director decided to take another step forward. Eight years after his graduation from film school he wrote his first feature-length screenplay, eponymously titled *Johnny Suede*.

The plot of the film is deceptively simple. It is set up like a modern, fractured fairy tale. Johnny (Brad Pitt) first falls in love with the girl of his dreams. Unfortunately he's too besotted by Darlette (Alison Moir) to see that she is even more confused and troubled than he is. She almost instantly leaves him, breaking his heart. Then he meets Yvonne (Catherine Keener), the girl not of his dreams. She's almost equally neurotic but much more grounded in reality, and as their relationship develops Johnny is forced for the first time in his life to confront his own fears, inabilities and lack of identity.

Johnny has created an alter-ego for himself, an anachronistic teen idol of the kind once-embodied by Ricky Nelson. Yet Johnny isn't a mere nostalgia freak. His immersion in this persona cloaks a multitude of hidden personality faults and insecurities; it is a facade. For Johnny, it doesn't matter that the 1950s ended thirty years prior, his vintage clothes aren't a uniform capturing a retro pop-culture zeitgeist, but they are a way of life, a philosophy of sorts. His towering pompadour and fashion aesthetic make him stand out in a sea of bland modernity, but his ultimate ego empowerment is derived from a pair of black suede shoes which literally fall from the sky. The discovery of these perfectly fitting, elegant suede shoes is not only the ideal aesthetic accompaniment to his wardrobe, but they become integral to his character, furthering the fairytale motif.

The film opens to the surf guitar twang of 'Hotel Loneliness', a blistering cut from Link Wray's 1990 album, *Wild Side of the City Lights*. The bent chords and palm-muted melodies accompany the camera as it drifts over a landscape of rippled suede fabric. The use of Wray's retro-contemporary 1950s timbre sets the tone for the film: surreal, romantic, distinctively offbeat and rebellious.

Gritty (or perhaps, *exotic*) in location and milieu, DiCillo early on juxtaposes the bland colour of Johnny's real-life situation with such moments as an elegantly photographed black-and-white fantasy sequence, rich in high-contrast chiaroscuro lighting and expertly composed close-ups of Johnny. DiCillo's chimerical leaps into fantasy and looseness with narrative trajectory often throw the viewer into moments of dream and illusion before they know it.

'I'm intrigued by the way film can shift you in and out of reality with nothing more than a whisper,' DiCillo admits. 'Most dreams in film are presented in some kind of ridiculous stereotypical manner. Real dreams are so intense for the very reason that you never know you're in a dream. It feels real. No one has dwarves in their dreams. No one has pink smoke or weird music in their dreams. But that's one of the great thrills about filmmaking; it can take you to a different universe in a split second. If you are careful, and you treat the audience with respect, you can take them anywhere. And people enjoy that, even if it's a journey that is painful or disturbing. There is a certain pleasure at being taken there and it's one of the things that I really love about film. So much so I think I've used that technique in every one of my films.'

With *Johnny Suede*, DiCillo crafts a world which is at once contemporary and timeless, a stylised and almost post-apocalyptic vision of New York. The exteriors are often barren and monochromatic, yet the interiors are rich in detail and saturated

Brad Pitt as the cinematic version of Johnny Suede, 1991

colour. The dichotomy of this world – cold and uninviting, yet warm and dreamlike – is that it harbours contrasting characters of both sides of the coin. For every richly-coloured setting where Johnny lies in bliss with his pseudo-sweet princess Darlette there is a dank, gritty and unpleasant world of clubs, subways, alleyways and grotty bathrooms where he meets bizarre urban creatures like Freak Storm (Nick Cave) who promise him sweaty handfuls of magic beans.

After three years in NYC, DiCillo had become familiar with them all. 'I used to see these neo-rockabilly guys stumbling home at night with their pompadours, their pointy shoes and sweat-stained sharkskin suits,' DiCillo explains. 'And I knew that was the world I wanted Johnny to live in. But by the time I got the money to make the film the Lower East Side had completely changed; condos, coffee shops, boutiques – wealthy people now buying their way into hip, arty edginess. So in order to capture the image of Johnny wandering through the rubble and desolation I recreated the Lower East Side in Williamsburg, Brooklyn, which was a complete ghost town then. Ironically, going out there enabled me to create a world for the film that was even better than the Lower East Side. I found locations that hadn't changed in sixty years, these really beautiful old buildings with paint peeling off like huge patches of skin. I loved the emptiness of it. There was no one around. It helped me set up my idea of Johnny being this guy who was kind of lost in time.'

DiCillo's years of studying acting, whilst performing in film and on stage, had served him well in determining his players. For the crucial part of the title character, DiCillo cast a then-unknown Brad Pitt, in his first starring role. 'We'd looked at every actor we could in NYC,' DiCillo explains. 'There was no one who came close to what I wanted for the part. So my casting director, Marcia Shulman, suggested a trip out to LA.' Casting and staying in the same budget motel in which singer Janis Joplin had died of a heroin overdose two decades previous, Shulman presented DiCillo with a multitude of up-and-coming LA actors. Among them was a young woman who would come to star in DiCillo's next four films.

Keener recalls auditioning in front of past and future Hollywood royalty at the motel, which resulted in her winning the role that would change her life. 'It was my agent's assistant – not my agent, but her assistant – who read and loved *Johnny Suede* and so she called me. She liked this script and I liked her so I went for it. I just thought the script was so good, so different. I could understand the part, and I could understand the world of the film, and I don't know why but I understood the character of Johnny, somebody who didn't really fit in. He was cool, because he felt like he should be; there was something innocent about him, but it was really the story and the writing that pulled me in, I thought the writing was great.'

Keener continues: 'I would have gone to the audition anyway, but this was really exciting. Brad wasn't even cast yet and he hadn't at that point done *Thelma and Louise*. So I went in and auditioned with Brad and Tina Louise at this old Hollywood motel, the Highland Gardens Motel. I was completely starstruck that it was Tina Louise! She was so beautiful. I actually found myself driving to the audition behind Brad, he was making the same mistakes on the road as I was, and we were both looking for this place. I kind of had a feeling that he was on his way to the audition as well. So I found myself in the motel room with Tom and Brad, which was funny because there was this guy that I was trailing behind in the car. The scene we auditioned was when Yvonne throws the shoe at Johnny. I was wearing loafers and I took one off and I threw it and I just hit Brad right in the leg, I hit him really hard, I just completely spazzed and threw it right into him. Of course the audition was completely broken by the reality of that but whatever we did to recover in trying to stay in-character was something Tom probably got a kick out of. And that's how I got the part of Yvonne.'

DiCillo acknowledges that the casting session was indeed one of unorthodox and spirited performance, that which left a haunting impression on him: 'Catherine's audition was like several strings of fireworks going off at once. She had an intense, whacky unpredictability that made you unable to take your eyes off her. But, right after her, another woman auditioned who performed the part almost letter perfect. And we kind of promised her the role. Then in the middle of the night, in that creepy motel – maybe it was Joplin's ghost who nudged my brain – I woke up and realised that it was Catherine's impulsive spontaneity, her inability to never do the same thing twice that was the crucial ingredient to bringing Yvonne to life.'

Johnny dreams of stardom as a rock and roll musician. So with his amiable best – and only – friend, Deke (Calvin Levels), Johnny starts a band, even though he can barely play the guitar. Enter Freak Storm, an albino rockabilly punk star, sporting a pompadour almost exceeding the dizzying height of Johnny's quiff. He is the man Johnny aches to be, albeit a doped–up, poisonous and altogether darker embodiment. Though he's dressed all in white save for red suede boots and oozing rebellious swagger, he is a tall, thin mass of pale, sickly heroin chic. This mysterious, dangerous allure which captivates Johnny is another example of his blind idealism. Freak promises to help Johnny get his first record made. The only thing he succeeds in doing is dragging the naive Johnny further down a rabbit hole of delusion.

Nick Cave as Freak Storm, serenading Johnny with a haunting rendition of "Mama's Boy"

The pathos of Johnny's character is informed primarily by his basic inability to survive in the real world. For one thing, he is unable to pay his rent, as we learn when his landlord comes by to ominously serenade him with 'The Rent Song':

Hey, hey, today's the day
Those that pay they get to stay
Those that don't, I hate to say
Got to pack their shit and move away.

Johnny's grungy fridge consists of a single carrot and might constitute a health hazard. He lounges around his semi-squalid apartment in his tattered white underwear like a child who is waiting the changing of its diaper by an absent mother. Therein lays an intriguing aspect of Johnny's character, that despite the bluster and bravado he seems in dire need of someone to nurture him, to guide him. In one of the film's most striking scenes, Johnny – regardless of his seemingly cocksure attitude towards women and sexuality – is taught the basics of female anatomy by Yvonne. When he attempts to please her manually she stops him, saying it feels like he is 'trying to pick up a watermelon seed'. The pure intimacy of this moment is immediate and revealing. Here DiCillo exposes his protagonist's basic flaw: his bravado is a front. There is an inherent mendacity to his image as a heartthrob and conqueror of female affections, yet the director doesn't make light of or crudely lampoon his sexual limitations.

DiCillo offers an insight into his method in making Pitt and Keener comfortable enough to perform the intimate scene: 'By that point in the shooting I'd earned their trust. This is where some of what I learned about acting really came to my aid. I wanted them to feel as safe and protected as possible. I wanted nothing to distract them or to make them self-conscious. So I cleared the set. It was just the three of us and the camera operator in the room. I suggested that together they determine a place on Catherine's upper thigh that would be the spot. Something as simple but specific as that helped them deal with a very intimate moment. I like the scene because it also provides Johnny with a great acting moment. He gets to be a little defensive but at the same time show this great pleasure in finally figuring something out, something that was so mysterious to him. He finally learns something! That was the intent; to peel back Johnny's carefully constructed facade and catch an uncensored glimpse into his unstable inner reality. It gave me a chance to completely dismantle the male psyche and I loved doing it.'

Yvonne's handling of the situation is direct and dignified, mentoring Johnny, not humiliating him or belittling his sexual inexperience. It is here the viewer becomes aware of the dual roles that Yvonne will ultimately play in Johnny's life, that of teacher and lover. Keener recalls the intimate moment: 'The "watermelon seed" scene is such a beautiful sequence and it's the moment where Yvonne really fell for Johnny. What Tom had wanted for that scene is what he got, to achieve this delicate balance of openness and vulnerability and honesty from Johnny. Tom is really so specific in his direction, which is what an actor wants so much; it's what a good director does: to bring you to where you want to be.'

For Keener, sharing such an intimate moment was alleviated by the genuine chemistry struck between her and Pitt off-screen, something that would mirror the burgeoning magnetism between Johnny and Yvonne. 'I can't really separate my experience with a character from my own reality,' she admits. 'I probably felt that way about Brad anyway, we were becoming friends. I had just gotten married and my then-husband, Dermot, and Brad became friends during the making of the movie. They goofed around with each other, and I liked Brad; I thought he was a good guy. That's always sort of a tipping point with me anyway. I didn't know him from Adam but I knew he was going to be a really good guy. That was Tom's intention and that's the thing about casting, Tom saw that in Brad and he saw that with me. We never had any anxiety about working with each other, there was never going to be any struggle to overcome something with each other in terms of our personalities or our behaviour. I was becoming friends with Brad, and so Yvonne was becoming friends with Johnny.'

Throughout the film Yvonne proves herself to be the antithesis of Johnny's first love, Darlette, and this terrifies Johnny. In place of Darlette's schizophrenic allure and physical beauty is Yvonne's guileless inability to be anything other than *who she is*, which is pragmatic, sincere, sympathetic and real. It is her infallible integrity that terrifies Johnny. Yvonne provides a potentially more stable future for him. But the harder Yvonne tries the further Johnny pulls away emotionally.

Johnny's true personality is buried so deep under his flashy alter ego that it results in a confused mess of destructive behaviour towards this one woman who actually cares for him. Johnny's all-consuming facade allows him to mask his fears and vulnerability but once it collapses all of Johnny's inner turmoil is revealed and manifests itself in rage and narcissism.

When Yvonne suggests they move in together it terrifies Johnny. The implications of intimacy and exposure are too much for him. In a scene that displays DiCillo's satirical comic sensibilities, Deke helps a perturbed Johnny construct a list to help him make the decision. One thing 'For': she has a colour TV; one thing 'Against': he'd have no privacy for 'things a guy does' like having to cut a fart. 'This idea of domesticity is a complete threat to Johnny,' DiCillo says. 'It means he'd be with Yvonne twenty-four hours a day, which means he'd have to work impossibly hard to keep her from seeing

Johnny and Yvonne (Catherine Keener) take a bath, the intimacy of which encourages Yvonne to declare her of love to Johnny

how much of him really is just an act. The list he and Deke come up with is absurd, but it really shows how fearful most guys are to fully expose themselves to a woman.'

Tellingly, Johnny's doubts about Yvonne increase after a quietly intimate moment with the two of them in the bathtub. While watching Johnny intently shaving her legs, Yvonne expresses her love to him. Johnny's response is a nervous, self-congratulatory 'thanks'. Instead of this moment of intimacy strengthening their relationship, it prompts Johnny to seek an escape from it.

Later, while riding the subway, Johnny catches the eye of a lonely woman, Ellen (Ashley Gardner) and follows her home. She's so lonely, she leaves her door open for him. The emotionless sexual embrace Ellen offers provides Johnny with another avenue of denial. This empty experience with a total stranger affords him a fleeting moment where he can stop masking his inferiority. Ellen accepts him for his surface appeal and asks of no more than that.

Yvonne's tolerance for Johnny's emotional limitations finally erupts when she sees Ellen's underwear fall from his pocket. The confrontation occurs in a stark and unflinching scene in which all of Johnny's constructed charm and illusion gives way to unveil yet another authentic, and more troubling, side to Johnny's persona. Yvonne previously brought out the real Johnny in a tender moment of sexual intimacy; now, in Johnny's desperation she reveals his potential for physical abuse.

Throughout the film Johnny endears himself to Yvonne when he peers through his facade and he reveals more of his true self. She encourages this in him. This is why she feels so betrayed by Johnny's selfish and destructive sexual encounter with Ellen. But Johnny's exposure turns him ugly and he attacks. 'You think I want to be stuck here with a chick that can't even put on fucking make-up?!' he yells. Wounded, Yvonne hurls one of his prized suede shoes at him, missing and sending the shoe out the window. She lunges toward him, grabbing his hair in the scuffle. Johnny responds with a frantic punch to the stomach, leaving Yvonne winded and writhing in agony as he exits for what will be a search for both his suede shoe and for himself.

Keener describes the moment when the intense scene momentarily crossed the line into reality for a nervous Pitt. 'Brad really felt uncomfortable doing that scene, trying

DiCillo, Pitt, and Keener confer on the set of *Johnny Suede*

to pull the punch, because that whole scene is so not him; it was tough for Brad. So when it came to shooting it he actually hit me for real by accident. He popped me in the stomach, if you listen to the soundtrack carefully you can hear the punch knocking the wind out of me, and Brad was just like, "Oh my God!" Our reality overtook the fiction of the moment; it was his worst nightmare come true. That burst of reality gave me what I needed for the scene.'

The final moments of the film find Johnny wandering lost and single-shoed. Stumbling upon Freak Storm only adds to his grief. Johnny discovers that Darlette and Freak are lovers. Freak whispers endearingly, 'There she is waiting for me like a little trained poodle'. At that moment the soundtrack is overtaken with the reverberated sounds of fluttering birds before descending into a discordant wail invoking Johnny's realisation that Darlette is gone forever. It is only then, with Yvonne left gasping on a bed clutching her stomach, that Johnny grasps he is completely alone.

In a powerful and surreal scene, Johnny joins the lonely denizens of a midnight diner. As he dozes off he is suddenly surprised to see Yvonne, who has retrieved his lost shoe. But just as joy and relief flash across his face the scene turns nightmarish. He sees a trickle of blood running down her leg and making a puddle on the floor. When Yvonne seems as bewildered as he is about the flow of blood, Johnny breaks down in anguish and regret. As he weeps uncontrollably DiCillo's camera pans to reveal a naked old man sitting at the counter watching them intently. It is only at this point that the scene is revealed to be a brief, sorrowful dream. Yvonne is not there. She has not found his lost shoe. The reality is that Johnny still sits completely alone.

As day breaks over the rain-dampened streets, Johnny returns to Yvonne. He stands before her silent, his hair a mess, his face unshaven and ridden with remorse. The facade is completely gone. His appearance finally reflects a real person. His coming back to face the brutality he unleashed on Yvonne reveals at last that he has some understanding of his actions. Nonetheless it is a moment that requires much from Yvonne. 'I don't think I rationalised the idea of Yvonne taking Johnny back after he hits her,' Keener admits. 'I think he was really sorry and it was so unexpected and out of character for Johnny to do. I think Yvonne saw it with eyes wide open. He was lashing out at a fierce internal struggle that he was having. Yvonne brought out these notions of domesticity to which he was so resistant. I think it was less about what their relationship was leading to but more about what he was letting go of. He was such an individual, with his style and his pompadour, his music, and along come I. And no matter how protective he was, reality just pierced through.'

The film closes with a shot of the coveted missing shoe being driven off atop the roof of a car. We leave not knowing what, or if anything, remains of Johnny Suede. But there is some hint he is finally accepting the real world and his place in it; he is finally allowing himself to be valued for the person he really is, flaws and all.

Johnny Suede endures as a stylishly inventive film that moves well beyond the limitations of a debut feature. The film is a journey of identity lost and found, a sumptuously gritty urban fairy tale which astutely examines a most modern malaise: finding love, while finding one's self. *Johnny Suede* is imbued with a sense of the avant-garde but framed within a seductively approachable narrative world populated with likeable and perversely intriguing characters. It is a film littered with pathos, absurdist humour and a deft touch of surrealism which is fuelled partly by a steady assortment of objects placed with skilful abandon throughout the shots. DiCillo instructed his design team to have a small truck accompany them on every exterior location. Inside was a wild variety of found objects, from stuffed animals to plastic Christmas ornaments that DiCillo and his art department had collected. At each exterior location DiCillo would set his frames and then place items from the Surreal Van in strategic positions to add his final touch of off-kilter absurdity. 'I found the old hairdryer chair that is the centrepiece of Johnny's apartment on the street one day,' DiCillo relates, 'I knew it was going in the movie somewhere. It sat in my apartment for six months before we could use it.'

The film has impressively managed to shift out of the context of its own time period and establish itself into the culture's psyche. Twenty-five years after its release *Johnny Suede* is still reaching new audiences. In December of 2014 Netflix included the film in its roster of indie cult classics.

For Keener, *Johnny Suede* is a landmark of professional and personal triumph, one that she admits she is fiercely protective of. '*Johnny Suede* definitely affected my career in a positive way, but more so it affected me positively,' the actress enthuses. 'Up to that point I hadn't found a place that I worked well in, in terms of what was available. But when I did *Johnny Suede* I found a place where I felt I could really work in, especially in that I like it. A good strong part can do so much for an actor … they just need to find that part. Those are rare. The thing about Tom is he always wrote such good parts that everybody in his films has a good part. There are certain things that I don't want fucked with, things that are precious to me, and not just because I'm in it or whatever, but *Johnny Suede* is like that for me, 'Don't fuck with this!' It's precious to me."

For DiCillo, looking back at *Johnny Suede* more than two decades removed from its production affords him the clear hindsight to acknowledge both the joys and the pitfalls of seeing his debut film come to life: "It's like your first child; you love it warts and all," the director confesses.

> I think I managed to find something original; which is pretty miraculous when you consider what the shoot was like. It seemed like disaster wandered by on day two and just decided to stick around. One day our wardrobe was stolen. Another day we arrived to continue shooting in Johnny's apartment and found that overnight the Fire Department had condemned the building. We had already shot half the scenes in the apartment. We had to find another one, in a day, paint it and hope that no one noticed Johnny now lived in an entirely different space. I had to fire my cinematographer after a couple of days upon finding out he did not want to be there and was deliberately sabotaging my film.
>
> But there were moments of great joy too. I was literally running from set to set I was so excited. I think the film's strengths are in the details of the interaction between Johnny, Yvonne and Darlette. Brad gives one of his most open and revealing performances. I got to know Catherine and developed a profound admiration for her talent. I was so grateful that something woke me up to cast her. That relationship lasted for four films.
>
> And eight years after graduating from film school I had finally made my first film.

* * *

Wayne Byrne: Johnny Suede *began life as a one-man show; can you tell me about the genesis of the character?*

Tom DiCillo: There is an autobiographical element in all my films but *Johnny Suede* probably touched most specifically on some things that I was personally struggling with. I was twenty-six and really had no idea who I was. I knew nothing about real intimacy and was frankly terrified of it. So instead of really looking inside I pretended I was fine and actually put more energy into making my outer surface more convincing. And with some dramatic exaggeration that complex balancing act became the essence of the character.

This idea is sort of familiar, you know; the guy who acts like he's got it all together but is really a fool. Usually though, this kind of character is presented as an awkward nerd, like many of Woody Allen's heroes. I wanted to try it differently, so that when you looked at Johnny you were charmed by him, attracted to him. The work he did on his surface was so good that at first sight you'd think this guy was fascinating. I wanted to have my fool be outwardly sexy, kind of cool like Marcello Mastroianni. I wanted

DiCillo on stage during the one-man stage run of *Johnny Suede*

there to be an edge to him, almost like the James Dean anti-hero in *Rebel Without a Cause*. I thought that it would be much more interesting to watch someone like that confront his weaknesses and literally fall apart.

In 1986 I gathered all the short monologues I'd written for Johnny in my acting class and shaped them into a one-man show. I don't know what convinced me to do that. Honestly, it seems like someone else was driving the car. I took it to a tiny Off-Off-Off Broadway theatre and to my utter astonishment they agreed to put it on. My first night I sat in this tiny broom closet that was my dressing room listening in terror as I heard the audience coming in. There was one little window that opened onto a parking lot and all I could think about was jumping out of it and just running as far away as I could.

So by the time the script got accepted to the Sundance Director's Lab in 1989, you'd been living with this character for...

... about five years.

Did the people at Sundance try to shape it or change it to suit their own aesthetic?

Some of them did; which was tricky because even though this was my first full-length screenplay I'd worked hard on it for several years, I'd put a lot of thought into it. But I readily admit there was a built-in obstacle or weakness, so to speak. It had started off as a monologue – not even a play – a monologue where all of the information was given through words and not action.

The first couple of passes at the screenplay were somewhat stymied by this, whereas if I had just begun it as a visual story I think it would have been different, and possibly a better film. But I did like the loose structure of it. At Sundance most of the advisors said to me, "Listen, I don't think you should make this movie because there's no Plot Point A and even if you had a Plot Point A there's no Plot Point B." I swear to God, the first time someone said that to me I said, "I'm sorry, what is a Plot Point?"

It wasn't until I sat down with Buck Henry [co-writer of *The Graduate* and co-star in *The Real Blonde*] that I received any kind of encouragement. He just looked at me with this crazy twinkle in his eye and said, "This is a good script." I said, "Really?" And he went on to tell me all the things he liked about it and why I should be proud of it.

That's a great compliment from the man who wrote The Graduate!

It was enormous. It gave me the confidence to make the film exactly as I had written it. Again, it's this schizophrenic dichotomy. You have to be completely open to criticism and new ideas because some might actually be helpful. But if nine out of ten people are telling you, "This is shit; you can't make this," it can really undermine your confidence. You have to be an almost impossible combination of totally vulnerable and hard as a rock.

So would you say your experience at the Sundance Institute was beneficial to you?

Absolutely. They were incredibly supportive, and they still are. For *Johnny Suede* they arranged for me to get a 35mm camera package from Panavision; for free! For my first film, it was incredible.

Did attending the Sundance Institute lead to financing?

It helped a lot. It gave the film just that little something extra to help separate it from the millions of other scripts just as desperate to be made. This then led me to my first encounter with a producer/financier. I signed a contract with him and we went into pre-production. I hired a casting director and started a very long and agonising search for Johnny. We ended up in a sleazy motel out in LA.

The actors would come in and audition in the tiny kitchen. We got so desperate we even asked some kid I saw in a burger joint to audition. He was terrible. Then Brad Pitt walked in and even before he said a word I knew he was Johnny. I'd found him! And the first thing my producer says to me is, "You're not making this movie with some nobody named Brad Pitt. You're not casting him!" I tried to convince him how great Brad would be but he wouldn't listen. He arranged for Timothy Hutton to read the script and he informed me I had to meet with him. I said, "He's got to audition." And my producer said, "No, he doesn't. He's going to meet you 'in character.'"

And that was one of the strangest meetings I've ever had. I mean I respect Timothy Hutton but whatever he was doing in character was beyond my ability to see it. I didn't see anything; just a guy sitting and talking to me. So I walked out of there and said to the producer, "I'm not casting Timothy Hutton." And, the producer took all his money and walked away. I couldn't believe it. I'd already spent over five years trying to get the movie made.

But there is a reason why people believe in magic in this business. The deal fell through on a Friday. On Sunday I had another deal. I had met this Swiss producer, Ruth Waldburger, who had expressed interest in the script. I somehow had been smart enough to keep in touch with her. She was the first person I called when my deal collapsed. I told her what was going on, showed her Brad's audition tape and she said, "Yes, he is a good actor. But you are the director; if you want to cast him please go ahead."

So she was coming from an auteur sensibility?

Yes. She had a European filmmaking sensibility. She'd produced three films for Godard, which was very flattering company to be in. And that's how I got the money to make the film, and cast it with the actors I wanted.

Why were you so certain about Brad?

I guess I just saw something original in him. It happened with Catherine Keener, Sam Rockwell, Peter Dinklage and Melonie Diaz. They all have something that makes them stand out. It's a kind of compulsive honesty; they can't help themselves. And that's what you want. You want an actor who is incapable of being false, or dishonest. Then, if you are lucky enough to find one that also has a rare beauty or attractiveness, well, then you've got it made.

DiCillo directing Pitt in Williamsburg, Brooklyn, 1991

All the guys who came in to audition for Johnny thought he was The Fonz, from the TV show, *Happy Days*. They played him as some kind of barely literate 1950s grease ball and no matter what I said to them about Johnny having some kind of grace or vulnerability they never got it. Brad was the only actor who walked in and presented the confused and unsure part of Johnny's psyche without my having to say a word. Brad had a grace and quiet intelligence; plus a very American, almost rural, sense of humour. He had an innocence that was real.

I think about it now and am kind of bewildered that even on my first film I wasn't thinking of following the Iron Rule for casting: getting stars. Maybe it was my years in acting class watching completely unknown actors perform brilliantly in scenes. I prefer discovering new actors because they come with a willingness and excitement and that brings such life and energy to a part.

So you finally got your cast, and I get the impression that you deeply admired Brad, enough that you cast him in the lead role of a film based on a character you nurtured for years. Why then, in the aftermath of Living in Oblivion, *did the rumour arise that Chad Palomino, your construction of a disruptive, bratty movie star, was based on your experience with Brad? How did some of these rumours get started? Was there any tension between you and Brad on set that could have led to this speculation?*

This is a sensitive issue and I preface it by saying that whatever ends up in the film is the director's responsibility. I had given Brad a note early on, saying, "Johnny's got the attention span of a child." What I meant was that a child can be interested in something very intensely and then instantly be interested in something else. There's no slow or deliberate transition from one thing to another; it happens abruptly and completely. I think Brad might have misunderstood me. He might have thought I meant him to have a child's *intelligence*. I think he gives an amazingly open and honest performance but by making Johnny less intelligent than himself it makes you question sometimes why Yvonne would be with him. I think if the character had simply been more like Brad himself – with his spontaneity, his quick wit, his sense of humour – it would have helped people understand why she stays with him, why she loves him.

In what way did you deal with this?

I remember feeling frustrated. I could tell the character was going off in a different direction than I'd written him and I was concerned that it was misshaping the film. The character became kind of a simpleton, and that was never the intention. Johnny was written to be sharp and wily; the way someone would have to be if they didn't want someone to see through their façade. I've seen people that way. I've been that way myself. If you think people are going to penetrate your veil of protection you put extra effort into maintaining it, not less.

Did you explain that to Brad?

I tried. Sometimes our communication was off. Part of that was my inexperience. Another part was a kind of distancing that Brad used. I've seen this since with other actors and usually it indicates an underlying insecurity about something. I didn't know enough at the time to help him unravel it. But with Brad it manifested itself by a quiet stubbornness that let me know he was not going to go certain places with me.

Like where?

I wanted him to tap more into himself and not work so hard on the "character". I know without a doubt if he'd brought the same sort of focused energy to *Johnny Suede* that he did to *Moneyball*, or even *Snatch*, *Johnny Suede* would have been a much different film. Instead, Brad felt he needed to add this layer of emotional immaturity which throws the balance off, especially the scenes with him and Yvonne. We're supposed to believe she cares about him deeply; that she invests herself completely in him. But the age Brad creates for Johnny makes it seem like she's dealing with a little kid. The innocence he brings is fantastic, but he doesn't offer her the crucial other thing: the real love, the charm and adult magnetism that would give her the reason to keep staying with him. What woman would want to invest her future with a man who seemed like he was just about to enter the sixth grade?

Did this bother Catherine? Did she mention any of it to you?

No. She and Brad became great friends during the shooting. And I was happy about that. It enabled them to build a real trust with each other that created some great work. I think some of their scenes together show enormous honesty and daring from both of them. Brad always committed 100%. And whenever he snaps out of the little boy

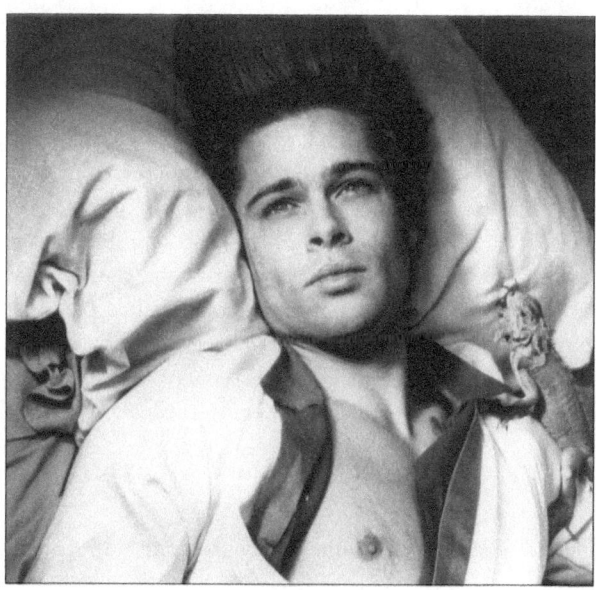

Idol: Brad Pitt as Johnny Suede

persona he is very strong. But it permeates the entire film and I think it made it hard for audiences to believe the relationship with Johnny and Yvonne.

Was there a sense that he'd already become a giant star?

To some degree, yes. Sometimes I'd get this feeling on set that even at this early point in his career Brad was already gone. On the final day of shooting, when we did Brad's last shot, I spontaneously embraced him in front of everyone. It had been a very tough shoot for everybody but we'd made it. I was grateful to him and I wanted him to know how much I appreciated all the effort he'd put into the film. He returned the embrace for a brief second and then subtly, but distinctly, he pushed me away. In that tiny little gesture I felt him slip into the stratosphere.

Did you try to stay in contact with him?

Absolutely. I liked him very much. During the publicity stuff for *Johnny Suede* in LA we spent a lot of time together, along with Catherine and Dermot Mulroney, and my wife Jane who'd also become friends with both Brad and Catherine. Brad and Jane went to the gym together one day and he had to borrow $20 bucks to get in. There was a surreal, drunken pool party we were all at up in the hills overlooking LA one night that is forever etched in my brain, like a scene out of Nathanial West's *Day of the Locust*.

I even had ideas of having him and Catherine doing another film together. But *Thelma and Louise* came out and changed all that. A few years later he was in NYC doing press for *A River Runs Through It*. Catherine and Dermot were in town and Brad had invited us all to the premiere. We spent the afternoon with him at his hotel. At one point Brad wanted to get cigarettes so I went down to the street with him. We went one block from the hotel and crossed the street. When Brad was in the intersection someone recognised him and yelled out his name. People stopped in the middle of the street and then started gathering around him. In seconds the whole intersection was a human traffic jam. We ended up running back to the hotel; without the cigarettes.

The last time I saw him was in LA back when he and Gwyneth Paltrow were together. They invited me and Jane over for lunch. They'd come to the premiere of *Living in Oblivion* the night before. I was a little nervous around Brad because of all the rumours surging at that point that Chad Palomino was based on him. Brad took me outside and led me into an old Spanish alcove behind his house. It was dark and cramped and the two of us were completely alone. I suddenly realised he had orchestrated the entire moment. The silence that ensued was so strange I can't even remember what either of us said. I think I might have mumbled something about the stupidity of the rumours and even mumbled some words of apology, but mainly I remember the look in his eyes.

He was angry?

No. It was as if he was telling me I'd hurt him in some deeply profound way. As if I'd betrayed him.

Did you?

Look, I handled the whole thing very stupidly. I should have killed all the rumours instantly. But I was a total neophyte with the press. It is in my heart that I know I didn't betray him. Hell, for two months he was going to play Palomino himself. But I don't think he ever forgave me. I've tried to address it over the years whenever it crops up. I've written several letters to newspapers and magazines endeavoring to set the story straight. I even wrote a letter to Brad himself a year ago. I told him how proud I was of him, especially his performances in *12 Monkeys*, *Snatch* and *Moneyball*. I told him how badly I felt about whatever estrangement there was between us and apologised with no ambiguity. I also told him Jane said he could keep the $20.

Did you ever hear back?

No. Since I had no direct contact for him I had to send the letter through his manager. Maybe he never got it.

I tried to get him to talk to me for this book. I made requests for over three years. There was at one point some indication that he was considering participating. But then word came that it just wasn't going to happen.

Yeah, I remember when you told me. It's too bad. I think his voice would have brought a fascinating perspective on *Johnny Suede*. Of course, I know he's a huge star with a life massively more complex than mine but part of me still remembers how I walked away from a completely financed film to cast this basically unknown kid in 1991. I remember running around the slums of Williamsburg, Brooklyn with him. And when we couldn't get the right look for his costumes I remember standing in front of my closet with him and being thrilled to see that my clothes fit him.

Did it piss you off?

It bothered me.

Did it hurt your feelings?

Yes.

In the end, how did Brad's performance affect the narrative and pacing in contrast to how you originally envisioned it?

I had to take so much out. The original cut of the film was two-and-a-half hours long and this was because the pacing of the dialogue was so *slow*.

Having read the original script it did seem to have a sharper rhythm to it.

It was a real lesson. In film the audience is always a little ahead of you and you have to sharpen things; impose a stricter rhythm in order for it to seem "natural".

In my case I should have simply said, "Keep the intention and focus that you have but just tighten up the lines." It's actually just a technical thing. I think it would have sharpened the film. Nonetheless, Brad brought something really beautiful and crucial to the character, a kind of genuine innocence and vulnerability; especially with Catherine.

The "Watermelon Seed" scene springs to mind. It's one of the best scenes in the film, there is such an intimacy there you rarely get in sex scenes in films. It's here that Johnny truly shows his complete sexual illiteracy.

That was the intent, to show that this guy, who so strenuously presents himself as an expert in all things regarding women and love, didn't even know the most basic thing about a woman's anatomy. I have such respect for Brad and Catherine in that scene. It was a fun scene to write but a difficult one to put on film. Actually, I've never seen a scene like that on film, where a woman instructs a man about her body – in that detail – yet with that much charm.

It's a very, very intimate moment.

I think it was a very courageous moment for them both. Catherine gave such a beautiful performance; she handles him with such patience and graciousness. It goes a long way toward suggesting there might be a future with these two.

In the original script there was a scene where Johnny fantasised about coming to the aid of a woman being hassled in the street. What were you getting at there?

Because Johnny doesn't know who he is he constructs an identity that he thinks will make him more interesting to women. Part of it is that he is a saviour of women. In his mind this gives him an almost medieval quality like the Knight trying to rescue the Damsel in Distress. The point about Johnny and his fantasies is that they help fuel his dream world, but in reality no woman really wants to be rescued like that, and if they do it gets boring after the second or third time.

So, what is Johnny really about?

He's a complex character, struggling to keep his intricate, very shaky facade intact. This is why I gave him Ricky Nelson as a role model. You could ask, "Why not Elvis?" Well, Elvis was too *dangerous*; especially in the first two or three years of his career when he was really pure and new. Elvis was threatening. Instead, Johnny chooses Ricky Nelson, who is this homogenised, almost anesthetised teenaged idol. Underneath Johnny is the exact opposite; he's a complete mess. I thought it would make a better contrast.

He has the potential to be dangerous.

Yes, and that is the irony. Here's a guy who purports to be a protector of women and what does he do? He hits one himself. The violence is to suggest how powerful that fear of exposure or self-awareness is; that when confronted with their own weakness people will lash out and they usually lash out at people who are physically weaker than themselves.

Is part of it to do with the fact that Yvonne is too real for him? He refers to her as having "a weird job"; she doesn't wear make-up and is physically and aesthetically at odds with someone like Darlette.

Darlette is his dream girl. When they first meet she confesses to him, "My boyfriend beats me!" We later learn this is completely untrue but it gives Johnny the opportunity to fulfil his fantasy of saving her. She's like a twisted troubled princess. She's perfect for him except for the twisted part. Yvonne confuses him because she presents him with no fantasies to fulfil.

There's nothing to save her from.

There isn't. And that's why I made her a teacher of retarded kids; you can't get much more real than that. That day-to-day reality is too disturbing to Johnny.

Which is surprising; as a teacher, especially one of mentally disabled children, you would think she'd be smart enough to recognise that he isn't treating her right.

In a way Johnny is more mentally challenged than the children she teaches.

Is that part of Yvonne's attraction to Johnny? That he is someone she can foster and nurture? Is it some kind of project for her perhaps?

I think she sees his potential. I tried to make Yvonne a real person, not just some "together" woman who tries to teach Johnny. She's a human being too, so she has fears and vulnerabilities of her own. She's alone. She doesn't quite fit in either. The one guy that she was seeing didn't look too promising. Johnny offers something different, something outside of her world. He's dressed differently, he's a musician, he's into the club scene. That life seems almost alien to her. Johnny seems to know more about putting on make-up than she does.

So they are both exotic to each other?

In a way, yes. They both seem puzzled by and attracted to each other which I think is a good combination. It always keeps you guessing.

In Johnny Suede *you played with classical narrative and illusion, with a taste for fantasy and the surreal. Is there a direct cinematic influence at work informing this aesthetic or is there something more relevant in there relating to how you perceive the narrative of life?*

Sometimes in life it only takes the slightest touch and something slips into the surreal and *un*-ordinary. To me the most interesting journeys into the surreal are the ones that also carry an emotional weight. To just present something that is "weird" or "heavy" leaves out something. But if the moment of exaggerated reality, or fantasy, reveals something more about the character, then it becomes really powerful and fascinating. Fellini was a master at this. Again, I go back to his intrinsic faith and interest in the things that make us all human. I think very few directors match his skill in combining humour and emotion.

For me, one of the most powerful scenes in Johnny Suede *is where Yvonne walks into the diner and sits down in front of Johnny after he has punched her in the stomach and she has blood running down the inside of her legs. It's an emotional blindside and it's a dream sequence that reveals something about Johnny: the guilt, the conscience.*

It reveals that he knows he hurt her; in the dream he acknowledges that to himself. That was a scene that Brad handled beautifully, with great honesty and power. He knew how crucial the scene was and he prepared himself for it for hours while we were lighting.

The suede shoes that Johnny finds echo Dorothy's Ruby Slippers in The Wizard of Oz. *They give Johnny a sense of empowerment and importance. He then loses one at the turning point of self-discovery. Can he survive without them?*

That's a good question. Obviously he's going to have to because at the end of the film one of his shoes is heading toward the sunset on the roof of somebody's car.
But yes; the point was that Johnny interprets the finding of these special shoes as an almost mythically divine event. They literally fall from the sky. They look so exotic and unique and they fit him perfectly. They are suede. Like him, they are "rough but smooth, strong but sleek". That's how Johnny sees himself. The shoes are part of the fable element in the film. When he loses one it is like he's losing some kind of power or magic. Or, in more realistic terms, he's losing some part of himself; something that he thought was crucial to his being. I think it does raise the question, "Who will he be without them?"

Is there something disocciative in Johnny's adoption of the 1950s teen idol image, something more than mere nostalgia?

I think so. Nostalgia does not really interest me. If you go back to any period of time you'll find human behaviour just as disturbing and horrific as anything happening in the "modern" world.

I was more interested in making Johnny look lost in time. That he didn't belong in the present but not in the past really either. The costumes were tricky. The costume designer had all these gaudy, cartoonish 1950s clothes, again out of *Happy Days*. And I said, "No, that's not the way I see the guy." As I said, we ended up going into my closet and choosing stuff from the vintage clothes I'd collected over the years. Luckily Brad was my size.

Halfway through filming, long after all the wardrobe had been established, someone left the wardrobe van unattended and all the clothes were stolen; all these one-of-a-kind pieces of vintage clothing I'd spent ten years collecting. The cops found the thieves but were told that if we wanted to continue filming in the rough part of Brooklyn we were in we should just forget about the clothes. The crooks liked them too much to give them back.

How did Nick Cave come to the film?

When I first wrote the screenplay I sent it to a friend of mine in Berlin, just to get his take on it. Then one day around three years later my phone rings about midnight and it's this guy with an Australian accent and he says, "Hey Tom. It's Nick Cave." He was staying with my friend in Berlin and he had seen the script lying around. He liked the part of Freak and was calling to ask if I would consider casting him in it. Of course I instantly said yes.

Was having Nick Cave on board good news to your financier?

Like I said, she wasn't overly concerned with casting stars or famous people. I know that when the American co-investors heard the news they were tremendously excited for two minutes because they thought that I said I'd cast Nicolas Cage.

I think I was actually more nervous working with Cave than I might have been with Cage. I was in awe of him as a musician. Plus, I sensed he was feeling a little anxious coming into the shoot. Now, the worst thing you can do to an actor who is feeling uneasy is to make them feel that they look ridiculous.

Nick had the idea of making Freak an albino Elvis preacher with a white rockabilly hairdo bigger than Johnny's. So he had to wear a wig. The production hired a make-up person who presented herself as a wig expert. On Nick's first day of shooting word came that there was some kind of trouble in the make-up room. I went over and found Nick sitting in the chair glowering while this expert was frantically spreading gobs of putty on his forehead and poking at it with a plastic fork trying to make it blend in to his hairline.

My biggest job right then was to keep Nick from walking off the set. Maybe walking isn't quite the right word.

He had spent so much time cultivating this image as a serious musician...

... and he justifiably didn't want to be seen looking like a fool; especially when he was already feeling nervous about acting. But to his credit he stuck around. We got a real expert to come in who fixed the wig and Nick did great.

Did you ask Nick to contribute any music to the film?

Not intentionally. The song I'd written for him to sing was called "Mama's Boy". It's a kind of pseudo-gothic murder tale that was openly intended to be a little stupid. Well, Nick thought it was a lot stupid. So he asked me if he could write his own lyrics. I said, "Please do."

A few weeks later a tape arrives with him singing a very heavy, dreary dirge. And about halfway through it, Nick stops singing and says on the tape, "You know what, Tom? This is pretty stupid too; let's just go with your version." I took it as a compliment.

This film required a certain style of music to compliment Johnny's musical influences as well as his fashion aesthetic. You worked with composer Jim Farmer on many of your films. What was it about his musical sense that you found intriguing?

Even on my student films I was fascinated by what music and sound could bring to the moving image. The right piece of music can do something as vital as save a scene or literally transport you to another realm. For my first film I was looking for someone who shared that enthusiasm. Jim was not just a composer; he also wrote plays and painted. So his ideas about what "film music" should be were just as open and irreverent as mine.

I mentioned Ennio Morricone to him and we both just went off. I think what Morricone did with film music has not been equalled to this day. I was completely in awe of his love of sound, his willingness to use anything that sounded interesting to him in a soundtrack – whether it was a bullwhip cracking, a whistle with echo and reverb on it, or a distorted surf guitar. Nobody was doing that. And nobody is doing it now. Jim loved Morricone as much as I did and that is where we started with *Johnny Suede*. We decided early on the film's sound would be like a spaghetti western shot in Brooklyn.

What was great about Jim was his openness to collaboration. He was very gifted musically but he did not feel threatened by other ideas. I had written all the songs that Johnny sings in the film. I didn't know much about music but I did know what I wanted to hear and where it should go. Jim welcomed me into his studio. There was no ego. We talked, we looked at cues, and we banged on things. Now, most of the musical ideas were his. He played all the instruments: guitar, bass, drums, synthesizer – all based on a kind of surreal surf sound which went very well with the source music I used in the film such as the Link Wray instrumentals and the sugary but haunting Ricky Nelson songs.

We had a great time together. And the score was simple but beautiful. What I liked about it most was that it sounded like nothing I'd ever heard before.

The film got accepted to the Locarno International Film Festival where it won the Grand Prize for Best Film. Did you feel at that point the sensation of, "OK, this is real!"? Was there a sense of reassurance that you had finally made a film and were a now a director?

I remember realising while we were shooting that being on set and making a film was something vital and instinctual to me. I really believe it is what I do best. Despite all the disasters, I was pleased with the film. I knew it had faults and they plague me to this day. But I also know there was a spark of something good in it, something true and original. And it was mine. I had written and directed it. That felt really good coming eight years after finishing film school. It did feel real, like I had actually accomplished something.

I never expected to win a prize at Locarno, let alone Best Picture. I think it was the first thing I'd ever won. I remember standing up in front of three thousand people and accepting the award, a large golden statue of a leopard. My Swiss producer Ruth was so thrilled she made me walk around the whole night carrying the Leopard. I tried to put it away when we went to a restaurant but she dragged it out from under the table and plunked it down right in front of me. All during the meal strangers would come by and congratulate me.

I had distant relatives in Italy who'd seen the awards ceremony on TV. They somehow found my parent's number and called them in North Carolina. My father was happy but probably a little more pissed off that he'd been woken up in the middle of the night.

Miramax, which was the Weinstein Company back then, bought the film for US theatrical distribution. Harvey's buyer at Locarno convinced him to buy the film sight unseen. So my first film was going to get released in movie theatres all across America. There was a sense, making *Johnny Suede*, that I was finally back where I wanted to be after a series of detours that at times seemed to be taking me nowhere but were actually extremely beneficial: the acting; the shooting; the writing. I came back feeling I was a director.

If I'd known what was going to happen later I would have carried that Leopard with me twenty-four hours a day.

CHAPTER THREE

Living in Oblivion

> 'It's your call, Nick. His acting or his face?'
> – Wolf

Films about filmmaking present the difficult challenge of breaking the wall of illusion that is cinema by enabling an audience to witness the very mechanics that bring the product before their eyes. In doing so, the audience sees the ego, the conflict, the stress, the labour, the heartache and, sometimes, the love that produces a film.

There are various approaches a director can take in getting us to contemplate the technical and artistic processes by which movies are made. Examples range from Stanley Donen's hilarious classic *Singin' in the Rain* (1952), to the dark, obfuscating examination of Hollywood in David Lynch's *Mulholland Drive* (2001). European filmmakers tend to treat the subject of film production with greater veneration than their American counterparts. François Truffaut's *Day for Night* (1973) examines the complex issues that arise in dealing with faded stars, undisciplined extras, illicit affairs and other on-set travails. Truffaut's depiction of such is successful without aiming venom at the film industry itself. However, very few, if any, of the more notable American works contend optimistically with the notion of film production. Predominantly, movies which deal with the art and craft of filmmaking and the bureaucracies of the film business have satirised, parodied or outright vilified the industry, often holding it up as immoral (Robert Altman's *The Player*, 1992), corrupt (John Schlesinger's *Day of the Locust*, 1975), harsh (Billy Wilder's *Sunset Boulevard*, 1950) and downright farcical (Frank Oz's *Bowfinger*, 1999). Even the more optimistic ones, such as Tim Burton's sanguine *Ed Wood* (1994), encourages one to question the sanity of those who commit to the pursuit of filmmaking.

"Films about the making of any kind of art are very tricky because the first thing you ask is, 'is the art or artist any good?'" DiCillo acknowledges. "I decided to just bypass that question. If you look at the film that Nick, the director in *Living in Oblivion*, is making I think you'd be hard-pressed to answer what the hell it is. I didn't want people to think about that; I wanted them to always be more aware of the process he was going through. That's why I had all the sets built much smaller than normal so you could always see off of them. This minimised their importance and gave equal weight to some of the other dramas taking place just off-camera.

But filmmaking is a group effort," the director continues, "and whenever you get more than two people working together on something, especially when there is a lot at stake and a lot of tension, then ego and neuroses all start working overtime. I had witnessed that and something made me believe it would be worthwhile trying to put that struggle on film. The nature of cinema is that things don't always go right and so bigger-budget movies have the luxury of using their money to solve problems, to reshoot if they need to. You don't have that opportunity on a low-budget movie. Film-making can be exhilarating but at times it can crush you. In my experience, when you are confronted with absolute disaster on a low-budget movie it is devastating. It's a miracle that any film ever gets made."

Few filmmakers, irrelevant of nationality, have dared to toy with the reverence of either art cinema or independent filmmaking. With *Living in Oblivion* DiCillo quickly burst this near-mythic bubble. The filmmaker himself comes from a background of working on some of the most respected independent films of the last thirty years. Add to this DiCillo's own low-budget feature *Johnny Suede* and the director was therefore in a perfect position to craft his film around his first-hand experience of life on the set of an independent film.

Living in Oblivion was born out of the frustration that comes from a business where a filmmaker's worth is relative to the amount of revenue his last picture generated. In DiCillo's case, *Johnny Suede* faltered financially, despite winning Best Picture at the Locarno International Film Festival in 1991.

"It is a hard rule in this business that everything you're trying to do is utterly dependent on what you've just done," DiCillo affirms. "There was great excitement about *Johnny Suede* after the Locarno win and the acquisition by Miramax. I got my first agent. We began working with Miramax on planning the release. They were thrilled because Brad was poised to become a massive star with *Thelma and Louise*. This was August 1991. The plan was to take the film to the Toronto Film Festival in September and then release it in early spring.

So I had a little time on my hands. I used it to finish my second script, *Box of Moonlight*. Ruth Waldburger read it and immediately said she'd produce it. So I had a film about to be released and my next film already set up. I was flying pretty high and in that mood I went to the first test screening Miramax had of *Johnny Suede*. Harvey Weinstein and I were sitting in the back and about two-thirds of the way through he catches my eye in the darkness and he gives me the thumbs-up. It was a good screening; people were attentive and laughing. Then the cards came in. The responses were not great; people liked the film but seemed confused by it. The numbers really disturbed Harvey. He had some very, shall we say, insistent ideas on how to 'fix' the film. I didn't really like any of them and I resisted them to the degree I could, but in the end some scenes were cut and a pretty useless narration was tacked on.

The release date was repeatedly postponed until finally it was set for August 1992; two full years after the film's initial appearance. On the night before the film was to open, my phone rang just after midnight. It was Harvey calling with the 'bad news': the chief film critic for the *New York Times* had just given the film a very strange review. Harvey read it to me over the phone: 'There's something going on in this film but if anyone can tell me what it is I'd like to know.'

The film played in New York for a week. Five years of work and it was gone in one week. The effects were immediate. Ruth had trouble securing financing for *Box of Moonlight*, especially from any American investors. Eventually, she pulled out. And that started a search for financing that went on for over four years. I was pretty down. Everywhere I turned there was a closed door. I didn't know what to do. I couldn't see the path."

The director continues: "Then, one night I went to a wedding. My wife's cousin was getting married. I had my first Martini. I liked it so much I had another, and another. Out of the shadows some guy comes up and says, 'Hey, Tom! Great to see you! I was in an acting class with you. Good for you, man! You made a movie! Lights! Camera! Action!' And I just erupted at him. Perhaps it was the Martinis talking with the four years of frustration pushing hard right behind. I said, 'Shut the fuck up! Making a movie can be nothing but a grueling and tedious nightmare.' And I went on to tell him all the things that had gone wrong while shooting *Johnny Suede*. I said, 'You can have an actress emotionally ready to do a scene and then take after take some idiotic accident will happen and it will shatter her concentration forever.' And right there, right at that moment, I saw the first half-hour of what became *Living in Oblivion*.

I gave this guy a nice part in the film, by the way. I went home from the wedding, got through the hangover and wrote the first thirty pages in about three days. It was so exhilarating; putting down on paper the raw, uncensored angst and frustration I'd been feeling for four years. To my amazement it was a comedy! It could very easily have been a horror film. I stayed close to the drunken wedding night epiphany: a gifted but certainly neurotic actress is primed and ready to do an emotional scene but through a relentless series of mishaps she has to keep doing it, over and over."

Living in Oblivion is an absurdly comic satire on the world of independent film production, imbued with a grinning disregard for the reverential stature independent cinema has seen hoisted upon it since the halcyon days of John Cassavetes (*Shadows, Faces*), Morris Engel (*The Little Fugitive, Lovers and Lollipops*), Robert Downey Sr. (*Putney Swope, Greaser's Palace*) and the like. The film charts the disaster-prone making of a picture called "Living in Oblivion", an independent feature directed by Nick Reve, a struggling filmmaker played by Steve Buscemi. The film is structured in three specific and sharply delineated movements. It opens with a static, slow zoom towards an isolated film camera, an apparatus of supreme engineering genius which has enabled cinema to become the most significant art form of the twentieth century. But this piece of inanimate equipment is only as good as those who utilise its powers.

"When Tom had written his script for *Johnny Suede* he wanted me to be a part of it but that didn't work out," Buscemi recalls, "but then he offered me the part of Nick in *Living in Oblivion* and I thought it was so funny and so brilliant, just an amazing part."

"I'd seen Steve perform these bizarre plays he'd written with his acting partner, Mark Boone Jr., in the early-1980s," DiCillo recalls. "We got to know each other and at one point I was considering playing Johnny in *Johnny Suede* and having Steve play Deke. Now, that would have been an interesting film. But this time I really wanted him to be in *Living in Oblivion* and he said 'Yes, I'll do it' and a few days later he asks, 'By the way, can I read the script?' He'd said yes without even reading the script."

Buscemi elaborates, "I remember being really excited about doing it. Tom and I had been working on low-budget films but there wasn't really much of an independent scene in the early-1990s. I remember when I got my first agent he was trying to get me commercial work in studio films, but then I would say, 'I got this offer for this film, it's a better part and I think I could learn more'. I would have preferred a more interesting part and to work with more interesting people than have a really small part in a really big film. The attitude was just really dismissive; they were just called 'little movies'. I remember the agent saying to me, 'So, you'd rather go off and do that little movie?' He didn't say that specifically about *Living in Oblivion* but that was the general attitude towards independent films at the time."

In Act One DiCillo adopts a grainy 16mm black-and-white documentary aesthetic to observe and capture the behind-the-scenes chaos. In contrast, once Nick calls "Action!" and we are looking through his own camera lens DiCillo then switches to gloriously saturated colour 35mm film. The scene being filmed in Act One is a moving exchange between Ellen and her mother, played by Nicole (Catherine Keener) and Cora (Rica Martens). Here, Ellen accuses her elderly mother of being ignorant to the physical and mental abuse she and her younger brother suffered at the hands of a now-absent father.

Scene 6, Take 2: Catherine Keener shooting the film within the film

For this scene Nick has devised a single setup which will dolly out from Nicole to reveal both characters in conversation. This simple attempt to capture Nicole and Cora's tender scene is foiled in a series of seven increasingly disastrous takes involving exploding light bulbs, inept focus pulling and forgotten lines. Nicole's escalating tension and frustrations are crucial to the arc of this first act.

Catherine Keener recalls the complex setup of the act's most dramatic scene, where Ellen actually breaks down in tears. "I was apprehensive about it. I have to repeat the same emotions over and over again but slightly different each time. We shot it all consecutively in one setup and it was very intimate. Tom was just dialing, dialing and dialing; then when it really had to happen when the camera wasn't there I was just present. Tom made it so that it wasn't a high-pressure environment; we had time to get where we needed to be. There was room to get where you want to be, it wasn't crowded with fear.

Tom gets so personally involved in the performance and you can see him becoming moved by what's in front of him while he's watching it. I just remember that he was incredibly supportive of me to just go wherever I needed to go with the scene. He doesn't sit by the monitor watching. I remember him standing beside the camera, almost in the scene and I was aware of his eyebrows rising and he was quite moved by the end of it."

Keener continues, "Tom is very present, like an actor. He's not detached; he's part of the scene. I distinctly remember filming that scene because I didn't know what I needed before that, but then I knew and ever since I know what I need or what is called for in order to do the same thing over and over again. With that scene it just built and by the end all that was left was to let go. It was kind of like magic, nobody planned for it, all of a sudden we're doing this final take where it's supposed to be when they get it just right but the camera isn't rolling, and it really mirrored the film. Rica Martens, who played my mother and whom I dearly loved, was this exquisitely sensitive woman, she completely surprised me when it came to shooting that moment.

Tom and the process by which he works allows for so many surprises for everybody, for you, for a viewer, for himself. He just loves the element of surprise and I think that's a really valuable lesson for actors for their confidence, because you never know. There are things Tom notices about actors that other directors probably wouldn't appreciate as something of value, or they think it is something that perhaps would detract from his or her storytelling; with Tom it's the opposite."

It is in this first act where DiCillo initially displays the destruction of the filmmaker's vision due to forces beyond his own control. The nature of film production is a wholly collaborative effort, yet increasingly frustrating mistakes on the part of the crew result in Nick's clear and simple single-shot setup being completely abandoned.

"One of my favorite moments with Steve is in this part of the film," DiCillo recalls. "Nick is watching Nicole and Cora do a run-through of the scene to make sure they have their lines. He's already had to force himself to abandon his idea for doing the scene in one take. Now, to his amazement, the scene suddenly comes to life. He wants to film it but no one is behind the camera. What Buscemi does with that moment is so profound. He shows his horror and disappointment but at the same

Nick Reve (Steve Buscemi) directs

time his eyes have an aching sparkle of pleasure in them; he can't help but marvel at the beauty of what he's seeing – and missing. That unexpected, beautiful colour is what makes the scene. You can make those kinds of suggestions to an actor but when they come up with them on their own it's like they're just bringing wheelbarrows of pure gold to your doorstep."

It's this moment that becomes the catalyst for Nick's tirade of abuse in which every single member of the cast and crew receives a searing personal critique, the culmination of which is a wrenching primal scream from the frustrated director.

"Even when he was losing it and taking it out on his crew, I found Nick really endearing," Buscemi admits. "He never gives up, so that anger comes from just wanting to do good work and wanting everybody to share his vision. Sometimes the reality is that you feel totally on your own."

Nick's yell of tortured anguish gives way to his alarm clock sounding off an early morning wake-up call. Here DiCillo pulls the rug from under us and reveals that the preceding half-hour was all Nick's nightmare; an anxiety dream the night before a real day of shooting.

Just as Act One ended with Nick waking up and a door closing on the audience, Act Two begins with a new door opening, this time in a different bedroom. This segment opens in colour, with assistant-director Wanda (Danielle von Zerneck) and cinematographer Wolf (Dermot Mulroney) getting dressed for work. DiCillo is revealing to us that the two are in a relationship. Wolf is suspicious of Wanda's pointed interest in arriving star Chad Palomino (James LeGros), who is in town to lend Nick's film some commercial clout. It is Chad and his calamitous effect on the cast and crew of Nick's film that is the central narrative device for Act Two, perhaps the most downright absurdly hilarious of the three segments. As a desperate Nick allows the Hollywood star's ego to run rampant, the film ascends to a comic plain that only Groucho, Chico and Harpo could have made more comically anarchic.

Brad Pitt, DiCillo's initial choice for Chad Palomino, was set to play the narcissistic star but was forced to pull out due to press requirements for Edward Zwick's *Legends of the Fall*. However, keeping in line with the production's unpredictable and serendipitous nature, DiCillo's adroit leading actress remedied the situation.

"I was on the phone with Catherine," DiCillo says, "and she was telling me the bad news about Brad having to pass on the role when she said, 'Hold on a second.' And I heard her yell out the window to someone walking by her house, 'Hey, James! You want to be in a film?!' And that was James LeGros and that's how we cast him."

"Brad was going to play Chad Palomino," Keener affirms, "the whole idea being that Brad was going to send-up the public perception of himself, but then he became unavailable. James was a friend of mine, and on *Living in Oblivion* everybody was a friend – Brad, James, everybody – and James was the right guy for the job, he brought his own twist to the role; he is fantastic in the film."

"I think Brad would have been great as Palomino," DiCillo states. "I was sorry to lose him. And as grateful as I was to James LeGros for stepping in at the last moment I really didn't know him. I had no idea what he was going to do with the character until his first shot and I called 'Action!' Everything he did with the character came from him. He'd just come off of *Point Break* and he told me later he based most of Palomino's self-absorption on Patrick Swayze."

The scene being shot by Nick in Act Two is a romantic drawing-room scene reminiscent of any number of melodramas of the 1940s. Replacing any combination of Joan Crawford, Bette Davis, Rock Hudson and Cary Grant are Nicole and Chad, declaring their love for each other under the fake moon and stars of a Hollywood-style background.

Nicole (Catherine Keener) and Chad (James LeGros) filming their scene, before it descends to all-out chaos on the set

The stage is now set for the real action to take place; where the presence of a 'star' can affect every aspect of the filmmaking process. With the lines between independent and mainstream cinema rapidly blurring into one artistic and economic aesthetic since the early-1990s, many so-called indie films are now star-vehicles in their own right. When DiCillo conceived the idea of *Living in Oblivion* the American independent film industry hadn't yet been consumed by the studio system.

"Having a big movie star working on your low-budget film can sometimes have a debilitating effect on the set," DiCillo suggests. "At the very least they put out this quiet little vibe along the lines of, 'You know, I'm doing you a big favour by acting in your film.' I've learned that no matter how big the star or how important you feel they are to the film, if they think they're doing you a favour you're in big trouble. You usually end up with a performance that's unusable."

As the tension between Nick and Chad reaches a peak, the actor snaps and publicly reveals to Nick his real motivation in taking the role: "I thought you were tight with Quentin Tarantino!"; DiCillo's timely reminder that *Living in Oblivion* was released in the midst of Tarantino mania. When Nick snaps back, "Go on and leave, you Hostess Twinkie motherfucker!" an all-out brawl ensues, dragging in almost every member of the cast and crew. The film set hasn't been this risky to one's health since Schlesinger's *Day of the Locust*.

After packing a punch-drunk Chad into a car and away, Nick joins Nicole on the set's squeaky bed and confesses his true intentions in writing the film. He has loved Nicole since the moment they met. Expertly mirroring the scene Nick had just been attempting to shoot with Chad and Nicole, DiCillo draws the act to a close with an intense kiss between director and actor. Just then the film cuts to Nicole awaking abruptly in bed, her alarm clock blinking 4.35. Act Two is revealed to be another dream sequence; this time it is Nicole's own anxiety dream.

For DiCillo, the attraction between Nick and Nicole meant the opportunity to utilise Buscemi in an area which the prolific actor had not much previous experience. While his most visible and widely seen performances are enraged gangsters, killers and oddballs, DiCillo extracts from Buscemi a rare sense of vulnerability here.

"There's a much deeper side to Steve that he is cautious about revealing," DiCillo discloses. "One day I noticed him in the shadows behind the set and I was surprised to see he looked really distraught. I went up to him, somewhat carefully, and I asked him if he was alright. When he looked up I saw he was on the verge of tears. We were about to shoot the scene where he and Catherine kiss. And Steve says to me, very quietly, 'This is the first time I've ever kissed a woman in a movie.'"

The director continues: "I think that did as much to endear him to me as anything in our history together. It was so real and human. Everyone always perceives Steve like he's a weirdo, that he lacks certain sexuality or an attraction. I've never thought of him that way; to me he's always incredibly interesting and appealing. And here he was about to do a scene that no one had ever considered him capable of, or appropriate for – but one that he was really longing to do."

When it came time to cajole Buscemi out of the shadows and onto the set, the director resorted to basics. "I just laughed and hugged him and told him he was going

Director Nick admits his feelings to his leading lady, Nicole

to be great," DiCillo recalls, "And he was. He and Catherine really liked and respected each other. I sketched out the blocking so it mirrored the scene Nick had been trying to shoot with Palomino, then turned on the camera and just sat back and watched in awe."

"The romantic element of their relationship was something that was already really evident and fully realised in the script," Buscemi says, "and made all the more easier for me that I was working with Catherine and Tom. It was certainly a lot of fun for me to play the intimacies of those scenes. It's nice, because I don't usually get to do that in films."

Any anxieties Buscemi felt were not evident to his co-star. "I wasn't aware at the time that Steve was nervous about kissing me during our romantic scene," Keener admits. "Steve didn't let me know that himself but I remember Tom at the time saying to me that Steve told him, 'This is the first time I win the fight and get to kiss the girl.' The thing is that Steve is so romantic, that is who he is. With me there was no problem; I was totally into Steve! I was a huge admirer of him as an actor and when I got to know him I found out he is such a great guy. There have been so many other people that I have had to kiss that were just work, with Steve it was play, it was just fun. You should have nerves about kissing a stranger, nerves are good."

The film's final act is set in reality and sees the crew filming a dream sequence. Nicole is having trouble finding the "truth" in a scene where she stands static in a smoke-filled room, wearing a wedding dress and reaching out to an apple held aloft by a circling dwarf wearing a turquoise tuxedo. Nick's battles with Wolf have intensified. Now he's arguing with his cameraman because he wants the scene filmed on the dolly, while Wolf petulantly insists on doing it handheld.

The dwarf, played by Tito (Peter Dinklage), is also having trouble connecting to his character. Nick wants him to laugh hysterically on cue, but the increasingly infuriated actor demands more motivation. Tito (repeatedly called Toto by Nicole) berates Nick

Behind the scenes of Act Three: Tito (Peter Dinklage) enters the dream world

publicly for his decision to have a dwarf represent the mascot of the nightmare world: "Have you ever had a dream with a dwarf in it? No!!! The only place I have ever seen dwarves in dreams is in stupid movies like this!"

The prevalence of this stereotype had been bothering DiCillo for some time. "It struck me that using dwarves as prototypes for weirdness, especially in dreams, had really become ridiculous," the director explains. "I felt it was time to retire that worn-out cliché. I loved writing that part; the truth of it was incredibly exhilarating. A kind of bombastic pomposity edged into the character that made the casting much trickier than I'd thought. I stupidly imagined that anybody who was less than three feet tall could play the part. But during the audition it quickly became apparent that I needed a real actor."

For Peter Dinklage, the role of Tito would prove a notable film debut for the then-struggling stage actor. "I was familiar with Tom's work as a filmmaker. I had seen *Johnny Suede* and loved it!" Dinklage enthuses. "I really admired the movies that were coming out of that period, so I wanted to be part of that world."

"When Peter came in to audition," DiCillo recalls, "I asked him to think of something personal that would piss him off. He said, 'Try patting me on the head.' That was one of those flashes of revelation that give an almost blinding insight into someone else's reality. In an instant I saw the years of larger-sized people reaching out and making that gesture to Peter, and well-meaning or not I could see how it would be infuriating. And when Peter did the scene he brought all that to it, plus the over-sized ego which gave it the unexpected twist of humour. I cast him immediately."

Dinklage is now a highly-acclaimed film and television actor, starring in the hugely successful HBO show *Game of Thrones*, while appearing in Hollywood blockbusters including various *Ice Age* and *X-Men* sequels, but on *Living in Oblivion* it was once again to be the friend-of-a-friend approach to casting that proved fortunate. "I did a short play about a year or two before with Kevin Corrigan, who is also in *Living in Oblivion*, and he knew a friend of mine," Dinklage recalls. "Kevin knew they were

Nick tries to inform Tito of his character's motivation, with little success

looking for someone my size and even though I'd only met him once or twice he remembered me and told Tom about me. I owe my career to Kevin Corrigan," the actor humorously admits, "I really should buy him a drink one day."

Prolific character actor Kevin Corrigan, who plays assistant-cameraman, Maurice, recalls recruiting Dinklage for the role of Tito. "Tom had asked me at the time if I knew any short people, and I remembered Peter from some Off-Broadway shows and I knew he was remarkable, a really versatile actor and who could be very funny."

For Dinklage, Tito's distress at being cast as an otherworldly aberration proved to be a cathartic release, the energy of which the actor utilised to produce one of the film's most memorable moments.

"Without sounding a bit arrogant, the material was easy for me; Tito's anger about being cast as this strange entity," Dinklage admits. "I totally understood where that was coming from, that anger and frustration about not being taken seriously as an actor. But I had the easier job in that big scene where I walk off the film. I will give all credit to Steve for the comedy there. I just had to get into an easily-tapped rage, which has never been a problem of mine. I just had to play it straight; most of the comedy in the scene comes about from Steve's reaction to me."

Aside from dwarf-induced surrealism, this segment also sees the shoot interrupted by the re-appearance of Cora. In this reality-based act she is revealed to be Nick's mother who has somehow miraculously escaped from her nursing home. Cora's no-nonsense attitude sees her spontaneously stepping in to replace Tito after he storms off in a huff. Considering the notions of familial dysfunction, having Cora in this scene makes for interesting thematic continuity. In Act One, the fictional character of Ellen yearns for a misplaced emotional connection to her mother, a response stymied by the mother's blatant denial of any aberrant behavior of the father. Here, in the climax of Act Three, Ellen grasps at and devours the fruit Cora offers. The symbolic intent of the

Tito and Nicole perform the dream sequence

gesture gives the audience, and perhaps Ellen, a sense of emotional closure, resolving the conflict of the fictional relationship set up in the opening third of the film. And so, with Cora's infectious enthusiasm and pragmatism, the scene works and Wolf's readiness with his handheld camera saves the shot for Nick, who only moments before was vowing to give up filmmaking for life.

DiCillo invites us to be privy to the collaborative effort it takes for a production to move forward. It is these elements of team effort, compromise and unity that are at the heart of *Living in Oblivion*. Much of the film's sadistic black comedy comes from the fact that the more love and care that Nick projects towards his film and his actors the more he is rebuffed of the pleasure of witnessing what he had imagined in writing the film come alive. It is a comedy of passion denied, of having what is closest to a filmmaker – artistic integrity – taken away for the sake of time, money and dwindling sanity.

The film's chimerical tone is reinforced by Jim Farmer's vibraphone-led score. In a nod to Nino Rota (Fellini's frequent composer), Farmer creates a surreal, carnival-like soundtrack which immediately sets the mood and atmosphere for the film. Much in the same way that Farmer's 1950s-inspired guitar score for *Johnny Suede* imbued that film with retro rebellious attitude, the composer's music for *Living in Oblivion* immediately informs the viewer that they are in a land of humour and fantasy. It suggests from the opening credits that the viewer is about to enter a world of fractured absurdity.

Despite *Living in Oblivion* being structured in three specifically delineated acts, DiCillo builds continuity in the film by providing his characters with an overarching narrative trajectory. He reveals a love and affection for his characters and empathy for their situation by restoring some equilibrium in the end. Despite the frustration and ineptitude endured in the first two acts, it would take a colder director to not have

Nick and his crew enjoy some kind of personal and aesthetic joy in getting at least one scene right, even if it wasn't quite what Nick had envisioned for his film. DiCillo wraps the film up with an emotionally satisfying closure yet doesn't dwell on it for mawkish sentimentality. The crew trudges on to set up the next scene. The film's narrative moves swiftly on before a final door is closed and the credits roll. It is a rhetorical closure rather than a literal one; life moves on after the final scene, like, well, *life*.

It's possible that some might see *Living in Oblivion* as a cynical view of motion picture production, but at its heart is a film that has more in common with the optimism and delight of Donen's *Singin' in the Rain* than many other films about filmmaking. Donen had his characters experience major technological breakthroughs in the art of cinema; DiCillo hasn't anything so grand in mind to deal with. The technology is already there as we see in the opening moments of the film, the camera sitting static and awaiting human manipulation, ready and able to capture light, movement and emotion on celluloid. If only the people behind the camera weren't so insane – so human. DiCillo's concern is that of the pain, the anguish, the anxiety, the egos, the absurdity and the pursuit of happiness of this group of individuals who are all working together towards the single goal of making a movie, while also confronting their own personal afflictions; these are the themes at the core of *Living in Oblivion*.

For Buscemi, these themes are universal. "I think people in the industry really like *Living in Oblivion* and can relate to it," the actor ventures, "but I think it transcends that too. It's about anybody's dream. Anybody who has a desire to do something where the odds are great and there are challenges, it's how you meet those challenges."

Living in Oblivion is a rare occasion in which a filmmaker utilises the medium to comically reprimand himself. DiCillo ridicules his own appropriation of certain clichés, such as having written a dwarf into the dream sequences of *Johnny Suede*. This sense of self-deprecating humour somewhat belies any criticisms which would suggest that DiCillo is merely critical of or lampooning other filmmakers. Perhaps it is this self-criticism which makes DiCillo an uncompromising liability in the world of independent filmmaking. The art end of independent cinema is built upon the notion that it is of higher cultural value and esteem than mainstream cinema, and thus taken very seriously. The acerbic nature of this film's comedy, which is directed at the whole process and practice of filmmaking, helps deconstruct the veneration with which the art and the industry are held, particularly by the filmmaking community itself.

"*Living in Oblivion* is about the phony mythology that has grown up around independent filmmaking" DiCillo asserts. "The filmmaker had become the celebrity wannabe of the Millennium. It's like one of the most fantastic Halloween costumes anybody could put on. I know several talent agents who quit being agents and tried to make their own films. The first thing they all did was grow a goatee and wear a backwards baseball cap because it gave them license to assume this cherished identity: the Director. But, veneration is for religion, not filmmaking. I see *Living in Oblivion* as aligned to the sensibilities of the Marx Brothers in terms of its willingness to look at the foolishness involved in making a film and I think this bugged anyone who had a sanctified reverence for film. A famous actor who'd worked with Cassavetes on several movies came up to me and Buscemi after a screening and said to Steve, 'I didn't like your performance; you were a bad director!' Not only was I stupefied but my feelings were really hurt. I thought he'd be interested in seeing a portrayal of honest human behaviour. There is nothing in *Living in Oblivion* that I haven't either done myself or seen on every film I've worked on."

"Some people just need to have a bit more of a sense of humour," Dinklage opines. "There's a difference between a serious film and a film that takes itself too seriously. At the end of the day, yes, *Living in Oblivion* pokes fun, but it's a movie that loves the art of making movies, it loves creativity and inspiration. I don't see a trace of cynicism in it. These characters are frustrated, they're upset, they're untalented – some of them – but the film certainly isn't any of those things. It mocks certain conventions of art cinema but in a joyful way."

DiCillo continues, "I don't see any difference between a Hollywood movie that forces golden sunsets and golden retrievers up your ass and an independent film that relentlessly focuses on a depressed artist toying sexily with razorblades. Life is much more complicated than that; in both instances. That's why I love what Peter Dinklage does when things fall apart during the shooting of the final dream sequence. He looks at the director and yells, so everyone can hear it: 'Is this the only way you can make this a dream sequence, by putting a dwarf in it?!' I don't think Nick Reve, as an independent director, has ever been faced with a question as brutally truthful as that."

Corrigan notes: "Tom is one of the authors of that whole independent aesthetic; to me he is an artist that represents the New York art world, and when I met him I felt a direct link to that world. That whole era had passed into legend by the time I made that connection with him. Tom has an insight into that world and knows it better than anybody; he has the absolute right to examine this kind of filmmaking the way he does in *Living in Oblivion*."

The general consensus of those who worked on *Living in Oblivion* is that what made it so appealing was the sense of family and unity that DiCillo was able to craft. This is an approach that has been serving the independent film industry well as far back as 1957 when John Cassavetes took his 16mm camera to the streets of New York and shot *Shadows* with friends and volunteers. This was an inspired aesthetic and fortitude not lost on DiCillo and his burgeoning cast of unknowns.

"I'm at a stage in my career where I have to go and do the big projects – hopefully I'll be smart and do the good big ones," Dinklage ponders. "But in my heart are movies like *Living in Oblivion*, films where you pull together with friends and family and everybody gets a part, that's the way to do it. Unfortunately it's so much more difficult to do that now. Everybody on this film, including Tom, the crew and the actors who were playing the crew all had similar experiences to draw upon to make it feel as real as possible. Tom wrote every single word, but I think that it's such a compliment when people recognise that chemistry and say it feels like the actors improvised or that it feels 'off-the-cuff'. That was definitely all in the script, and yet it feels so real and immediate."

It is not generally known that the film actually started as a thirty-minute short that DiCillo wrote with Keener in mind and it was her initial attraction to the script that spurred much of the film's financing.

Keener recalls: "After I read the script I just said to Tom, 'let's do it!' He was having a hard time getting his second movie off the ground, which was to be *Box of Moonlight*. So with *Living in Oblivion* the aim was to just fucking do it on our own; shoot it cheap and let it be whatever it is. And that's what happened. Dermot, my husband at the time, was in Texas shooting and I brought the script to him and afterwards he was just crying. He said, 'let's do it, I'll kick in some money'. And so that started the ball rolling of people going, 'I'll give some money!' The boom guy, Matt, he was Tom's wife's trainer! You could buy your way into the movie, it was ridiculously fun."

Buscemi recalls his realisation that the film was destined for greater things. "The fact that it started out as a short film meant that there wasn't that element of pressure; it felt like we were really making it for ourselves. We thought it was going to be a lot of fun and we'd have a nice little film and that maybe it would play at some festivals. That was the idea going into it, but by the third or fourth day – of a five or six day shoot – all the actors started talking about it and wishing that it was a feature-length film. We started saying to Tom, 'you have to make this into a feature.'"

"It was like being in a pilot episode for TV and having the series get picked up, it was a great feeling; I've never been on a project like that since," Corrigan enthuses. "Everybody on that film had their own incentive and many of them contributed funding to the film. There was a great feeling of camaraderie and chemistry. And this continued when James LeGros joined the cast when he replaced Brad Pitt at the last minute as Chad Palomino … 'Chad Palomino'! That's another thing I love about Tom: he is the best creator of character names that I can think of, perhaps beside J. D. Salinger. I remember when he came up with a name for me. When we did the short I was just called The A.C. (Assistant Cameraman), but there's a scene with me and Bob the Gaffer and as I'm preparing to shoot it Tom comes up to me and says, 'You guys are going to go up to Chad Palomino with a script and it's about a tsunami hitting New York; I've just told James LeGros to call you Maurice' … Maurice!!!"

DiCillo shot the short in five days. On the last day the mood of the cast eventually struck the director. "Everybody was walking around depressed," DiCillo recalls. "Nobody wanted it to end. I remember Catherine coming up to me during one of the last shots and saying, 'Geez, Tom, it's too bad you couldn't make a feature out of this.' And I thought, 'She's right! That's the only way anybody's going to see it.'"

A few months after the short was completed DiCillo committed himself to writing the two additional acts that would make the film a feature. Drawing on the relationships that had evolved in the half-hour short he crafted a complete screenplay that carried them full circle. Time, however, was of the essence.

"Steve got a role in a big film," DiCillo remembers. "Dermot got one. Catherine got one; and I'm watching this little movie, which I knew was the best thing I'd ever done, just slipping away from me. I was on the phone one day, about to sign a deal with some guy who'd never made a film but he wanted to start with *Living in Oblivion* and make a big name for himself. He wanted to change all the casting, get bigger stars in it. 'I'm gonna run the whole show,' he said. Just then my call waiting clicked in. It was my wife's cousin, Hilary, whose wedding had birthed the entire idea. I had given both Hilary, and her husband Michael, parts in the film. She plays the Script Girl

DiCillo directs Keener on set of *Living In Oblivion*

and he plays Speedo, the soundman. Her father had died and left her some money. Now she was calling me offering to finance the entire rest of the film. I hung up with that other producer and a month later we were shooting, just like we'd started; no producers, no financiers, no distributors – just us."

And so, with financing now in place from people working directly on the film, DiCillo was finally able to re-assemble his entire cast. During the winter of 1994 he shot the rest of *Living in Oblivion* in fifteen days.

"I was holding my breath the whole time," DiCillo confesses. "It was like a dream. I was terrified I was going to wake up and the whole thing would just evaporate. It felt that good. There was such a sense of the miraculous. Everything; the script, the money, all these wonderful people were coming together at the perfect time. It was an almost overwhelming rush from beginning to end."

Living in Oblivion has become DiCillo's calling-card film, and remains one of his finest achievements to date. His acute and at times downright farcical portrayal of the making of an Independent film identifies a director who is a candid observer and storyteller with a fascination for the offbeat, the absurd, the dramatic and the surreal details of life a few inches right of the camera lens. For the actors involved it remains a treasured moment, just before Hollywood came knocking.

"*Living in Oblivion* is one of my favourite films," Dinklage sincerely acknowledges. "I got lucky it was my first one out of the gate. You get a little bit spoiled because of it; you think they're all going to be that good. They certainly aren't. Tom was instrumental of course; I didn't know what the heck I was doing, because I was so new to it. Tom is such a great director, and considering the pressure a filmmaker is under when shooting an independent film I was so grateful for him to take the time out to help me. He loves actors and it shows in his films. You can tell Tom's loyalty with actors, look at his work with Catherine Keener and Steve Buscemi. That those guys love working with him says it all."

Dinklage continues, wryly recalling one particularly absurd moment of miscalculation. "I remember I was invited to the premiere – this is kind of a sad story – and I didn't really look at the date on the invitation. Being the non-Hollywood guy that I was, I assumed the premiere happened on the day that the movie opened. So I brought my mom and my dad all the way in from New Jersey, I had invited them in to go to the premiere, and we showed up at the Lincoln Plaza Cinema, the venue for the event. So me, my mom and my dad arrived and there was nobody there ... we thought we were early! Then I looked at the invitation and realised the premiere took place a week earlier. I was devastated! But it was my first film, there was such a great reaction to it and to my performance; it was such a positive experience. I really hold *Living in Oblivion* down deep in my heart; it's like a first love kind of thing. I'll never forget that film."

"It was a pretty special atmosphere," Corrigan admits. "On *Living in Oblivion* it was so exciting to be going to work and seeing everybody. Each character was so clearly and specifically sketched out, they were so distinct. And Steve was really coming into his own as an actor at the time. I was kind of in awe of him; I idolised him. All of the promise and potential that he seemed to represent all came together on *Living in Oblivion*. Tom's films are sophisticated and sometimes it's hard to find an audience for sophisticated films today, I think his films would have been more recognised had they come out a generation earlier. All you have to do is look at the cast he assembles, or to look at the way his films are shot, they always look really beautiful. Tom always has an abundance of ideas. His films are so deeply layered, with so much going on in them; they're richly textured."

For Keener, *Living In Oblivion* has become something of a cult phenomenon, haunting her from set to set. "After all these years later people still quote this film on shows that I work on. I just worked with this director of photography and she knew every line of *Living in Oblivion*. It took a few days for us to get to know each other but once she was comfortable around everyone she started blowing out all of these lines from the film, the whole camera crew knew everything about that film, it was hilarious."

Dinklage concurs. "Always! Every single time I work with people. And seeing that they know about *Living in Oblivion* then I think, 'Oh, boy, you've got something right!'"

For Buscemi, *Living in Oblivion* astutely captures a period in independent cinema prior to the movement exploding and being consumed by the mainstream. "Tom made *Living in Oblivion* before independent film itself became a genre and mini-industry," Buscemi explains. "Having worked on a lot of these low-budget movies I feel that Tom's script really nailed what it was like to actually make a film with very little money and very little time and with all the things that can and do go wrong. It's a film with a lot of humour and a lot of heart. Everybody working on it was there for all the right reasons and it shows on screen."

For its creator, *Living in Oblivion* is a feat greater than the sum of its parts. It represents a goal that every artist aspires to achieve within their chosen medium; that it will reach out and touch someone, somewhere, somehow. No matter how complex or obfuscating a work, audiences will relate to basic human emotions. And here, within the milieu of an independent film production, Nick Reve and his engaging crew spoke to more than just cineastes and industry insiders. DiCillo recounts one such unexpected revelation.

"I went to France to do publicity for *Delirious* a few years ago and I ended up in a small movie theatre deep in the South of France," the director recalls. "Suddenly a woman in the audience stands up and says, 'I am a high school teacher and I show *Living in Oblivion* every year to my students!' Her comment really moved me. Even though it does deal with the mechanics of filmmaking *Living in Oblivion* is also very much a film about human beings; this crazy group of people caught up in this tense, mysterious struggle. That's what fascinates me about filmmaking, the same way any communal effort does; this idea that any tiny movement by one of the group can throw the entire thing off or could bring it to absolute success, like Wolf's idea that the final shot should be handheld. It turns out he was right all along! He gets the chance to redeem himself.

One of the things I've learned about filmmaking is that it is essentially trying to capture the impossible. You can't plan it. You can say, 'Well, this is what I'm thinking…' and you can toss the balls in the air and run and get the camera, but you never know where the balls are going to land. And then suddenly the gods smile on you and everything becomes magical for a brief moment. The beauty is if these moments of spontaneity and absolute accident are captured on film they can live forever."

* * *

Wayne Byrne: *Tell me about writing this film. Because it was born of your frustrations and personal experiences in filmmaking, how easy did you find writing the script, from a technical point of view, compared to your other films?*

Tom DiCillo: In some ways it kind of wrote itself. I did a huge amount of re-writing on *Johnny Suede*; with *Oblivion* I did very little. Maybe it was because I knew that world so well. Everything just fell into place: the harried, frustrated director, the arrogant cinematographer, the good-natured but humbling crew. It's a comic film, no question about it, but there are also several elements in it that go deeper. Those elements took some thought and work. For example, if you didn't believe Nicole had an intense emotional experience with her own mother then that moment during the run-through where she suddenly recalls her last moments with her mother wouldn't have any meaning.

Catherine Keener came to stay with us for a few days just as I finished it. I gave her the script and I will never forget the howls of laughter coming from her room. It wasn't until then that I realised I'd written it for her. As she left the next day we stood in the doorway, me, my wife Jane and Catherine and we just kept saying, "We're going to make this."

I really believed it. At that point I was ready to shoot the film on Super 8 or on a roll of paper towels; I didn't give a shit. Thanks to Jane, Catherine, Dermot and bunch of other crazy benefactors, we raised $37,000 in three weeks. It felt so good to really be doing something after all those years of phone calls and rejections. None of the actors auditioned. Anybody who put up money got a part. Dermot put up $5,000 for which he deserved a really good part. He wanted to play the director. I saw him more as Wolf, the cinematographer. He said OK and instantly suggested Steve Buscemi for the director.

So, you got Steve, Catherine Keener, Dermot Mulroney and you made a short film.

We shot a half-hour film in five days. Everybody worked for free. Jane and I provided food. I finally embraced the utter poverty of it all and found a way to enjoy it. I mean, there were no producers around, no agents, and no money people. There was no money! It was just us, doing whatever we wanted; like when you were kids putting on a play in the garage.

You didn't consider entering it in festivals, perhaps for short films?

I did but short films are more easily digested if they're under ten minutes. Festivals don't really know what to do with a film longer than that. So I sat down and started writing Act Two.

Act One was complete?

Yes. That first thirty minutes we shot is frame for frame what appears in the final film. It gave me a great base to spring off of. I already had actors that I knew something about and I had a sense of what the key relationships were. I knew I wanted to put on film a scene where the director gets into a fistfight with his star actor so that became the major theme. Nick's love for Nicole grew out of that. I switched the use of black-and-white to what Nick was filming; this time it was a love scene between Nicole and Chad Palomino.

Did you have any idea what Act Three was going to be?

No. And I was really starting to freak out about it. Both Steve and Dermot were getting offers from big films and I knew if I didn't get this thing written and shot very soon I might lose both of them. It was Jane who came up with the idea that inspired the final act. One day I was bemoaning my frustration to her and she said, "Act One is Nick's anxiety dream. Act Two is Nicole's dream, so why don't you have Act Three about them really shooting a dream sequence?"

As soon as she said that I saw a scene with a dwarf who gets pissed off that he's playing a dwarf in a dream sequence. And that sparked the whole last movement. To my astonishment I had actually written a full-length feature script incorporating the entire first part.

Did you try to raise the money again yourself?

Yes, I sent the script to all the independent distributors and they all passed. Some had seen Act One which I'd made a finished print of. And these people said, "You want to make a feature out of this? Why?" They couldn't comprehend it.

Did you set out to make a film about filmmaking?

No, it just happened. But, even in film school I had a fascination with what was going on just two feet off-camera. It intrigued me that the attention of the entire film was almost blindly focused on the 'scene' that was being shot while so many more interesting dramas were being played out just off-camera.

But you also used the opportunity in the film to examine the whole technical process in almost relentless detail.

DiCillo framing the scene

That's because this fabulous medium, which is generally perceived as being something magical and romantic, can turn disastrous in a heartbeat. You're trying to capture genuine emotion which is by nature fragile and fleeting. If you see it and you miss it, it's agonising. Several moments from the shooting of *Johnny Suede* found their way into *Oblivion*. There was a scene where Darlette breaks down and reveals something painfully truthful to Johnny. Alison Moir, who was not a trained actress, was halfway through this one incredible take when the cameraman pulled a filter out of the camera; while it was running. And the take was ruined. Alison tried so hard but she could never get that emotion back again. It was gone.

Another moment was the scene in *Johnny Suede* where Yvonne finds Johnny in the coffee shop at the end of the film. As I said, Brad knew the weight of that scene and began preparing at least an hour before. He was sitting in his seat for lighting, we didn't have stand-ins, and the cinematographer just kept lighting and lighting. I finally realised that the guy was running hundreds of feet of cable to light a building ten blocks away, out of focus and barely visible through the window Brad was sitting in front of.

What was that cameraman thinking about? His whole purpose on the film was to provide *vision*, yet he couldn't see Brad sitting there right in front of him, prepared and waiting to do an intensely emotional scene. I was both horrified and fascinated by these random acts of accidental violence, so to speak. It was like the process itself can turn completely against you. And usually, none of that stuff ever gets spoken about.

It sounds like the basis of any number of anxiety dreams.

I've had hundreds of them. That's why the first two acts are revealed to be dreams coming from the fevered brains first of Nick and then Nicole. These are annoying during shooting because the day is usually anxiety-ridden enough but then to waste precious time reliving the whole thing?! You wake up exhausted. And so the entire filming experience is a barely conscious haze. That's partly where the title came from.

Earlier you defined film as "the language of dream". Living In Oblivion *is a film about cinema, and also a film about dreams. The film ends by giving us a glimpse into each character's yearning and aspirations; a snippet of what inspires them: stardom, artistic recognition, regret, power, or even the hunger to just eat the juiciest damn hamburger ever made.*

The films ends, as does every day of shooting, with a long moment of silence as the sound man records the general ambience of the room for sixty seconds. This sound is crucial because it helps smooth out the ambient tone under the dialogue when the film is being edited. The very first time I experienced Room Tone I immediately thought how surreal it was. Everybody stops and just stands in silence, like living statues. You're usually exhausted and the frame of mind you're in is very fertile ground for thoughts both existential and completely human – like "what is my life?" and really, really wanting a hamburger.

To me, both are equally valid. But again; film is so beautiful in the way it can transport you into someone's inner world. And that moment at the end of *Oblivion* is really kind of complex. It is a final, very intimate visit with everyone we've come to know during the film.

Much of the film seems like it is literally being written on the spot. How much of it was improvised?

Actually, very little. There are a couple of moments where Buscemi goes off but all of it was scripted.

How do feel about improvisation in general?

I like it, just as much as I like a really well written scene. But not everybody is a great improviser. Buscemi is one of those rare actors that know how to experiment with a scene but still keep the arc of the entire film in his mind. His rant at the end of Act One was completely improvised. I needed some shots of the crew reacting to Nick's breakdown at the end of the first act, and as these kinds of reaction shots are actually hard to do I had Steve stand just off-camera and come up with real things to yell at the crew. Well, Steve started making up stuff to scream at each crew member individually that was so brilliant I told the cameraman to just turn the camera around and film him. Of course the guy said, "I can't do that; there's no light." And I just yelled, "Do it!"

And we got it. It was a little dark and out of focus yet it was one of Steve's most incredible moments in the film. But the whole shoot was that way. Just as disaster seemed about to crush us, some miracle happened. It felt like whatever demon was stalking me on *Johnny Suede* had somehow gotten distracted and was leaving us alone. We managed to wriggle out of every calamity until we shot the scene of Nick's mother Cora saving his film. I'd originally written it as a long dialogue scene between Rica and Catherine Keener. As we started shooting I could tell instantly it was completely dead. One by one all the crew started quietly leaving the set. But the pressure to get the scene shot was intense. So even though I knew it was terrible I shot the scene as I'd written it.

I was lying in bed that night, exhausted and depressed because I knew this key scene did not work. And somehow I came up with this idea to cut all the dialogue and just shoot Cora coming in, taking the apple and simply performing the scene as she'd seen Tito do it. With the exception that this time she would laugh.

I told Frank Prinzi, my DP, the idea the next morning; thinking he would say yeah, well, we already shot the scene. To my still amazed gratitude he looked at me and said, "That's a great idea. Let's set it up and reshoot it."

And we did. I couldn't believe it. Once again, we'd managed to slip out from beneath the crushing train wheels and keep the film alive.

Independent films are already fraught with anxiety, with dwindling budgets and time limitations, etc. How does having a Hollywood star like Chad Palomino on set affect the actors and crew?

This is something I was very interested in exploring. And it's not a simple answer. Palomino is a star. He is a famous Hollywood actor and no matter how passionate someone is about only being interested in art and integrity, being that close to this image of success has an effect on you. I mean, even Bob the Gaffer takes the opportunity to slip Palomino his script called *Tsunami*. It's an addictive, complexly seductive energy. Nick clearly feels that casting Palomino could help his film. Anybody would feel that way.

So people defer to Palomino and he uses it entirely to his own benefit. You'll often hear an acting teacher say to an actor having trouble in a scene, "You're only thinking about yourself; take the attention off of yourself and put it on the other person." Well, Chad Palomino is all Me, Me, Me! I wanted to put Nick into a situation where he hated this guy but he had to grovel a little bit. Chad's a Movie Star and he needs him. It throws Nick off his game. It makes him doubt his instincts. His integrity goes right out the window.

Throughout Living in Oblivion *we see several intimate relationships that result in disaster for the production, such as Chad and Nicole's regretted one-night stand, Wanda's infatuation with Chad which distracts Wolf, as well as Nick's own affection for Nicole. What's the role of a director when it gets personal on set?*

At the very beginning of the film I set up these two sleepy production assistants preparing the breakfast food table for the arriving crew. One suspects the milk might be bad but they both are so exhausted they just leave it and hope for the best. And it's that tiny, insignificant moment that ultimately results in disaster. Nick misses the best emotional scene from his actors because Wolf has drunk the bad milk and is in the bathroom puking his guts out.

Was there any way that Nick could have known the milk was bad? Is it even his job as a director to oversee the serving of food and coffee? No. But if something as catastrophic as that could happen with sour milk imagine what the complexities of intimate, personal relationships on the set can create. For example, if an actor tense with self-doubt overhears people talking about her dismissively right before a take, or the cinematographer is being tormented by fears his girlfriend is sleeping with the star actor.

It disrupts the flow of communication and creative ideas. It creates confusion and tension. Now sometimes this confusion is caused completely innocently. The results are hard to deal with but at least you don't have to worry that the destruction was intentional.

Other times, it is intentional! There's something about this business that attracts a disproportionate amount of neurotics and nutjobs. But everyone's human. Everyone has weaknesses or vulnerabilities. If you get a group of people working together for long hours, no pay and bad food, conflicts are inevitable. And part of the director's job is to always have his eyes and ears, all his senses actually, keenly attuned to what is going on around him. You're trying to put out fires before they get out of control.

It sounds like you're always on the edge of chaos.

You're right. As soon as you yell "Cut!" everything falls apart until you drag the whole machine up to the next shot and you shout "Action!" Once, while waiting for a shot to be set up, I noticed the sound man whispering intently to his boom operator and pointing to the cameraman. This went on for so long that I went over and asked what was going on. It ends up the cameraman's lighting was making it impossible for the boom guy to position his mike without a shadow in the frame. I suggested that if one light was moved two feet the boom guy could do his job. They moved the light.

Now, was that the director's job? It was to me because I knew how much I had to do that day. That's why Nick Reve is in a constant state of anxiety. Fellini said once that all he asks from crew and actors is that they are *willing*. That's such an amazing word: *willing*. If everybody is willing then you can find a solution to any problem. It means everybody is open to any idea that can potentially benefit the film. It is only when someone becomes unwilling that the trauma sets in.

Speaking of willingness, Living in Oblivion *has a great sense of vibrancy and life to it. It looks like people were having a good time. Were they?*

I think so. On most films it is specified the exact days actors are working. You hire somebody and their agents make it very clear they're only going to be there on the dates in the contract. So you shoot their scenes and you try to get everything you can because they're not coming back.

Well, because of the way *Living in Oblivion* was made, with all the actors being friends and putting up money, there were no dates or restrictions. Everyone was on set all the time. They wanted to stick around and watch what was going on. And I think we all felt that something *was* going on. At the very least, we felt we were making something truthful and different. It was one of the purest cinematic experiences I've ever had. Again, I can't stress this enough: it was just us. There was no one telling us what to do.

That sense of joy and freedom permeated the whole shoot. It completely affected the way I thought about shooting. Some days I'd look over at the group of actors and I'd grab three of them and throw them into a scene just to see what would happen. That kind of spontaneity is rare but so crucial to a film.

And it came from the crew too. You have to remember most of them were working for free. Frank Prinzi was working for less than free; he actually contributed money to the budget. One of his most intuitive ideas was to have a sliver of crescent moon hanging outside the window of the bedroom set with Nicole and Chad Palomino. It added this beautiful touch of whimsy and artifice that brought a sparkle to the entire scene.

And Therese Deprez, the Production Designer, brought her own sense of humour and beauty. Something as simple as making the door Tito walks through in the Dream Sequence cut on an angle brought an immediate comical mystery to the set. It's like a door out of a strange fairy tale, and Therese painted the back of it with a blue and white cloud pattern straight out of Magritte. It was an incredibly deft and inspired touch. It made you not want to leave that world.

The film won the Waldo Salt Award for Best Screenplay at Sundance in 1995. What was that experience like for you?

When I was at Sundance with *Johnny Suede* the reception was so cold it was like being in Siberia. With *Oblivion* something sparked right from the beginning. The screenings were sold out. We had several offers from distributors; the press response was strong. And most of the cast was there to enjoy it. It was an amazing experience; especially watching audiences react to the film. It was the first time it had screened in public. I never took the audience reaction into consideration while editing. Sometimes the laughter was so long and loud whole sections of dialogue got missed. The whole experience was like a dream, really.

The sense that the film now had a life of its own, it was out of your hands and into the world?

Well, it made a little splash. People saw it. Most people don't even know I made *Johnny Suede*; they think *Living in Oblivion* is my first film. It did very well in New York and LA and around the world actually. But not everyone got it. Some guy from the *New Yorker* wrote it was a "one-joke film only for filmmakers". That always puzzled me. Does it mean that *Apollo 13* is only for astronauts?

While at Sundance there were urgent whispers about an award. I met Janet Maslin, the chief film critic from the *New York Times*. She happened to be at one of the sold out screenings and she loved the movie and gave it a great review. I met several financiers who wanted to invest in *Box of Moonlight*. We sold *Living in Oblivion* to Sony Classics. My wife's cousin Hilary got her money back. We did win an award, for Best Screenplay; which I'm very proud of. I worked so hard on making that screenplay seem like it was all of one piece and not just three disjointed stories. I think more I was just proud of the film. It came out of one of the darkest places I've ever been and literally saved me.

CHAPTER FIVE

Box of Moonlight

'It's not where you're going in life; it's how you get the hell out of there.'
— Al Fountain

The numerous accolades *Living in Oblivion* was awarded at some of the most prestigious international film festivals, including Sundance and Deauville, meant that in the mid-1990s DiCillo was a hot property. People now knew who he was; more importantly investors knew who he was. And yet, despite one or two offers from Hollywood, DiCillo chose instead to succeed *Living in Oblivion* with an unlikely follow-up, the gently off-beat rural fable, *Box of Moonlight*.

"I was getting more attention than I'd ever dreamed possible after *Living in Oblivion*," DiCillo admits. "Perhaps I should have used the opportunity to make another crazy urban indie comedy in the same vein. I was certainly tempted. I'd formed very intense bonds with all the actors and it was such an incredible experience on *Oblivion* part of me didn't want it to end. *Box of Moonlight*, as a concept, is vastly different from *Living in Oblivion*; literally worlds apart. And I did think about that disparity. But I'd been trying to make the film for six years. And the Hollywood offers were really rather lame; one was about a happy, sexy prostitute who dies and comes back to life as a shepherd-collie mix. So when a company offered me $3 million to make *Box of Moonlight*, which was my biggest budget to date, I said, 'you know what, I think I'll take that.'"

The film follows the strange journey of Al Fountain (John Turturro), an electrical engineer building a turbine in a remote production facility that will eventually manufacture windshield wipers. Al is a strict and regimented boss whose by-the-book mentality places him at odds with his fellow workers. Even when stripped to his underwear his posture remains tight and rigid as though still encased in his uniform of crisp white shirt and ironed blue slacks. But cracks are appearing in his foundation. He starts having fleeting visions: a glass of water flows backwards into a pitcher, a boy on a bicycle pedals by in reverse. Given his structured nature these images make him distinctly uneasy.

Despite Al's diligent work, news comes through from corporate that the company is pulling the plug on the factory job. While the labourers are happy to accept their bonus severance pay and go home, Al surprisingly calls his wife, Deb, and tells her the job is still going on. During this conversation DiCillo offers us a glimpse of how Al's inflexibility spreads even towards his family. When his son Bobby realises it is his father on the phone he quickly turns off the violent video game he is playing and proclaims to be studying. Al is fooled for a moment. But as he continues to quiz his son on his math tables Bobby's wildly erroneous answers give him away. Al is furious and demands to speak with Deb, insisting she have the child start working with giant, absurdly oversized flash cards.

"I was terrible in math," DiCillo confides. "I actually loved geometry but my brain just could not get algebra or trigonometry. And so, my dad – who was a math whiz – took it upon himself to 'help' me. I had many excruciating encounters with him and flashcards. I made the flashcards Al forces Bobby to memorise in the film gigantic, even to the point where they fall on him and crush him because that's how they made me feel."

This disappointment in his son is the final push that prompts Al to sever the only connection he has (his family) and to grasp this opportunity to step out into this unexpected void of free time. Instead of returning home to Chicago, he rents a car and takes to the road. His journey sees him moving through uncharted emotional territory, a lost weekend in which the shackles of his strict adherence to routine are severely rattled.

Thinking he is courageously venturing into the unknown, Al's journey is actually circular; it is no accident the rental agency is called Circle Rent-A-Car. Like a figure in an Escher print he ends up right back where he started.

"I never trust movies where people have massive life changes," DiCillo observes. "Real change happens in micro-movements. And any soul searching, whether through religion, therapy or drugs, always comes back to the basic idea that revelation always comes from within – not from some outside source. It is always there."

Al's sole destination is an amusement park he'd been to as a kid. But he finds no comfort in the nostalgic expedition. The park has long since been abandoned and has fallen into disrepair. It seems his impulsive journey has come to an abrupt end until he literally runs into Kid (Sam Rockwell) whose car has broken down in the middle of the road.

Dressed curiously in a dingy Davy Crockett costume complete with coonskin hat, Kid is a tangle of unchecked optimism and energy. With relative ease he convinces Al to tow his broken-down car home. Kid's abode turns out to be a mobile home sawn in half and sitting in the middle of the woods. But Kid isn't merely living out some ideal, non-conformist hippy dream; there is something more troubling beneath the surface which the film sets out to explore.

Al Fountain (John Turturro) and Kid (Sam Rockwell) in *Box of Moonlight*

DiCillo sees the two men as the flip-sides of the same coin, with Kid defining everything Al morally and ethically opposes – he's the anarchic antithesis to Al's steadfast, responsible citizen.

"I wanted to present Al with something that would be the most antagonising and disruptive to him," DiCillo says. "Kid doesn't pay taxes; he sells stolen lawn ornaments for income. Compared to Al his life is total chaos. The challenge was for Al to see something of value in this troubled young guy and against all odds find tiny moments of connection."

"Kid is an incredibly lonely and isolated person," Sam Rockwell recalls. "I think what he takes from this connection with Al is the bond with a kind of father-figure or an older brother. There are a lot of poignant moments in the film that I was able to personalise and bring those emotions to the scenes. There was this sense of hero worship there already; John was a hero to a lot of young actors of that time and he was someone I looked up to. So I was able to channel that energy into Kid, because he looks up to Al for that similar kind of approval."

Though he continually disapproves of Kid's irresponsibility, in his company Al gets an unexpected taste of life "off the grid", Including a swim in a secluded, pristine rock quarry, as well as the simple pleasure of tasting a tomato plucked from the vine. But DiCillo dispels the preciousness of these moments by instantly breaking the idyllic tone. The police pull up to the remote tomato field seeking the vandals who are stealing tomatoes. When the cops venture out into the field Kid sneaks into the patrol car and releases the handbrake. As the driverless car picks up speed aiming straight at the backs of the unsuspecting officers, Al is horrified to see Kid cackling with glee.

The car misses its intended victims but Al has had enough. As he gets in his car determined to leave for good his departing words are, "Good luck and I hope you get your life squared away." It is the perfect analogy to what Al considers a responsible life to be, squared away in a box, a coffin of conformity. But Al isn't going anywhere yet; he's lost his car keys.

And thus begins the journey to the heart of the film. As he waits for his new keys to arrive Al takes an unintended detour into Kid's life and the world he inhabits. Despite Kid's facade of comically absurd abandon, Rockwell details an influence behind Kid which comes from some of the darker periods of American history.

"Tom gave me a book on the plight and eradication of many American Indians, and I think it informed the character of Kid with a subtext," the actor recalls. "He is an oppressed figure and he identifies with these people. Also, I had read about a whole group of people in America today who want to live 'Off the Grid' and so that was helpful because the Kid really considers himself to be living this alternative existence."

"Yes, there is a great sense of freedom in Kid living alone in half a trailer out in the middle of the woods," DiCillo says, "but we learn that he's terrified of living in town because there are a few people that enjoy beating the shit out of him. He doesn't live out in the woods because he wants to, but because he has to. He's actually a very troubled, vulnerable and lonely person."

Kid's mortal enemy is a local maintenance worker, Wick (Dermot Mulroney). He and his sidekick, Doob (Mike Stanley) a looming, hulk of man, share an intense aversion to Kid's very essence. Yet, despite Al's protective presence, Kid stumbles into an unavoidable confrontation with the two. The scene erupts into sudden violence that is shocking but thematically inevitable. Al and Kid do not fare well. Back at the trailer Kid collapses under the weight of his emotions and Al is startled to find himself consoling this distraught young man who only a day before was a complete stranger to him. Al's embrace is hesitant and awkward – possibly the first time he's hugged another man in his life. It's an intense moment, immaculately acted by Turturro and Rockwell.

There are numerous similar shifts in tone, yet the film proceeds and unwinds with an unstrained, unified ease. Literally bringing a ray of sunlight, two local women appear at the rock pool, sisters Floatie (Catherine Keener) and Purlene (Lisa Blount). Neither seems concerned that both Al and Kid are only in their underwear. Playing a forest Cupid of sorts, Kid invites the sisters over for a cookout, and it is here, after some chemical courage dispensed by Purlene, that Al Fountain finally steps out of the box.

Catherine Keener recalls Al and Floatie's sexual encounter and why she considers it the catalyst for a possible shift in Al's emotional rigidity. "My character Floatie is almost like a wood nymph," Keener offers. "She has this fairy quality and Al has to overcome this obstacle, and her presence helps him. Al finds himself in this strange place and whatever happens in this forest never leaves this forest and whatever happens between Al and Floatie becomes part of this trip that Al requires to overcome his problems."

John Turturro concurs. "Sometimes you can have an experience which has human ramifications rather than just physical. I think Al was having something more than just purely physical, but he wasn't going to be there forever. I always thought of it as

Fireworks: Floatie (Catherine Keener) and Al get intimate after the 4th July celebrations

something positive for someone like him. It is an encounter with another person in a completely different way from which he is used to."

"It's not just a guy away from home getting his rocks off. He truly makes love with her," DiCillo affirms. "The idea was that something was exchanged between these two strangers who will never see each other again. No one is taken advantage of. The sex is a mutual decision. And really, my only question is, 'Why not?' Nobody is being hurt. In fact, the connection helps both of them."

And this mutually beneficial connection also applies to the central relationship of the film, that of Al and Kid. As Al leaves for home the next day he shakes hands goodbye to Kid. Both seem uncomfortable. DiCillo offers this insight:

"I think they realise they'll never see each other again. I've always been interested in that moment where two strangers meet, share something and then move on. That is what happens in the film. Not every encounter results in a massive life change but in this case two very different people actually came to know each other for a moment. You then learn that Kid orchestrated the entire event. He stole the keys to Al's car and pretended he had no idea what happened to them. Why? Well, to me it was because he was desperately lonely."

Box of Moonlight is an intensely personal film for DiCillo, some of which must come from the fact that Al Fountain is a direct composite drawn of the director's father, Col. Frank DiCillo. "It ended up that Al Fountain became almost a mirror image of my father," DiCillo reveals. "In fact, I had Turturro meet my father to help him understand the character. John took a couple of things from him which brought some interesting colours to Al. It's a little strange for me, even now, to see those elements of my father on the screen. Although his own control and tyranny was much more destructive than Al's, we did use some of it in the film. But my father was apparently oblivious. He saw the film and later told me it was one of his favorite movies of mine."

Turturro explains that meeting the Colonel not only assisted him in drawing upon the influence behind Al's creation, but also helped the actor understand his director that bit further. "After meeting Tom's father I realised you can see pieces of Frank in Tom too, even though Tom isn't that way in his personality. But we all have those remnants of our parents inside of us. Tom talked a lot about his father and from everything he told me I was able to get a real sense of the conflict in their relationship."

Any actor assuming the role of Al Fountain needed to bring a certain sense of power and authority to the character, for despite his personality shortcomings, Al is anything but meek and acquiescent. In Turturro, DiCillo found something more than an astounding acting prowess. The actor's demeanor and physicality reminded him of the powerful screen presence of one of Old Hollywood's preeminent figures of masculine virility and vigor. "John has an unquestioning self-confidence and strength," DiCillo says. "It's actually something that could easily become unyielding and dictatorial. But I knew that Al Fountain needed to have this kind of stature. He couldn't be just an uptight, annoying nerd. To me he could have been Burt Lancaster; stoic but with a real power, a sense of dignity and integrity. When someone like that starts to lean and tip over, then you have an event. If a tiny twig starts to lean, who really cares or even notices? That's why I cast John Turturro. It took a long time to get him to say yes but the wait was worth it. He has an amazing presence and commitment. No matter what role he plays he's a force to be reckoned with."

"I had to get into really good shape," Turturro confirms. "Tom was talking about having a similar appearance to Burt Lancaster, really coiled and tight, and so I put a lot of work into it actually. Tom wanted Al to be tanned and fit; he was very, very specific about how he wanted Al to appear. I think that shows nicely in the film. Al's a regimented guy so I figured that applies to his diet and appearance as well."

Turturro recalls the unconventional approach that DiCillo took in pursuing him for the lead role. "I didn't know Tom personally but I knew of his work. I had seen *Living in Oblivion*, which I thought was a hilarious movie about the film business. I was also aware of his work as a cinematographer. I first heard from Tom when he wrote me this really nice letter about his father and how he thought that I could bring all the contradictions to the character. And he mentioned it was sort of inspired by his father's life." Turturro continues, "I was working on a lot of things at that time but I read the script and I thought it was interesting; I don't think I got it immediately at the time but in the midst of being so busy with so many different things it was the letter that intrigued me, and I kept saying 'ah, I don't know if I can do it' and blah, blah, blah and then we talked about it. I read it again, then we did a reading of it, and that helped a lot. It took me a little while to come along, I have to say. But once I started working on *Box of Moonlight* I realised it was very rich material."

The crucial role of Kid would be one that would prove to be a potential showcase for any young actor. Sam Rockwell envied the part from the get-go. Rockwell had previously provided memorable supporting appearances in Victor Salva's horror film *Clownhouse* (1989), as well as *Last Exit to Brooklyn* (Uli Edel, 1989) and *Strictly Business* (Kevin Hooks, 1991). Rockwell is loaded with vigorous energy and a likeable, adolescent demeanor; attributes which have stayed with him to this day. The actor became the first to be cast in *Box of Moonlight* and remained attached to the project throughout the initial woes of securing financing.

"I was attracted to it because it was an amazing role, a killer part," Rockwell enthuses. "I was just dying to play it; a lot of actors were up for the part. I guess Tom saw the goofball in me and wanted to stick with me. That's why Tom had such a hard time getting funding, because I wasn't a name at the time and he was being forced to

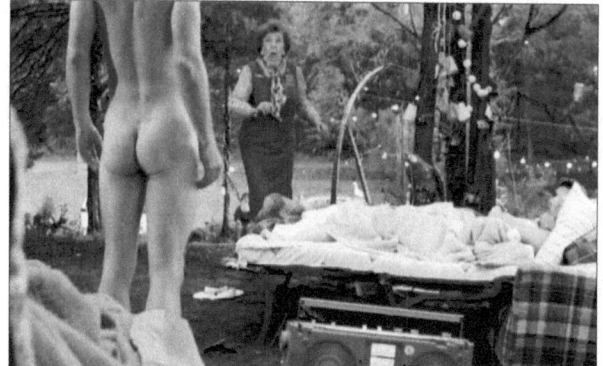

Off the Grid: Kid surprises Doris (Rica Martens)

get somebody else, someone more famous. He had turned down a few actors, Jason Priestly, Ethan Hawke ... I actually auditioned for Tom before, for *Johnny Suede*. I read for Brad Pitt's part. Later on I went to see *Johnny Suede* when it came out, and then I saw *Living in Oblivion* a few years later; so because of those films I was dying to be a part of Tom's work."

Once he had his desired leads DiCillo's next and most challenging task was to ensure that the chemistry between the two was authentic. "The biggest risk making a film about two people forming an intense bond is that the actors playing them need to make you believe the bond," DiCillo reveals. "John and Sam did get along but their acting styles were polar opposites. John is a very concentrated actor. When the camera rolls he is committed entirely; that's what makes him great. Sam's distinction comes from his imagination and his refusal to do anything the same way twice. This can add great life and spontaneity to a scene. Many times I never knew what Sam was going to do. But this style can also pull you out of a scene. I mean, sometimes a bird would fly by and Sam's attention would vanish."

The director continues candidly: "John had some issues with this. He wanted Sam to be more 'responsible'. Sam resisted this and developed a sense that John had too many rules. This was actually really rich ground for them as actors because it almost perfectly mirrored what was going on with their characters. But it also led to some added conflict and tension on the set."

Turturro elaborates: "Sam was with the film a long time, and I like him but you know ... sometimes I think I pushed him a little bit, but then sometimes I'd be protective of him because Tom would be a little rough on him sometimes too. But I have a lot of affection for Sam. I thought he was a very good actor; he was doing a really good job and I remember that certain scenes were more challenging than others.

It took a while for Tom and I to get to know each other," Turturro admits. "Sometimes we had a little friction but that can happen from time to time. When you're making a movie the schedule can make people tense and can do a lot of things to you. But I didn't feel that way throughout the whole of filming. I enjoyed working with Tom; he's an intense guy and I can be that way too. When you're under the pressure of the schedule you have to get to work, but there was a great joy to it and Tom's distinct sensibility is there throughout the whole movie."

DiCillo concurs: "Shooting on location is really, really difficult. After the first two days I was wishing I was back in NYC shooting an entire movie in a tiny apartment. So, yeah, I was feeling the pressure. But I think some of my original awkwardness with John came from the differences in the way we saw the actor/director relationship. He's very proud of his acting instincts and it took a while for him to trust me and allow me to make small adjustments to his performance. It wasn't until we shot the scene where he dances around the fire that he saw the pleasure of what Al Fountain could really be. He kept thinking that it was some kind of joyless character outside of him and that meant he had to lock himself in a box in order to do it. In essence, I was just trying to get him to be himself. If Al was such a constricted and compulsive person then nobody would like him; why would his wife even be with him?"

Shooting the scenes at the rock quarry required the actors to be barefoot. One day Turturro stumbled on a sharp piece of gravel and broke his toe. DiCillo recalls the moment distinctly. "The first words out of his mouth were, 'Goddammit! I knew I should never have taken this part!' To his great credit he went on to finish the scene," DiCillo continues, "but, it bothered me he felt he had to yell so loud the other actors and all the crew heard him."

Tensions reached a peak one afternoon on a deserted country road. In a scene where Al and Kid discuss how to tow his car back to his trailer, suddenly Turturro exploded. "John reached out and punched Sam in the chest," DiCillo reveals, "which of course really disturbed Sam. On some level John was saying to him: 'If you're going to be in a scene with me then be in a scene with me.' There's some truth to that and I can in many ways understand John's frustration. Sam had the script for four years and he'd devised a myriad of tiny actions for each scene. Many of these were brilliant but they took his focus off the other actor in the scene. However, the first rule of acting is that no actor can dictate how another actor should act. And, more importantly, I would never condone using physical force to get somebody's attention. Everything is discussable."

Rockwell confesses that it wasn't an easy task in bringing such a complex performance to Kid. "I was very nervous at the time about having this big role. Tom guided us very nicely. He was all about what motivated the characters emotionally. Tom has training in acting so he knows about the vocabulary of acting and how to achieve a certain kind of unique performance."

One could argue that it is this very hyper-intensity that Rockwell brings to the film that works so deftly opposite Turturro's stoic reserve. Surely the film would have ended up playing differently had the actor reined in his performance under the weight of his nerves?

"It could have," Rockwell admits. "Looking back, I think I could have been a bit more relaxed, but then again, perhaps you're right, if I had been more relaxed it wouldn't have the same energy that it has. It was a case of having the first-day-of-school fear throughout the whole picture; I had that fear pretty much every day on that shoot. I was working with one of my heroes in John Turturro and I also didn't want to disappoint Tom for giving me this big shot. There were two passionate Italian men – Tom DiCillo and John Turturro – and there were strong opinions on the set and I got caught in the middle of that sometimes. John taught me a lot about acting and Tom wrote me this great part, so I wanted to do my very best."

Rockwell reveals that in bringing Kid to life in all of his complexities he was under the influence of several seminal performances from films of the New Hollywood era. "I was originally thinking of a young Gary Busey but then Tom advised me to watch the Errol Morris film *Vernon, Florida*. There's a turkey hunter in the film, and I watched him; and I watched the Michael Cimino film *Thunderbolt and Lightfoot* and studied Jeff Bridges in that movie. I also looked at the character of Joe Buck in *Midnight Cowboy*. Kid was really an amalgam of those characters, and Davy Crockett."

"I did mention *Midnight Cowboy* to Sam," DiCillo confirms. "I wanted him to look at Jon Voight's performance for the idea of somebody who could bring a completely believable innocence and naiveté to an adult role. Voight's Joe Buck looked at the world as if he were a child and there's an element of that in Kid's psyche; it's one of the reasons he lives by himself. He can't deal with the real world; he's like a child lost in this environment he can't fathom."

Box of Moonlight would prove to be another collaborative effort for DiCillo and Catherine Keener. This, their third film together, was a particularly special one for Keener, who plays Al's fragile and slightly dented love interest, Floatie Dupre.

"I loved making *Box of Moonlight* so much!" Keener earnestly enthuses. "I loved playing Floatie. I think she resonated with me more so than the other three characters I've played for Tom because they were sophisticated urban city girls and somewhere in *Box of Moonlight* I found the true me. Jumping off that rock into the water, that was me. Floatie was a little bit more country, and it had more to do with my own childhood and my outlook, my awe of things and how naive I was and still am. She's not about knowing; she's about doing, more along the lines of how I am. I definitely have a soft spot for that character."

In the early-1990s, when most independent directors were establishing themselves in a milieu of hip, fashionable urbanity, whether it's the ironic blue-collar prosody of Hal Hartley's Long Island, the retro-laden nostalgia of Quentin Tarantino's Los Angeles underworld, or Gus Van Sant's hustler paradise of Portland, Oregon, with *Box of Moonlight* DiCillo went unfashionably rural, filming on location in Knoxville, Tennessee. This venture south allowed the director to engage in the physical and

Catherine Keener
as Floatie Dupre

aesthetic challenge of shooting outside of the controlled concrete confines of New York City, that which he is most familiar with.

The shift in tone is immediately evident in the opening credit sequence where the film's spirit rushes in with a sweeping helicopter shot. The film welcomes us into its quasi-realistic world with images of rolling hills and lush green landscapes of a lost and forgotten America. Jim Farmer's score, an indescribable musical mélange spiced with banjo and harmonica, hints at the surreal, whimsical adventure that lies ahead.

"I'd always been interested in getting out into America," DiCillo states. "Because my dad was in the Marine Corps I had moved around this country every two years, from the East Coast to the West Coast; to the South – wherever my dad was stationed. I had some really developmental experiences as a kid growing up in small towns and thought I could draw on those.

Filming in the city tends to really focus you visually," DiCillo continues, "it focuses the eye on the compositions. Shooting in nature is very challenging. It's not like being on a small city street or a set where you can manipulate colour and light to accentuate and exaggerate visual ideas, especially when you're making a low-budget film. You're pretty much restricted to the weather and what you see. If you wanted to shoot a scene on a sunny day and it's cloudy, well, you end up with a cloudy scene. That can be tricky when the whole point of the film is to make the environment Al is in look as inviting and mystical as possible."

Cinematographer Paul Ryan had worked on Terrence Malick's *Days of Heaven* and Robert Redford's *A River Runs Through It*; films celebrated for their natural aesthetic beauty. "That's one of the reasons I hired Paul," DiCillo admits. "I loved the great mood and lyricism he was able to capture with available light. One of my favourite visuals came during a simple shot of Al's car driving through town. I was annoyed at an assistant-director who was rushing me, so just to bug him I dragged an old stuffed chair into the shot, doused it with lighter fluid and right before the camera rolled I set it on fire. It added this amazing element of mystery to the shot. I remember how excited the flames made Paul and how they really pissed off the assistant-director. I like the way the film looks. Considering the budget we had and what we were trying to do I think we accomplished something."

DiCillo continues: "One thing I talked a lot about with my production designer Therese Deprez was this really wonderful tacky, cheesy world of rural America. Whenever we'd have a question about how something should look we'd always remind ourselves of the 'cheese factor'. This enabled us to manipulate reality a little bit. I didn't want the film to look completely naturalistic or precious. I wanted the things that had beauty to be perceived very strongly, almost mythically. The quarry where Kid takes Al for a swim looks almost prehistoric. The woods look almost primeval. Yet when they go into town, the supermarket, the gas station, they all have an over-saturated colour, almost a garishness. There is a strange beauty in the way colours and shapes clash. Some of my favourite experiences shooting a film were on *Box of Moonlight*," DiCillo confesses. "The tomato fight, the opening aerial sequences, all the stuff jumping into the quarry, the strange world of Kid's half-trailer – these were extremely rewarding filmic moments for me."

"I really loved working in Tennessee," Keener admits. "It was great being on that location. Sometimes it can present challenges depending on the individual performer, but for me, I love it, it's sort of a gift. Working with Tom on location, it gives you a whole other perspective on what these experiences can be like and an admiration for what people do in pouring their hearts out, especially when under tremendous scrutiny. I have an especially soft spot for the making of that movie because I saw how hard everybody worked."

Shooting on location also meant a more arduous physical effort on the part of the film's leading man. In some instances Turturro came closer to confronting fears than he'd expected. DiCillo wryly recalls shooting a scene in treacherous snake-infested water, a fact initially kept from Turturro. "Being a city kid John wasn't a strong swimmer," DiCillo relates. "I'd told him we were going to shoot that scene in a shallow river or a mountain stream but we ended up shooting at this abandoned rock quarry that was 350 feet deep. We got him into the water for the dialogue scenes with a lifeguard in a boat just three feet out of camera range. But for the shot of John jumping into the water we had a double for him. John was sitting next to me by the camera as we were lining up the shot. Knowing he was going to have his clothes off a lot in the film he'd worked hard to get in good shape. The double we had looked like John from behind but he also had some rather prominent love handles. I could see John looking at them and getting increasingly uncomfortable. Next thing I know he stands up and says, 'You know, Tom, I think I'll do the shot myself.' So we set up three cameras, John goes to the edge of the cliff and I shout, 'OK, action!' Ten seconds go by, thirty, a minute, and he's still standing there willing himself to make the leap. And finally, he just does it. I had such affection and deep admiration for him at that moment. Here's a guy who couldn't even swim and he jumps forty feet into an almost bottomless rock quarry. Also, I suspect the fact that Lisa and Catherine had both jumped in countless times with no hesitation might have been some motivation. But John's commitment to the part was unshakeable."

After thirty-five days on location the film finished principal photography on budget and on schedule. Five years after he'd written it DiCillo now had his third feature in the can. A brief bidding war for the film had ensued, with Bob and Harvey Weinstein at Miramax making an offer that pushed other buyers out. Then, at the last

Left to Right: Al Fountain (John Turturro), Kid (Sam Rockwell), Purlene Dupre (Lisa Blount), Floatie Dupre (Catherine Keener)

minute, Miramax passed on the film. The film was effectively seen as damaged goods in the eyes of other interested parties, resulting in those other potential distributors walking away. The film sold to a small US distributor at Sundance, but the minimal marketing budget allotted to its release meant the film didn't stick around in theatres long enough to find its audience. The lukewarm critical reception didn't help. Despite the distinctly subversive undertones of the film, it may have been a little too human for a mid-1990s independent scene infatuated with cynicism, post-modernism and ironic bloodshed. DiCillo stands as one of the few maverick directors of that decade interested in defying this trend.

"Few people took the time to try and understand why I made *Box of Moonlight*," DiCillo ventures. "The same critic from the *New Yorker* who said that *Living in Oblivion* was a 'one-note film for filmmakers only' said of *Box of Moonlight*: 'Where's the dwarf when we need him?' It was quickly dismissed as a goofy hippie film, which is the last thing it is. It's not about Kid introducing Al to his sunny world of 'Total Freedom'. In fact, I intentionally wrote a scene of Kid's reality that Al would definitely *not* want to participate in: the moment where Wick beats Kid up. There is nothing flower power about this. There is no 'peace and love' answer to the deep trauma both Al and Kid feel at that moment. It seemed the film came up against a growing fear or reluctance to invest personally in anything real or emotional. That's a little tough for me because it is the only language that I speak."

While *Living in Oblivion* was a masterwork of formalist subversion, seeing DiCillo playing with cinema's traditional modes of narrative continuity and reality, *Box of Moonlight* unfolds in a deceivingly traditional trajectory, wherein DiCillo orchestrates the proceedings with subtle surprise and revelation as he unveils the harsher truths beneath the fairy tale veneer. The film isn't obviously oblique at first glance; DiCillo eases us into it with the tools of classical narrative cinema, but the deeper into Kid's world and fractured psyche we rove, the more the film reveals its intricacies and unorthodox nature with delicacy and nuance.

Al Fountain's particular *ennui* is that of every man who lives and dies by the clock, his journey into the unknown akin to Dorothy's sojourn to Oz. There is an element of danger and peril to Al's personal expedition, yet it ultimately results in a series of small, but significant enlightenments. DiCillo dares to be optimistic in confronting daunting questions about our anxieties and morality, even challenging traditional ideas of loyalty and ethics that we bring to family, work and relationships. The director presents some notions that may disturb a more conservative audience – how many of us use fear to structure a "normal" life of restraint and inner seclusion? Do we want our hero to get away with having an affair while his wife is home minding the kid? How can we embrace our loved ones when we cannot embrace ourselves?

Box of Moonlight is an enchanting, delicately natured yet thematically significant comedic drama illustrative of DiCillo's unique cinematic aesthetic as well as his idiosyncratic personality. Among the film's myriad qualities are the riveting multi-layered performances of the lead duo, as well as the densely rendered and exquisitely detailed rural milieu in which the characters truly come to life. It is DiCillo's quietest film, but also one of his most sincere and intimately personal explorations.

"There is a sense of whimsy to *Box of Moonlight*, but cinema is whimsy," Keener offers. "We get all the tools to craft this magic trick. We go to these dark theatres to experience this trick that the filmmaker is pulling on you, to get you sucked into this fictional world, this illusion. Tom has the power to do this with his movies. His films are grounded in reality but there is an illusion in there that pulls you out of reality just slightly, it's just a little off-real. There is this delicate line and I think it's where Tom gets tickled and that's his reality, that's where he lives and what truly sets him apart. It's how Tom sees things, with this sense of the absurd, or with this sense of humour that's just a little different. It's why I adore *Box of Moonlight* so much! I talk to friends about that film and I hear how much they love it. I always recall how much fun it was to shoot, especially working with Sam Rockwell, Lisa Blount and John Turturro. It was amazing to watch Tom directing that film, he was clearly in love with it, and when he loves something you get caught up in it, it makes it very easy to admit that you love it too."

For Rockwell, his performance as Kid proved to be a pivotal moment, leading to a prolific and critically acclaimed career in both independent and mainstream cinema. "When they screened *Box of Moonlight* at Sundance I was blown away by it. It was a big deal. It literally opened doors for me. It changed my life," he sincerely admits. "While we were at the festival there was an article in the *New York Times* about my work – all this stuff was happening. Other films like *Lawn Dogs*, *Confessions of a Dangerous Mind* and *Moon* have had a big effect on me too, but *Box of Moonlight* really provided a springboard for my career. I'm really proud of it." The actor continues: "When you're making a film that is a little off-kilter you still have to keep it real and Tom is a very good director at keeping his films real while retaining that tilted quality to them."

"Tom got really good performances out of everybody on *Box of Moonlight*," Turturro fondly recalls. "And if you look at his other films, especially *Living in Oblivion*, you can see he got amazing performances out of everybody on that film. I have to say I have always regretted that I never worked with Tom again since *Box of Moonlight*. He certainly got a really good performance out of me. It shows that Tom has a real eye for talent, look at how well Sam has done and how well Catherine has done; he cast them before all of that. I haven't seen the film for a while but I talk to my son about it and I said I would show it to him. It was one of those experiences where I felt like I was in a film that really meant something and where I did something different, and it was Tom who gave me an opportunity to do that. There are a lot of films that I've done that I wouldn't give an interview about, but *Box of Moonlight* is special. When people see it they always tell me they really like that film. It's something I'm really happy to have been part of. It's a performance I'm very proud of."

"*Box of Moonlight* is a strange, contemporary American fable and I had a blast doing it," DiCillo admits. "If we'd had a little more time and money the shooting might not have been quite so intense. But I stepped out into a different way of storytelling and I believe I accomplished something with it. I'm still amazed at the number of responses I get from total strangers telling me the film changed their lives."

* * *

Wayne Byrne: *You had the script for* Box of Moonlight *kicking around for a few years before you got to direct it. Just how far back had the idea for the film developed?*

Tom DiCillo: One day during the editing of *Johnny Suede* I passed some guy selling records on the sidewalk. One album cover that caught my eye was with some martini glasses gleaming in the moonlight. It was a cheesy orchestra mood music thing from the early-1960s called *Moods of Moonlight*. It cost fifty cents, so I bought it. I thought I might use it somewhere in the film.

I took it into the editing room and one of the assistants transferred it to tape and put it in a box. About two months later I was working on a scene and I thought of that music. I said to the assistant, "Where's that box of moonlight?"

We never used the music but something about that phrase stuck in my brain. I knew one day it would be the title of something. The image of actual moonlight somehow being captured in a box, even jokingly, struck me as an interesting symbolic idea.

So you didn't even have the story?

I had only the most basic idea. It was about a guy who was very rigid and structured and who falls out of his comfort zone, but he's courageous enough to take advantage of it. He steps out into this void of free time which is a great risk because most people live their lives in a very strict and ordered way. We take comfort from routine and familiarity.

Were there some personal experiences as a kid that you drew upon?

I had a prolonged juvenile delinquent period that I would highly recommend to everyone. I think it is a crucial part of childhood. As a military kid I moved around the country a lot, mostly to small towns. One day I stumbled with my best friend into this vast tomato field full of ripe tomatoes. We ate about a half a tomato apiece then instantly launched into a tomato fight that lasted for hours. It was amazing. We were so intoxicated by the joy of running madly up and down the rows hurling big, fat tomatoes at each other we didn't see the cops pulling up. When they called out to us over their megaphones we just hit the dirt and crawled down into a ravine. They kept calling down to us to come out. We didn't move an inch. They finally left when it got dark and we were able to crawl out of there.

You ended up shooting in Knoxville, Tennessee. There is something of an off-kilter vibe with the small town, it's anywhere but it's nowhere, and a little eccentric.

I was looking for a slightly fictitious America; one that had a sense of mystery and myth about it – like in the very early days of this country. We got to Tennessee and I saw these run-down towns and cities nestled in landscapes of lush, rolling hills and I was struck by the great contrast it presented. It suggested an America that existed long ago, before the Europeans came over. It had something magical, almost out of *The Wizard of Oz*, but with a slight sense of danger and uneasiness.

Is that America for you?

I think this country has enormous potential for freedom and liberty but it also has something darker that it was born with: a stiff, stubborn resistance and suspicion of anything new and different. The idea was to try and look at both. That's why I had Kid dressed in a Davy Crockett outfit – which he'd stolen. The idea was he represented something about the promise of this country. The problem is that this idea of America has become so twisted and misunderstood by Americans themselves that it has lost its meaning.

How did it feel going back out into that America? Was it the America that you grew up in?

It was, pretty much; which is interesting, because we shot in the south. It's typically a much more conservative part of this country but there were things that deeply impressed me, some charming things about the Southern way of life. For example, the owner of the tomato field lived in a little house at the top of the field. We talked and in a matter of minutes he said, "Sure, you can shoot here. I'm going away for a couple of weeks but I'll just leave the door open. I've got some good video tapes in there; go ahead and watch my TV." He was completely serious. I guarantee you that would never have happened in NYC.

It was genuine Southern hospitality?

Absolutely genuine. On the other hand there was some serious racist tension going on with a few of the locals and some members of the crew. It was very disturbing to me because it was so instantaneous and unquestioned; like nothing had changed since 1865.

I want to ask you about Al and Bobby's relationship, the father/son theme running through the film. I get a sense of intrusion in Box of Moonlight, *Kid intrudes upon Al, but in a constructive way. Al's relationship with his son is more fractured ... did Bobby intrude upon Al's life?*

Interesting observation. Bobby exists in a world that is completely alien to Al. As a child he is the opposite of Al, and this makes Al very uncomfortable. Bobby has needs, he's unsure of himself, he cries; Al doesn't know how to deal with it. And ultimately that was affecting Bobby which would then affect the relationship between father and son. As the years go by the layers of protection and defense get thicker and thicker.

Does Kid act as a form of surrogate son for Al while he is away on his weekend?

Yes, I would say there's an element of that. I just this minute realised something underlying my impulse when I wrote the character of Kid. Basically, he is extremely adept at fucking with Al's brain. He scopes him out immediately and he quickly learns how to keep him off balance – he's very skillful at it. If he does become like a surrogate Bobby it's a very healthy one, because that's what Bobby needs to do. It actually makes him an equal of Al's. That's one of the biggest struggles I had with my father. I never felt that he treated me as an equal.

I do think that what Kid and Floatie do for Al is offer glimpses into another world. He is so blinded, so in a box, and to see these characters that seem to enjoy life despite their problems opens his eyes a little bit. I doubt he's ever met a woman like Floatie; someone working in the sex trade. But she's actually not very good at it and her insecurity forces him to have some real connection with her.

It could be said that Al and Kid are flip sides of the same coin; this brief friendship throws Al out of whack with his routine.

Well, actually that's true. Certainly, you wouldn't want to live your whole life like Al. The guy is so uptight and regimented that his whole life is like an instruction manual. But something of that discipline and commitment is what makes him successful in his job. I tried to show that a series of events had thrown him off balance a little bit. And that is a great state for any character to be in.

How did Turturro like being off balance?
I think he really liked it. He understood the value of a role that allowed him to be confused and bewildered at times. I'd seen him in many films but it was his performance in *Quiz Show* as Herbie Stempel that convinced me he could bring humanity to someone as structured as Al Fountain.

John's commitment was absolute. We'd be in the middle of take and someone's walky-talky would go off and John just focused harder and stayed in the scene. Afterwards he erupted like an enraged bull and I didn't blame him. But he was incredibly professional and solid as a rock.

Killing Time: Al rampages through the empty factory with a BB gun

It is a bit strange to see Turturro as such a pedantic guy. His rigid demeanor comes across in the early scenes with his workers. Then they invite him to play poker and we see he has to practice his banter with them in the mirror.

He needs to practice because he doesn't know how to do it naturally. And on top of that, he overhears the guys calling him an "asshole". That shakes him to the core; especially since he never suspected they felt that way. Hearing that is what sets up his willingness to take his journey.

The Splatchee Lake sequence is quite powerful and emotionally resonant. Everyone envisions a place from their childhood that is untarnished by nostalgia but usually when seeing it again the reality can be devastating, time having taken its toll.

If you are feeling that your life is a little bereft of joy one of the things you do is hold on to the moments that gave you pleasure. Splatchee Lake was one of those places for Al. It was written into the script as a way for him to justify why he's taking this time off. It gives him a place to go; a destination. It's the first step of his journey out into the unknown and I wanted that step to have a little bit of familiarity to it.

So it isn't so much Thomas Wolfe's idea that a man can never go home again?

It's really more about memory. Al's thinking, "I don't know who I am. Why am I seeing water going backwards? Why am I seeing a kid riding a bike backwards?" It is very disturbing to him. He thinks, "Here was a place I was once where I really knew myself and the world. Let's go there and see if I can find some *meaning*." In the haze of his memory he thinks he had a great time there when he was younger, he says that a number of times: "I had a great time there as a kid."

And now it's polluted and crumbling...

It has changed, like he has. It's not that he can never go back there. More it is like someone is saying to him, "You know what, Al, sorry to tell you but it might be time to find some more current things in life that have value for you. Like your wife and your son." Al has a very hard time being in the present moment. He doesn't know the most basic forms of connection.

Neither does Kid really.

Kid can't survive in the outside world; it is literally hostile to him. But part of his isolation is his own doing. It baffled me that some people categorised the film as a kind of "hippie" flower trip. I don't see it that way at all. In fact, if you look the "wisdom" that Kid tries to impart upon Al you see most of it is complete bullshit.

He doesn't know anything about Indians. He claims that the "Crows Feet were the first to tame the wild dog". There is no such tribe. It is either a jumble in his brain

Farewells: After an eventful weekend, Al says goodbye to Kid

of the Crow and the Blackfeet or a convenient misappropriation of the word for lines around your eyes. Nothing that he tells Al about how to live an enlightened life has any validity.

Does Al learn anything from the time he spends with Kid?

I don't know if he learns anything but he certainly allows himself to experience things that are completely new to him. Real change in someone's personality takes years and even then only manifests itself in tiny increments. Al is who he is. He's not going to suddenly turn into some ideal father. But he does bring home some "illegal" fireworks for his son. So the idea was that the box has been cracked open just a bit.

I think Kid learns something from Al.

Al has some pretty solid ideas about how to function in the real world that apparently no one ever taught Kid. When he gets upset with Kid it shows he cares about him and that is something rare for Kid. The same thing happens with Al and Floatie. She's a phone-sex operator who has a severe inferiority complex. Partly it's because of a large birthmark on her cheek. But Al never mentions it. In fact, it doesn't seem to bother him at all. When he makes love with her he seems genuinely interested in a mutual give and take.

The soundtrack to the film is wonderfully eclectic. One of my favourite moments in the film is the montage sequence where Kid is towing Al in his disabled car. You have a great sequence of music where Wall of Voodoo's 'Mexican Radio' segues into Peter Murphy's 'Cuts You Up'.

The idea of Al finding someone else's mix tape in his rental car gave me a whole range of styles to play with. I credited it to some guy named "Eddie" whom we never meet. I just put some of my favourite music on there. That's why there's this lush, mysterious surf instrumental called 'The Wayward Nile' by the Chantays along with tracks by Nick Cave and Wall of Voodoo. It was a great way to utilise actual music and have it serve as a score.

The helicopter shots really accentuated that feeling of freedom and soaring through that beautiful wideopen countryside.

Getting those shots was a miraculous accident. I knew I needed them in order to open up the film. But on the day we were to shoot a storm blew in for a week. You can actually see it in several muddy scenes around Kid's trailer. Suddenly the sky cleared. It was on a Sunday and it was our one day off but we grabbed the camera and took off in the helicopter about four o'clock in the afternoon.

The camera was fixed underneath the helicopter and I was sitting in the back seat looking at a little monitor. As we flew I'd say, "OK, now go down! Now go between those trees!" And the pilot would execute the move instantly with amazing fluidity and precision. He was a kind of whacked Vietnam vet. Just for laughs he'd fly straight at a mountain until I thought we were going to crash right into it. But the light was just incredible. The rain had cleared the air and the afternoon sun was like this rosy orange sherbet dripping over everything. I was in a state of absolute ecstasy. It was like a dream. I simply could not believe we were getting this footage.

That was one of the more magical moments I've had making films. When things like that happen you just have to sit back and say, "Ok, someone is smiling upon us now," because you couldn't have planned the shot like that. It was completely accidental; the weeks of rain, the break in the weather. And those shots, especially the one that opens the film, set the kind of mysterious, slightly magical tone of the whole movie.

Not every day of shooting was quite so magical was it?

No, and when the bad things happened they struck with a power that almost crushed me. It might have been being away from home for so long, or the exhaustion. We were shooting six-day weeks which I will never do again. We shot for five weeks with only five days of rest.

But every shoot has its own nature. And once it's established it is very hard to change it. This one had a sense of unpredictable incompetence that was relentless. We shot all the underwater scenes in an outdoor swimming pool. The weather that day was cold and rainy. At one point I noticed all the actors shivering in their wet bathing suits. They all looked miserable. Then I saw the entire wardrobe team sitting wrapped in down coats and scarves. I asked them to get some coats for the actors. They said there weren't any. I said, get some sound blankets. They said they're all wet. So I had the DP set up his biggest light at the end of the pool and all the actors stood under it to keep warm. Steam was coming off of them but they were laughing together now and I managed to salvage that joy from them I needed for the scene.

The worst thing happened just as we started all our night shooting around Kid's trailer. Shooting all night is like entering a strange twilight zone where you are out of touch with the entire world. At about 7pm I walked up to a camera assistant and asked jokingly, "So, do we have enough film?" Next thing I know there is this very tense silent huddle by the camera truck and someone comes up to me with the news that actually there is *not* enough film. Someone had forgotten to order it. I kicked a tree so hard I almost broke my foot.

I'll never forget having to walk up this long hill to John Turturro's trailer and break the news to him. Just an hour before I'd sat there assuring him there would be no more interruptions, no more abbreviated takes. Now I had to tell him for the entire night we would be forced to shoot with only short ends; bits of rolls left over that were two to three minutes long. I think my utter sense of dejection affected John. He was a prince. We worked that entire night and he never complained once.

I'm sorry for asking but how could someone forget something as basic as ordering film?

That question was never answered, and that only freaked me out more. Because you're right; if something as basic as that could happen well then, nothing was secure. Anything could happen. And honestly, when you start to think that way it makes you very uneasy and it's hard to dig yourself out.

Did you?

I had some help. My wife Jane came down for a few days. She instantly picked up on the heavy vibe permeating the set. And before she left she pulled me aside and said, "You know, Tom, your mood, although somewhat justified, is affecting everybody. Whether you like it or not, you are the captain of the ship. People are looking to you for guidance, for a way to continue, for a purpose. No one wants a captain who looks like he wants to jump overboard."

Did things change after that?

Actually, they did. It was still a tough shoot but an element of heaviness was taken away. Like the scene of everyone dancing around the fire in the middle of the night. It was about 5am and we were rushing to finish before the sun came up. I put this great thumping Mexican-flavoured surf song in the boombox and just cranked it. The soundman was furious because it meant that any actually spoken dialogue, or sounds made during the scene would have to be looped since the track was saturated with the music. But I didn't give a shit. I wanted the actors to really be able to cut loose. And I remember standing deep in those Tennessee woods, watching in amazement as John, Catherine, Sam and Lisa Blount just gave over completely to the scene. It was very surreal and deeply satisfying to see them all dancing through the trees.

It was certainly a wonderful surprise to see Al Fountain letting go like that. He's actually a good dancer.

He is. And he's very, very funny. If I have any regret it's that I couldn't have found a way for him to use more of that part of himself; it could have been very useful for Al. It's a lesson, for me really. Al is pretty much shut down; he's shut down from his wife, from his son and from himself. But that doesn't mean he's a robot. He's still human and I think a little more of John's own humanity would have helped open the character up to people.

Do you think it was a tricky move having Al being so alienating towards his wife and son?

Yes. And again, I take responsibility. That is why this job is so hard. You have to be so clear all the time and then on top of that be willing to engage in very difficult and complex discussions with the actor for as long as it takes to get them to see what you're thinking. Bottom line is, if you question why Al's wife loves him it throws the whole film out of balance. Even my father, who this is based on, has moments where he's very charming and appealing.

When the film was finished you hired a composer who you ended up falling out with; what attracted you to him in the first place, why not Jim Farmer this time around?

I was feeling the urge to get more specific with the score. As much as I love Jim and his sensibility, I felt that the films could use more musical cohesion. I wanted a score to be a force drawing things together, giving it shape and emotional identity.

Like what a classical composer would do?

To a degree, yes. It was a painful discussion telling Jim I was going to try a different composer. I know it hurt him and I did not feel good about that. But he was very gracious, which was part of why I liked working with him so much. So I tried someone else. Egon Friske. He had done some other scores and was well known in the independent world; he was a performer, sort of a celebrity and I'd known him for years.

What do you think contributed to things going so wrong?

I just don't think he was the right person for the job. Whatever your opinion is of *Box of Moonlight*, the fact is it is a very human story driven by simple and basic human emotions – like joy, like pleasure; like loneliness and the desire for connection. Unfortunately, all the music Egon wrote was oppressively sour and gloomy; like someone strung out on heroin, which he was.

Nevertheless, I called him one night and said, "I just want you to know you're doing a really great job and I appreciate it." There, that's part of the thing Billy Wilder talked about; the things you have to do and say just to try and keep the film alive. Because, the truth of it is he wasn't doing a great job and I didn't appreciate it and the only fucking reason I said that was because we'd paid him a lot of money and I needed to get my film scored.

He said to me, "Yeah, I am doing a great job. The hardest part is I'm coming up with all this great stuff and I just give it to you." I said, "What do you mean you're just giving it to me?" He said, "It's like a gift, it just comes to me and something about giving it to you really bothers me."

That's what I mean about this business attracting more psychotics than any other profession on the planet. I went all the way to the mix blindly thinking I could somehow salvage Friske's dreary score. But it all came crashing down when I realised it was beyond saving. It was killing the film. So I fired Egon Friske and called Jim Farmer.

Did Friske get to keep his money?

Every cent. And I didn't use a note of his music. Tom Rosenberg, my producer at Lakeshore Entertainment, couldn't believe that I had even hired him. I was intensely grateful to Tom for trusting me and even coming up with a small amount of extra money to pay Jim. Still, it was a weird, disorienting time. We had to just shut down for a month. And it was back to me going down to Jim's little studio which was basically just his computer, a keyboard and a couple of guitars. Jim absolutely understood the emotional needs of the film and he really came through with a wonderful score that had this beauty and mystery, and that crucial touch of whimsy.

Do you always get so involved with your scores?

It all depends. I'm more than happy to just sit back and let someone amaze me. That's what you strive for. You don't want to tell someone what note to play and where. But as the writer and director I have a sense of the strengths and weaknesses of the film. Sometimes you realise that maybe you just missed a colour or emotion in a scene; or that the meaning is not quite clear. That's where I see the power of music as almost a final stage of writing the film. It's the last chance you get to imbue the film with more *meaning*. But I'm not suggesting that I use music to fake something, or create something that isn't there. I'm only saying that a sound or series of notes carefully slipped in can touch something slightly subdued in the film and bring it to life.

Not every composer likes to have the director being so involved. But with Jim, and later with Anton Sanko on *Delirious*, their own egos were so assured that they allowed me into their playground, so to speak. And I cherished that gift. I say without question that in each case the scores were entirely the work and creation of both of them; they just let me poke around a bit.

The film screened at some of the most prestigious film festivals around the world. What was the response to the film at those screenings?

To my astonishment the film got accepted into the Venice Film Festival. This is generally held to be the second most influential festival after Cannes. *Box of Moonlight* had just been invited to Locarno, where *Johnny Suede* had won Best Picture several years earlier but I felt it would be more of a step forward to try for Venice. When the head of Locarno heard I was graciously passing he was so incensed he said to me in a seething Swiss accent, "If you sink your feelm vill get into Wenice you must still beleef in Santa Clowze!!"

Look, I never believed in Santa Claus, but I couldn't help wondering why he so desperately wanted the film for Locarno if he felt I was such an idiot for thinking it could get into Venice. The fact is; the film was accepted to Venice. And I sat through a screening in front of about 2,000 people in this magnificent Italian movie theatre. The film was projected on a huge screen and it looked incredible but the audience was completely silent throughout the entire screening. And I was drenched in sweat, thinking, "My god, this film is an absolute failure." Then the film ended, the house lights came up and the next thing I knew the entire audience was on its feet giving me a standing ovation.

The Venice audience really got the film and especially appreciated Turturro's performance. There was pressure to get him to fly in from New York because there were strong rumours he was a real candidate for Best Actor. I called him from outside the theatre. He sounded a million miles away but there was no mistaking the real pleasure in his voice, not just for himself but for me personally, and for the film.

I thought it might be a turnaround moment for the film. But it wasn't. Nothing really changed. Very few people saw the film and of those very few understood it.

CHAPTER FOUR

The Real Blonde

'Sometimes it just feels like the world is getting stupider and stupider.'
– Mary

Tom DiCillo's fourth feature film, *The Real Blonde*, is an inspired ensemble piece; a thought-provoking dramatic comedy and sharply written battle-of-the-sexes in which the lives of several main characters intersect throughout their search for meaning in their professional and personal lives. DiCillo intimately examines the dynamics of relationships that are complicated by love, success (or lack of it), sexual politics, identity and ego. Never one to prop his characters up on a moral high horse, DiCillo portrays flawed everyday people whose integrity and sense of self are severely tested throughout the film.

The Real Blonde centres on Joe (Matthew Modine) and Mary (Catherine Keener), an unmarried, childless couple fighting the survival game in NYC. Joe is a struggling actor waiting tables for a living, while Mary works as a make-up artist for a high-end fashion photographer. The difference in their income is becoming a sore spot for the both of them. Joe is thirty-five, well past the age of being 'discovered.' Yet he still resists seeking more lucrative acting jobs, like soap operas, because he considers them crap, hack work; "not real acting".

Mary has respected his choice and sympathised for years but the strain is beginning to show. And when Joe brings up the idea of having a child, the tension peaks. DiCillo uses this theme to structure the film into three movements, each closing on sharp, complex arguments between Joe and Mary about sex, money, children and the unspoken chasm of where their lives together might be heading.

DiCillo contrasts their domestic identity crisis with the largely sexual escapades of Joe's best friend Bob (Maxwell Caulfield). Bob is a handsome leading man on a daytime television soap opera called "Passion Crest". His looks and confidence attract him to many women but underneath his cocky surface is a strange compulsion that inspires the film's mockingly serious title. Bob is on a quest to sleep with a woman who is truly a real blonde. It is an absurd quest and DiCillo frequently lets us know this. But it reveals a dark, complex aspect to Bob as well as alluding to the themes at the heart of the film: illusion, identity and reality.

While the film is on the surface a romantic comedy, DiCillo uses the genre to craft a satire on the entertainment industries of television and fashion – cultural institutions that feed off the public's appetite for illusion and artifice. In so doing, DiCillo digs into the struggle of those trying to find success in these treacherous, elusive worlds while also attempting to preserve their integrity.

Matthew Modine recalls the qualities that attracted him to the role of Joe Finnegan: "When I met Tom I could feel his own struggle and the personal pains that come with being a filmmaker. What I understood deeply was Joe's desire to maintain a sense of self. Dignity, pride; in an industry or business that is ultimately about, at its most base, tits and ass."

"I was an admirer of Matthew's work," DiCillo affirms. "I particularly liked him in *Short Cuts*. Because of the bigger budget my financier, Lakeshore Entertainment, was pretty insistent on casting names. So I met Matthew, we talked about the part and I felt he had a strong connection to Joe. We offered him the role and that was that."

Casting his leading lady didn't quite work out so smoothly. "The biggest battle I had," DiCillo continues, "was over Catherine. I'd written the part for her but Lakeshore wanted me to cast names like Nicole Kidman or Julianne Moore. I knew no one could play the part like Catherine but Lakeshore wouldn't approve her. I was in agony. Every night I'd lie awake asking myself, 'Is this what it takes to move ahead? Rejecting all the wonderfully talented people I've worked with who actually helped get me to where I am?'" Tom Rosenberg at Lakeshore was particularly resistant but DiCillo kept pushing. Finally, Rosenberg relented, saying he could cast Keener on two conditions. DiCillo was instructed to tell Keener that she needed to commit to a six-week workout regimen with Rosenberg's personal trainer as well as consult with a "professional make-up artist" of Lakeshore's approval.

DiCillo was elated. At long last he was free to cast the actor of his choice. Still, he hesitated calling Keener with the good news. He went back again to Rosenberg, asking him to reconsider his conditions. The Lakeshore exec refused to budge; it was the trainer and the make-up artist or no Keener. Desperate to get his first choice in this crucial part, DiCillo finally picked up the phone and started to dial Keener.

"Then I thought of Catherine," DiCillo says. "I imagined her hearing the words I was about to say to her and I knew there was no way I could make the call. What actress could ever commit to a film knowing the producers were questioning the way she looked? Also, it would have destroyed our friendship." DiCillo hung up and made another call instead. "I called Tom Rosenberg and said, 'That's it. I've put stars in every other role. I'm casting Catherine Keener, without your trainer and your make-up

Catherine Keener plays Mary in *The Real Blonde*

artist.'" DiCillo continues, "I don't know; maybe he heard the craziness in my voice but he kind of laughed and said, 'OK, Jesus fuckin' Christ, you can cast her!'"

DiCillo's persistence paid off. Keener once again excels with an ebullient, sparkling performance that balances shrewd pragmatism and fortitude with her delicate, enchanting femininity; traits which mark her as one of the most remarkable breakout stars of the 1990s independent movement. With Mary, Keener informs the role with a required practicality, willfulness and passion, yet skillfully never renders Mary as truculent or resentful. There is an inherent hope and optimism in Keener's countenance that belies the heavy load the character bears across her shoulders.

"Mary was a really great role," Keener enthuses. "I had personal reasons for wanting to play this part, but I also think that, artistically speaking, it was appropriate. Tom writes for women beautifully, it's just immediate. When you work with him you realise that he has a great deal of respect for women and that's important to me."

Maxwell Caulfield chuckles at his being cast in the role which coincidentally reflects his own experience, having waited tables while a struggling actor before finding success in television soap operas such as *All My Children* and *The Colbys*. "Tom and I actually both worked for the same catering outfit in NYC but we never met each other," the actor recalls. "They hired all these pretty-boy actors in New York, as long as we had tuxedos to pass ourselves off as waiters. We basically sauntered around with canapé and champagne and were often hit on by these society women who were there with their older, richer husbands."

Caulfield brings a crucial charm and flamboyant decadence to Bob, a deeply troubled character underneath his easygoing demeanor. Straying from his girlfriend, the faux-blonde model Sahara (Bridgette Wilson), Bob seeks out his elusive holy grail in his "Passion Crest" co-star, Kelly (Daryl Hannah).

Filming the soap opera, Passion Crest: Kelly (Daryl Hannah) and Bob (Maxwell Caulfield)

"I love the way Maxwell brought this sense of ease," DiCillo states, "making it seem like Bob could skate through anything. To me, Bob has got a lot of potential. He's attractive, charismatic, intelligent, but deep inside there is something missing. What is it about him that makes him feel he has to conquer every woman he meets? It's a ridiculously impossible task and one that makes him completely alone. He gets no happiness from it. He likes to devour things. That's his way of dealing with the mass of turmoil and confusion inside him. Kelly knows exactly how to turn him into a helpless infant. That's where Daryl Hannah really tapped into something personal. She is amazing in those scenes. Sex is a very practical thing for Kelly. She's extremely knowledgeable about how to get what she wants with certain men. She knows, especially with Bob, that by moving away from him he will want her even more."

The film's three main arguments between Joe and Mary crackle with sometimes brutal honesty. Keener offers an insight into her process of keeping it authentic, rendering her character all the more intense by evoking real-life stresses and strains when shooting scenes that called for many personal insults to be hurled back and forth between the actors,

"Matthew and I really relied on each other for shooting those heavy scenes of us arguing," Keener recalls. "We knew we could go as far as we needed to for the scene and it would still be okay between us. I didn't have to worry about hurting his feelings if I inadvertently said something stupid while being in character. That happens in real arguments; it's not scripted, you say stupid things and then you think 'How can I take that back?' ... you can't."

"A real argument is an intricate series of developments, with specific moves and counter-moves," DiCillo says. "I love listening to people in a real argument. Their dialogue is riveting. Someone says something to attack and the other person has to recover and instantly think of a response that hits just as hard – or harder. A real argument is like striking a match in a fireworks factory."

To see Joe's quandary from Mary's point-of-view is to see a different picture of their domestic and financial dilemmas. Joe's petulant inability to face basic adult responsibilities on a practical level makes him almost entirely dependent on Mary. This conflict becomes more complicated when it is taken into account that Mary perhaps loves her man for the very reasons that make him a liability in the first place. It is a debate over Starving Artist vs. Dependable Provider. What perhaps initially attracted Mary to Joe (artistic personality, boyish demeanor, good looks, a sense of abandon) is now straining against the steel edges of time and reality.

"I wanted to tell that story from both sides," DiCillo says. "From Joe's side, he believes he's a good actor and he doesn't want to give up. But Mary is equally justified in thinking, 'He's talented, but what's our future? Why do I always have to be the responsible one?' She's right. If a disaster hit she's the one who would have to handle it financially. Everybody at some point wants to feel that somebody can protect them – not all the time but at least once in a while. And all of this is intensified when both people really love each other."

A test of Mary's loyalty to Joe is presented in Doug (Denis Leary), Mary's self-defense instructor. He charms his female class with a prepossessing demeanor, his virility and vanity. Doug is all that Joe isn't: confident and successful. Behind Doug's benign veneer lurks a mighty ego, one which offers him an advantage over the demoralised and vulnerable women in his class; especially when their guards are down. Mary very nearly falls for his calculated maneuvering; she is, at this stage, at a low ebb in her relationship with Joe. Communication has broken down save for the basic survivalist questions of "do you have your half of the rent?" and the customary "how did the audition go?" which of course is a thinly-veiled "will you be getting paid this week?" It is therefore not thoroughly surprising that both halves almost venture into foreign sexual territory. These other partners offer them an escape, an illusory moment away from confronting that which is very much real, to address the cracks in their relationship.

Keeping it real informs the whole film. A key scene takes place between Joe and Bob late in the film. Joe feels his life is going nowhere; he humiliated himself by taking a part as an extra in a Madonna video and was further humbled by being fired from it. Meanwhile, Bob's career is taking off. During the scene the two men keep trying to keep their ego balloons afloat with results that resonate in tragic silence. Joe boasts that Madonna actually called him and even pulls out the crumpled piece of paper with her number on it that he's been carrying around with him for weeks. Bob laughs and tells his friend that it was actually him who asked some girl to call Joe and say she was Madonna. The entire facade of Joe's naïve hopefulness collapses on screen before our eyes.

Caulfield recalls a moment of DiCillo's guidance that helped craft the scene. "Matthew and I were having trouble making the scene work. I was playing all the darker shades and making choices that weren't informing the scene with the colour that Tom was after."

DiCillo explained to the brooding actor: "You're playing the guilt and the awkwardness. Go the other way. Make a positive choice about how great your life is now and

Madonna body double, Tina (Elizabeth Berkley), takes a break between shooting the music video

see where that takes you." This shift in focus awakened Caulfield to a different perspective on this complex moment. "Tom's words made both Matthew and I come alive," Caulfield admits, "and suddenly the friendship between us was reignited in that very brief scene. It was now infused with a lifeforce which up to that point was absent because both of us had been going at it from a darker place. As a result the scene has a wonderful ebullience that counterbalanced the underlying pathos to it that ended up making it one of my favourite scenes in the film."

Joe's struggle to find balance between realising his dreams and survival in the world resonate with several other lead characters in DiCillo's films. DiCillo seems to be saying that you require immense passion and sensitivity to be a great artist but in the real world those very necessities are what make it almost impossible to survive. "Integrity is not necessarily a virtue in today's world," Modine says, reflecting on Joe's moral dilemma, "Joe has integrity. Agreeing to take a job in a music video was not a goal of his."

At the Madonna video shoot on which Joe has landed a part, the Queen of Pop herself turns out to be nothing more than a body double played by Tina (Elizabeth Berkley). If we can't trust our false idols, who can we trust? Joe is momentarily fooled, spellbound by both Tina's intense beauty and the striking illusion she offers.

The symbolism of the Madonna music video is playfully satirical. Like the scenes in the fashion studio where Mary creates fake bruises to distract from Sahara's real black eye, its impressions are sexy, decadent, subversive and a little cheeky, but most of all, striking in their presentation. One image was distinctive enough to become the poster of the film; a pop art rendering of Elizabeth Berkley as Madonna in a polka-dot bikini.

Working with Lakeshore Entertainment and Paramount Pictures, *The Real Blonde* is DiCillo's first and only film to be handled by a major studio. Having been vehemently – and successfully – independent in spirit and in aesthetic on his previous three films, DiCillo would be permanently altered by this association with the Hollywood machine where marketing is based upon test scores and corporate unanimity.

Caulfield considers this process with bewilderment: "The studios use these test audiences to determine the fate of the film, and it's terribly brutal for the director. If

Erotic reflections: Bob (Maxwell Caulfield) satisfies his quest for a real blond at a peep show

the scores don't come in well and the early word from the press is not strong the studio starts to back-pedal furiously in terms of its commitment to the picture, the number of prints it puts in circulation, and the advertising dollars."

It was this industrial mentality that compromised DiCillo's early cut of *The Real Blonde*, which according to the original script was defiantly and humorously more subversive. A notable scene that was actually filmed but later omitted at the whim of studio executives who deemed it as far too controversial for Middle America saw Bob return to a porn-shop peep show hoping to witness a real blonde. "Beautiful ... like Madonna", the proprietor of the store informs Bob who enters the booth to see a large, middle-aged woman reclining in an attitude of depression and bored, professional indifference.

Caulfield recalls shooting the scene: "We went to a real peep show and there they had a woman as you just described to me: large, middle-aged and unkempt. It struck me as having that wonderful irony that marks Tom's films. But the scene didn't make it into the final cut of the film, unfortunately."

Another scene regrettably discarded with was the hilarious and surreal dénouement that saw Bob and Sahara getting married. In the scene Bob is enraptured to see that Sahara is really blonde. Almost blinded by the sight, Bob wakes from this dream to find real brunette Sahara making breakfast. He becomes furiously agitated at her repeatedly asking him how he likes his eggs.

"Tom crafts these films very painstakingly and very meticulously," Caulfield continues, his voice informed with indignation, "and to have some integral parts of the film cut by forces beyond him confounds me. Omitting these scenes did something to my character's arc and removed a unique ingredient from the film."

DiCillo considers this to be part of the dance between an independent director and a major studio. "I knew what I was facing going in. I wasn't innocent or naive. I felt the give-and-take was part of the battle and although I was compromising by having scenes omitted, I was still winning because the best scenes were still in. But the compromise battles started right from the beginning."

A few weeks before principal photography the studio suddenly insisted that to save money the entire film had to be shot in Canada. "I fought very hard on this one,"

DiCillo affirms. "This was a script I wrote specifically about a city I live in, a city that I know intimately and I'm being told I can't even shoot here?! I looked at a couple of locations in Toronto that were supposed to be 'New Yorkish' and they looked so unmistakably Canadian I knew I couldn't shoot there. I finally worked out a deal where all the exterior scenes were shot in New York in a week."

And why was DiCillo so adamant about that? "The exterior scenes really give the film a sense of place," the director states. "I think audiences get confused and uneasy when they don't know where they are. It was incredibly exciting shooting on the NYC streets. You get such life and drama in every frame. People were watching the scene where Catherine Keener has a fantasy revenge on some jerk that's harassing her on the street. At the end of the take a whole crowd of people just erupted in cheers."

The Empire State has certainly given birth to a variety of filmmakers who craft their films around the city that has shaped their perception of the world, from Martin Scorsese to Spike Lee and Woody Allen. Utilising his three decades as a resident of Manhattan in combination with the grace and style of his own cinematographic eye, DiCillo gives us in *The Real Blonde* a bustling, wide-open, lushly rendered Manhattan in sharp contrast to the derelict and gritty world of *Johnny Suede*.

"This is a very intense city," DiCillo says. "The only movie I've seen that even comes close to touching the acid-trip electro-shock impact of NYC is *Midnight Cowboy*." The influence of Schlesinger's film is certainly apparent in all of DiCillo's urban films, from *Johnny Suede* through *The Real Blonde* and later *Delirious*. These are works of a filmmaker still awed by the possibilities of shooting on the vibrant streets of his adopted hometown.

"In New York people's lives are always intersecting," DiCillo observes. "I once saw the same complete stranger three times in one day, in three totally different places. Out of millions of people, I ran into the same stranger three times. I put an element of this in the intersecting lives of the characters in *The Real Blonde*. The energy of New York inspires me. This is a city where people are literally pressed together. Basic human drives and instincts are right on the surface. And because of the city's structure they are forced into sharp focus, thrown in your face. It makes what people do much more immediate and dramatic. I couldn't have imagined shooting this film anywhere else. It's a battle I'm very glad I won."

The Real Blonde ends on a note of fragile resolution for Joe and Mary. While many of the other main characters have spun off into new tangles of delusion and dysfunction something real flickers back to life for Joe and Mary. While not offering a clear resolution or direction for them, DiCillo focuses instead on something simpler; their genuine love for each other. It has persevered. DiCillo notes this briefly, values it, and moves on.

The release of *The Real Blonde* brought DiCillo once again to Park City, Utah for the 1998 Sundance Film Festival. Caulfield recalls promoting the film on the most prestigious of festival circuits: "We went to Sundance with the film, the whole cast. At that point Paramount appeared to be behind the film, and we were opening night in Park City, where Sundance really gets cooking. With Tom being something of an uber-Sundance director we had *Vanity Fair* taking our pictures and the whole experience had that kind of rush."

But the rush was short-lived. Audiences and critics seemed perplexed by the film. Caulfield continues: "Perhaps what happened with *The Real Blonde* was that the die-hard indie crowd had thought that Tom had sold out – there were so many A-list actors there for our film – they could see that this time he had more money. *The Real Blonde* was perceived to be too much of a mainstream film for Tom's audience, or for the Sundance audience of the time."

Caulfield's speculation brings up the question of the film's desired market. Even without the rawer elements that were in the earliest cuts of the film, *The Real Blonde* remains an adult film, thematically speaking. The seeming problem for a major studio is finding ways to successfully market a film to such a demographic when the most valuable audience is the teenage audience. DiCillo's comedy is subtle, biting and more refined. It tackles the complex tangles of gender equitability, career quandaries and domestic politics.

It is possible to argue that commercially viable adult cinema was snuffed out at the dawn of the 1980s, after Michael Cimino's troubled epic *Heaven's Gate* effectively killed off the New Hollywood movement, an auteur-led period of American film instigated in 1967 with *Bonnie and Clyde* and *The Graduate*. DiCillo shares the same auteur sensibilities as the best writers and directors of the New Hollywood – Robert Altman, Milos Forman, Mike Nichols, Buck Henry, Paul Mazursky, Hal Ashby – satirists and dramatists who worked within a social-realist milieu that was shot through with an absurdist comedic filter with an empathy for human frailty.

Why any studio could have imagined selling a watered-down version of *The Real Blonde* to a broader audience is perplexing. It is a complex and textured film which ruminates, albeit in a humorous context, on the intricacies of deep relationship issues, moral and ethical concerns, unfulfilled careers and conflict over having a child. The youngest of the ensemble cast, Bridgette Wilson, as Sahara, was twenty-four years old at the time of production; there were no teenagers selling this film to other teenagers. The film is also littered with a superb supporting cast of faces from pop and film culture such as Christopher Lloyd, Buck Henry, Marlo Thomas, Dave Chapelle and Kathleen Turner. Steve Buscemi also appears, delivering a hilariously self-aware cameo reprising his character Nick Reve from *Living in Oblivion* who is now directing Madonna music videos; same leather jacket, but with fashionable dangling earring and a stylish haircut.

Catering boss Ernst (Christopher Lloyd) instructs Joe (Matthew Modine) at work

What made the travails of cutting his scenes and going up against the bureaucratic adversity even worse for DiCillo is the fact that Paramount eventually released the film on the East and West coasts only, then dumped the film after a couple of days. Devastatingly, DiCillo learned of this on the Sunday afternoon of its opening weekend via two phone calls from top-tier Paramount executives. The first came from Sherry Lansing, then-President of Paramount Pictures, ringing to confirm her support of the film and the company's contentment with how it was performing on its opening weekend. DiCillo was ecstatic, for all of one minute. No sooner had he hung up and begun to celebrate when the phone rang once more.

DiCillo describes the scene, "This time it was Rob Friedman, Paramount's Head of Distribution. He says, 'Hey, Tom. I just want to tell you how sorry we are about your film.' I said, 'Wait a minute, I just got a call from Sherry saying…' He says, 'Right. Well, that was essentially a courtesy call. We're pulling the film from all theaters on Monday.'"

After all was said and done, Middle Americans never did get to see the supposedly safer, pedestrian version that the studio imagined they could sell to them. "It was a very difficult time for Tom," Keener wistfully recalls. "The stakes are always high for him; he always wants to achieve excellence in his work. It was so disappointing for all of us that the film didn't get a better release, because we all loved that film. Despite the bigger budget and bigger cast it was still a close personal film to Tom and he had to hunker down and get what he needed. When we did *Living in Oblivion* it was just us, it was a laugh, it was bliss. *Johnny Suede* and *Box of Moonlight* had that same feeling too, but *The Real Blonde* had a different dynamic in terms of money. It had a budget from other people and money just makes people crazy; you have more responsibility to a third-party that you don't know. The bigger the budget the more neurotic those other people can get. I never saw that pressure affect Tom during production, he was just focused on making the best film that he could."

For DiCillo, it was a hard lesson, an incalculable influence on him to never again let his films to be trifled with at the expense of artistic and aesthetic integrity. As a filmmaker of auteur sensibilities and the man whose name is on the final work, DiCillo sometimes blames himself for what happened to the film. The director was accosted at a post-screening Q&A for the film at the Deauville Film Festival by a woman who questioned some of the casting choices: "This woman said to me, 'Doug is cute and sexy, why doesn't Mary leave Joe and just go off with him instead?'" DiCillo recalls. "It showed me there was something off in the chemistry between Matthew and Catherine. It is neither of their faults. If anything, I'm responsible – I cast them both. But if audiences are going to be drawn to your main characters there has to be something vital about them together; something charged, sexual and alive. You want to feel that they should stay together, that they have something unforgettable. No matter what, there has to be something about them that touches your heart, otherwise when they go off into the deeper parts in the script that are questionable or even annoying it makes the audience reject them and they'll never come back."

Despite the director's soul searching *The Real Blonde* remains a powerfully smart and stimulating showcase for his ability to inform his work with relatable and iden-

Glass Tears: Man Ray's iconic image watches over Joe and Mary

tifiable characters and situations, expertly weaving a complex network narrative that keeps the film's pacing brisk and alive with a punchy rhythm that rarely lets up. DiCillo achieves this within his deeply textured yet audaciously humorous rendering of the lives of his characters. They all harbour aberrations and eccentricities, yet he doesn't make them any less-attractive, or less-identifiable.

"What I was trying to get at was this sense we all have regarding happiness," DiCillo admits. "Some of what happiness is comes from ourselves; some of it comes from the relentless bombardment of the world around us. But there is this general belief in most of us that if we could only have that rare and elusive thing over there, then we would be truly happy. And we spend most of our lives trying to attain this thing that is unattainable and usually completely meaningless. This ferocious energy and interest goes in exactly the opposite direction it should. Instead of looking within to seek some simple and basic truths about ourselves – which is really what would set us free – we look outside."

Warm, witty and rich in humour and pathos, *The Real Blonde* is a film which, perhaps with the appropriate marketing and support of the studio that financed it, might well have appealed to audiences on both sides of the cinematic divide, containing both the shimmering aesthetic glow and viable ensemble cast of a commercial picture, and the subversive, intellectually nourishing qualities of a serious art film. It is a film where the expanded budget allowed DiCillo to embellish some of his most sophisticated and elaborate visual ideas.

"It wasn't a lot of extra money," the director relates. "But it was enough to let me go a little wild visually without the terror the whole film was going to collapse. I had a great time with the Madonna video shoot, creating this giant beach set with twirling umbrellas and a hundred guys in tiny yellow banana slings."

The worlds of fashion and entertainment are rich in detail and this is where the director wisely directed his extra funds. The observant viewer will notice the posters in Sahara's apartment feature her in an ad campaign for a fragrance called Depression. "We were able to set up a whole photo shoot just for those posters," DiCillo recalls with some wonderment. "They're a little absurd but they also add a great element of credibility. And I really enjoyed being able to recreate the whole world of a TV soap opera with "Passion Crest". We had sound people, camera operators, wardrobe assistants; all the great, juicy fun, sweat and tears of a real soap opera. I just love that world, I guess: the set. In front of the camera, behind the camera – it's all infinitely magical and fascinating to me."

Maxwell Caulfield suggests that *The Real Blonde* has resonance in the current milieu of a media-preoccupied and image-obsessed contemporary world. "The film was reflecting society and it is more relevant especially now as we are becoming more and more obsessed with our packaging, what's on the outside, rather than the content." The actor continues: "Tom is an auteur filmmaker who is committed to his vision and you can see that in the recurring themes throughout his body of work. No matter what adversity he goes through in getting these films made, it's always his vision that remains."

"When you work with Tom he just makes you feel like you want to do the right thing," Keener states unequivocally, "because he's investing in it emotionally and you'd feel like a fool if you didn't. He's not a detached director, he gets involved and he wants to engage with you. When he talks to you as a director you have to get into his world and see it how he sees it. Tom and I share the same sense of humour. I think he's hilarious, and you can see that in his films."

The actress continues: "There's just a connection there between us, and you never know who you're going to meet that you will find a connection with, particularly artistically. I can think of other people whose work I love yet on a personal level not really feel a connection with them. Tom is a completely honest artist and that's his way; he has a real strong commitment in being truthful to his work. I was lucky that I fell under that umbrella. My chunk of work with Tom has been a very significant portion of my career."

DiCillo concludes: "I think the central idea of *The Real Blonde* has some continued resonance and meaning. How do you survive in a world where everyone is fascinated by the false and artificial and all you have is your integrity? The work from all the actors is strong, filled with play and imagination. I think the script has some great turns and surprises; like how Bob manipulates the story arc of "Passion Crest" to lead to Kelly's 'suicide' in order to make up for his humiliation in front of her.

And I believe my faith in Catherine Keener paid off. Once again, she brought something sparkling and amazing to the film. I'd written the part for her, knowing how crucial her talent and essence were for it and I was kind of proud of winning that battle with Lakeshore. A strange little irony is that halfway through the shoot all the Lakeshore execs came to adore her and wanted her to be in several more of their films.

But there is a hint of moralising to the film that bothers me. My films work best when they are the sharpest and clearest. Unfortunately, the 'moral element' was given more importance than I intended when some of the more provocative scenes were cut."

The director pauses, before continuing: "Every film takes three to four years of your life. That's a long time. It takes a massive amount of focus and commitment to follow the idea all the way through. And if I missed the target on a few things it doesn't mean I focused any less nor had any fewer sleepless nights than on any other films. Sometimes the results are clearer than others. It's all the same amount of work."

* * *

Wayne Byrne: The Real Blonde *feels more elaborately constructed than your previous three films; one can immediately feel the effect of you working on the larger canvas here. You truly capture the feel and energy of New York City and showcase how it affects your characters.*

Tom DiCillo: After being out in the world of rural America for over a year with *Box of Moonlight* I wanted to get back to New York.

I wanted to get back to some ideas that were connected to me in a more immediate way like the day to day reality of a relationship; specifically where one person has artistic aspirations and the other has to be the support system. What happens when the romance of the starving artist starts to wear off? You love someone but they're not bringing in any money. That can get pretty tedious and annoying, especially as the years keep going by and there is no real indication that success is coming.

I wanted to explore the relationship from the point of view of both Mary and Joe. She's the main bread-winner; Joe isn't bringing anything to the table financially. He is going through his own problems with his career and his sense of identity. He is getting older and the breaks are getting harder to come by. But this existential crisis can't pay the bills. So the cracks in the relationship are under the added pressure of Joe's basic inability to provide for Mary.

That gave me the idea for the main relationship. Then I started to sketch in other kinds of relationships, ones that were equally intense but with no real love involved; which is the essence of Bob's relationship with both Sahara and Kelly.

What made you choose the title?

It had struck me long before I wrote the script. It's a phrase people use a lot; it's very common. "She's a real blonde." "Is she a real blonde?" "Yeah, she's a real blonde." I liked it because without really saying it what it is referring to is the phenomenon of a woman's hair matching her pubic hair.

Personally, I've never been colour coordinated. But it struck me as a good title for a story about people who are struggling to tell the difference between what is real and what is false.

Those ideas and the title itself, they all relate to illusion.

The basic theme of the film I think is the power of simple honesty. For many people that power is either too simple, or too complex to grasp. They're not interested in it. Illusion holds much more power. For many people truth is terrifying. It's a very simple concept. It takes great courage to really see ourselves and to see the world around us.

Those themes are heightened by setting the film in the worlds of fashion and television, which you duly satirise.

I have nothing against fashion, television or any of the pop cultural institutions. I love pop culture. I think it is necessary and healthy. But the shift in its importance interests me. It's almost like escapism has lost its intended artificiality and morphed into reality. We're putting massive amounts of value on things that were never intended to be taken literally. I chose these worlds because it helped me define the characters of Joe and Mary more. Their instinctive honesty places them in sharp contrast to what's all around them.

I would place The Real Blonde *as the second of a tetralogy of your films that deals somehow with the machinations of the entertainment industries. The first being* Living in Oblivion, *the third being* Delirious *and the fourth being* When You're Strange. *What attracts your attention to scrutinising these industries, be they film, television, fashion, etc?*

All I know is that even from the beginning, on the sets of student films, something struck me about what was happening just off-camera. On a film your focus is always fixed intensely on your little scene: the shot, the actors, whatever tiny artificial fragment the camera is pointing at. And that focus is relentless. Everyone on the set is caught up in it. But if you turn your head just a little bit you might see something off-camera that gives some accidental glimpse of real human behaviour. The simultaneous co-existence of the two worlds fascinates me.

The same little shift of focus can apply to every aspect of the entertainment business. I'd love to do a documentary watching how people act in front of cameras, like on a red carpet. I've witnessed episodes regarding slights to a celebrity's perceived status that would rival anything out of *Macbeth* – I mean, life and death intensity all because someone is standing two feet from where they think they deserve to stand.

Having discovered some young talent who have gone on to have very successful careers do you see that change in those actors, now celebrities?

In some. It takes a very strong person to not let it go to their head. When you have a million people telling you that you're incredible you end up believing it and not only that but you want them to keep saying it. And that's where the disease creeps in. That kind of attention becomes addictive. I don't think there's anything in the human psyche that can protect us from the impact of such massive adulation.

You had quite a few real, established stars in The Real Blonde. *This was a first for you.*

It was. Lakeshore Entertainment, the company that had financed *Box of Moonlight*, liked the script so much they immediately agreed to make it. And I was thrilled. I'd had a very positive experience with them on *Box of Moonlight*, especially in Tom Rosenberg's support during the whole Egon Friske catastrophe.

But they made it clear to me right from the beginning that they saw the film as something bigger. They didn't want to make a tiny, low-budget art film that showed in two cinemas around the world. They told me straight out they wanted me to cast stars.

Return of the Reve: Nick (Steve Buscemi) from *Living In Oblivion* makes a cameo appearance, directing a Madonna music video, conferring with assistant director, Zee (Dave Chapelle)

I don't hold that against them and I completely understand their reasoning; especially since they were putting up around five million dollars.

I also don't have any qualms about working with stars. There are many who are very gifted and brilliant performers and who don't bring the whole movie star baggage with them. This was our starting point; trying to find these kinds of actors. And I think the stars that I cast turned out very well. It was a thrill getting Buck Henry in the film. We'd stayed in touch since his life-saving advice to me at Sundance back with *Johnny Suede*. He's a brilliant writer but I think he's also a brilliant and quite underrated actor. His scene as the hotel clerk in *The Graduate* is a classic of timing, wit and absurdity. So I thought he'd be great as Dr. Leuter, the whacked-out shrink Catherine Keener's character is seeing. He wasn't really a marquee name to Lakeshore but they let me cast him. I'm sure if they'd thought about it a little more they would have insisted I cast Anthony Hopkins.

Working with Christopher Lloyd was a dream. He did his first take, a very long scene, and when it was done I was speechless. I literally had nothing to say to him except, "That was fantastic." It actually kind of threw me. The same thing was true with Kathleen Turner. She was completely willing and committed. She allowed herself to be a little foolish which is rare from some actors. And I still can't believe I got Dave Chappelle to do a small part. I rarely use the word genius but I've got no other word to describe him. He's one of the most talented people I've ever worked with.

Daryl Hannah really blew my mind. Word came from her agent that she wanted to be in the film. I reacted stupidly, thinking, "Do I really want a mermaid in this movie?" Then the agent called back and said that Daryl would come in and meet me. I still didn't see it. Then the agent said Daryl was willing to come in and read for the part. This got my attention right away. I said, "There must be something she's reacting to very strongly in the part if she's willing to come in and audition."

I can't stress how unusual this is. Most successful actors will not audition; they feel it is humiliating. Yet Daryl came in very calm and professional without a trace of desperation and I felt an immediate respect for her. Her reading was so amazing I gave her the part right there in the audition room. And she dove into the role in the film. She just wallowed in it, enjoying it and taking huge risks. I never knew what she was going to do next. At times her ferocity was really startling.

There were moments in the script that were more explicit than anything in the finished film. How much of this is your own editing and how much of was Paramount or Lakeshore?

Unfortunately there were several really strong scenes that ended up being cut. Some of those decisions came from Lakeshore; some came from me. Ultimately, what became very clear was that Lakeshore and Paramount wanted a movie they could sell to the largest number of people. My mistake was being surprised by that. I kept trying to find the strongest movie I could in the editing room, the movie that was closest to what I'd originally had in mind and what excited me.

There was a scene I shot that is one of the most disturbing, and actually most beautiful, scenes I've ever put on film. The character of Bob, played by Maxwell Caulfield, is obsessed with finding a woman who is a real blonde. I shot a scene where he sees one in a sleazy peep show off Times Square. The fact that the woman in the booth was overweight, somewhat homely and decidedly depressed did not deter from his obsession. That was the point of the scene. And Frank Prinzi lit it beautifully; this heavy woman with pasty white skin, rotating on a blue dais while in the darkness around her where glowing rectangles of light from the tiny windows the men were looking through. Lakeshore insisted I cut it. They said they wanted the film to play in Middle America. I refused. I said I would take my name off the film. They said go ahead. Finally, after seeking the advice of every person I knew in the business, I capitulated. The advice was, "It's just one scene. Just do it."

That was such an important scene in Bob's development as a character. He has sunk so low in his quest for a real blonde, abusing and then ignoring the relationship he's in with this beautiful woman, Sahara, only to be vaguely satisfied by this? It's a crucial scene.

I know. I still think about it. And after all the shit that went down and after seeing how poorly the film was released I have to ask myself, "How did cutting the scene benefit me?" It didn't affect audience reaction to the film in any way. I could have, and should have, left it in. At the very least I would have felt I'd made the film I wanted.

There are three main arguments between Joe and Mary that structure the film.

I wanted each act to end on one of their arguments. I wrote them so they increased in intensity and venom as the film progressed.

The line that Mary says to Joe when she mentions the rent is due and he hasn't handed over his half, "Yeah, it sort of works that way. You know, once a month?" That really stings.

Yeah, it's a dig. And the point was to show that they both are right. She needs his share of the rent. It's a fact of life and she's a little pissed that she has to remind him. And he's broke; so immersed in trying to make it as an actor that he dreads the first of the month like it was a death sentence.

Joe is reading an article to Mary about the Virgin Mary appearing in some guy's bird bath and she responds with a genuine question: "If God didn't want Mary to go through the actual act of sex why did he force her to experience the pain and trauma of childbirth when he could have just handed her a child?" Is this saying something about Mary's own reluctance to have a child with Joe?

I hadn't thought of that connection but that's a very interesting question. In its simplest terms the scene was meant to examine Christianity's insistence that the conception had to be *immaculate*, in other words: no penetration; no real, "messy' intercourse. For God to have gotten that intimate with Mary is just a little too real for most people. In the film all Mary is asking is, "If God could conceive with Mary immaculately then why couldn't he just as immaculately have popped a baby into her lap and saved her a lot of trouble?"

So why is she so resistant to having a child?

Because she feels it would bring in more insecurity than the relationship could bear. The fact is, Joe's not making any money. How could they survive if Mary had to stop working?

So it's less a religious malaise and more a practical one?

I think it's practical and emotional. On a gut level Mary fears that Joe can't survive by himself. That's a tough thing to face, especially when you really love the person. Equality in a relationship is a very fragile thing. I think most relationships flourish when both people are feeling the best about themselves. If Joe is having doubts about his ability to make money and therefore survive in the real world, his sense of self is shaken.

At times Joe is quite irresponsible and negligent; he can't afford a child yet he persists about not wanting to use a condom. This only antagonises Mary further.

He certainly can't afford a child. And even though he does raise the question, "How do other people do it; people without money have been having babies since the beginning of time?" he still can't answer his own question. Joe is like a child in some ways. That is part of what Mary loves about him. But it also drives her crazy. I think maybe the real issue between them is their hesitancy in creating a concrete bond that would mean that their being together was *real*. Creating a life together, raising that child; stating clearly their willingness and desire to be with each other. I think they both were afraid of that.

Mary would have had to give up her life and career for something she is uncertain about.

Her career is her only means of support; they have no money other than what she earns. These are very real issues; just as Joe's desire to accomplish something artistically as an actor is very real. It would be very difficult for him to just put that away and forget about it. So what are they going to do? That's what I was interested in examining; problems in a relationship that have no easy answers.

Is Mary cutting off a potentially conflicted family even before it begins, by deciding to not want children?

Perhaps. On a very real level she might be completely justified in saying to him, "Joe, you're thirty-five years old and you don't have a job." But by the same token I sympathise with Joe because he is doing all that he knows how to do. To me, that's where the juice of the conflict comes from. But also I don't think Joe really knows what he's saying. All he does know is that there is some unspoken and very complex distance and silence beginning to develop between him and Mary. In his soul he knows that Mary doesn't trust his ability to provide as fully as she does, so he's probably grasping at straws, thinking that if they have a child it will help their connection. In his brain he's going, "Wow! This child could be some magical fix for us" and he doesn't think about what the real consequences are.

One of my favorite scenes in the film is in the bohemian restaurant in which Joe and Mary are having an argument with their successful hipster friends, Alex and Raina, about a movie called Il Piano. *I found this a fascinating discourse on cultural capital and how it so quickly can veer into elitism.*

The film title is a fake; it's a combination of *The Piano* and *Il Postino*. Both films had just come out and were hugely popular, especially with critics. The scene was intended to show what might happen if Joe was the only one who disagreed with the mass of public opinion. His argument is that on some level *The Piano* is really not that distant from romance novels with long-haired, tattooed, bare-chested pirates looming behind love-starved heroines with ripped bodices and Olympic-style cleavage.

Alex is a successful artist, they have a child, they have connections – Raina knows Madonna – they seem happy together as a couple and as a family unit. To me, Joe sees their championing Il Piano *as an extension of this lifestyle that he is somehow envious of.*

That's the crux of the scene right there. Both Alex and Raina are successful. They appear happy and content with their lives. Alex is getting a lot of attention, and actually making a lot of cash as an artist. Raina is close with Madonna. They've just adopted a black baby. For them, their lives are perfect. And in comparison Joe feels completely inadequate. All he can really say about his career at that point is that he's working as a waiter.

I think a lot of people have been there. You're not where you want to be and you don't know how to get there, or if you're ever going to get there. Also there is the element that Alex and Raina may be a little condescending to Joe who perceives this and is saying some of this out of spite.

You reference Death of a Salesman *several times in the film. Joe uses a famous speech from Willy Loman's son Hap as his audition piece. There is a similarity in their situations: both have hopes and aspirations but feel they are compromising themselves by accepting mediocre and limiting jobs.*

It's that inability to compromise, to lower his ideals, that is the real connection for Joe to Hap's speech. Hap says, "Every day I've got to take orders from those petty sons of bitches…" It's a great speech. We've all been there too; doing demeaning jobs and having to take orders from bitter, mean-spirited morons. That used to be my audition piece when I was trying to find work as an actor. Joe doesn't feel that soap opera acting is really acting. Is he wrong? A million people feel that way! He's working hard trying to find work but his moral compass is just a little more sensitive than others. He has a sense of integrity, and that's a big problem in this business. Bob has no integrity and it serves him well. When he gets a job on a soap opera he laughs it off and says, "OK, it's a piece of shit, but I'll make some money."

Joe, because of who he is, can't make that adjustment. He's simply telling the truth when he tells DeeDee Taylor soap opera acting is beneath him. Now, that's also part of his problem because the world doesn't always operate that way.

The film has great comedic appeal and a strong cast of familiar actors. It's approachable, it's not obfuscating. Why do you think it struggled to find an audience?

The film was test screened on the Paramount lot and I knew I was in trouble when the last shot of the film came up. As the lost dog started walking toward the camera someone started laughing. That's when, for whatever reason, I knew audiences were going to resist the film. I am still deeply moved by that scene. I put a lot of effort into how it was filmed. The dog had the frayed end of a dirty rope around his neck, as if he'd been tied up for weeks. We made him look matted and dirty like he'd really been through hell. I told the trainer that he should not run; he has to walk *slowly*, as if he's exhausted and can barely move. The point to all these details was to shift the moment away from cheap melodrama; to try and make it real. Here's a woman who's lost her only real companion and somehow, some way, he finds his way back to her.

But the test audience didn't go for it. We were on the lot after the screening; one of the Paramount executives comes up to me and gives me one of those limp, three-fingered handshakes…

The Dead Fish?

Yes, it was literally like a dead fish in my hand. And I could tell he was keenly aware of how the audience had reacted. He was not optimistic about the film's potential. He says to me, "The first thing we're going to do is change the title." And the first thing I said was, "No, I don't think you are." Tom Rosenberg, the producer from Lakeshore jammed his elbow into my kidney. The exec said, "Yeah, we're changing our pitch. We're going to make it like a movie version of *Friends*."

That is about the most inappropriate analogy I could think of for your film.

You have to remember this was my first experience with a major studio. It took me a while to see that they all operate on the lowest common denominator. "How do we alter the film to the point where the most people will understand it?" That's how they think. They're businessmen, and to businessmen that makes perfect sense.

Was the film too mainstream for the indie audience, yet too indie for the mainstream audience?

I heard that from several people. Maybe it did turn into some strange hybrid. I think you either commit completely to making a Hollywood film or you make an independent film. There is no middle ground. People get too confused. Why did *Living in Oblivion* strike a larger chord? In a way, it's because that is perhaps my simplest film. There's a tone to the film that is consistent and which maintains itself throughout. *The Real Blonde* has some pretty massive tone shifts between buffoonery and absolute tragedy. But to me that's the way life is.

Did this experience affect how you would conduct the business of making your films from here on in?

It made me vow to never put myself in a position where someone else could tell me how to make my film. Some directors can deal with all the maneuvering and game playing that it takes to work with a corporation. I can't. It's too exhausting and it is such waste of time. A film made by committee is a generic film. You want a pizza with something on it for everyone? To me it ends up being inedible.

I realised after the experience of working with a studio on *The Real Blonde* that the only thing that matters to me is the natural and spontaneous flow of ideas that come to me and my collaborators on the film. That is where the vitality is, the real joy of creation. If it means scaling way down to doing a film for nothing then I would do that in a second. No amount of money can take the place of the thrill that artistic freedom brings you.

CHAPTER SIX

Double Whammy

'Why are you talking like that? Dope, fresh, whacked ... nigga, you ain't black!'
– Cletis

While *The Real Blonde* would be the closest to a studio film Tom DiCillo would ever make, his next move would be yet another exploration of unfamiliar terrain: the crime film. DiCillo's fifth feature, *Double Whammy*, is a markedly original, postmodern take on the classic genre, featuring a burnt-out cop who becomes entangled in a web of lies, deceit and attempted murder. However, the film is not merely a police procedural; DiCillo's tale is also a trenchant satire on media exploitation and a humorously critical discourse on contemporary film itself. The step was not accidental.

"I realised that some of my favourite films are crime films, especially some of the more intense films noir of the 1940s and 1950s," DiCillo admits. "I think *The Asphalt Jungle* is a masterpiece, and not just of that genre. John Huston brings out the small, human aspects of the characters so clearly you feel like you can smell them. Sterling Hayden dies over the last fifteen minutes of the film. It's a slow, quiet, very real death. I'd never seen anything like it. It actually was one of the early inspirations for *Double Whammy*."

DiCillo's film literally opens with a bang. A crazed psycho drives a truck through the window of a fast-food joint, then jumps out and starts mowing people down with an AK-47. NYPD Homicide Det. Ray Pluto (Denis Leary) happens to be inside. He has a clear shot at the shooter when suddenly his back goes out so violently he lurches backwards and is knocked unconscious when his head hits the floor. An eight-year-old

Detectives Ray Pluto (Denis Leary) and Jerry Cubbins (Steve Buscemi) in *Double Whammy*

boy picks up Pluto's gun and approaches the killer from behind. With his eyes closed in terrified anticipation, Ricky Lapinsky pulls the trigger. A loud shot rings out as the screen goes black. From the darkness a voice bellows out: "Do I have your attention now?!!"

Ricky Lapinsky becomes a national hero and Det. Pluto is publicly humiliated. As he limps back to the tenement where he lives, the threads of DiCillo's intricate narrative begin to interweave. Ray's superintendent, Juan (Luis Guzman), has a sixteen-year-old daughter, Maribel (Melonie Diaz), who is incensed when her father refuses to let her get a tattoo. In her ill-judged despair she hires two lowlifes, JoJo and Ping Pong, to murder Juan.

Pluto spends his evenings zoning out on hash, with the buzz helping to relieve him from the guilt he feels about the death of his wife and daughter. On the recommendation of his only friend, Det. Jerry Cubbins (Steve Buscemi), Pluto goes to a chiropractor for his back. He is not expecting Dr. Anne Beamer to be Elizabeth Hurley. Yet Pluto finds more than a skilled physical therapist in Anne. Over the course of his sessions, he encounters an attractive yet lonely woman with whom he shares a profound bond and an immediate sexual chemistry.

In an obvious nod to Hitchcock's *Rear Window*, the film observes two young hipsters living in the apartment across the hall from Pluto. Cletis (Donald Faison) and Duke (Keith Nobbs) are near completion on a script that will be one of the hippest and most violent films ever made. Their efforts seamlessly intersect with Maribel's quickly developing murder plot. In the film's terrifying (and equally hilarious) climax, Jojo and Ping Pong burst into the screenwriters' apartment thinking Duke and Cletis have witnessed their stabbing of Juan. They discover Pluto there as well, tied to a chair in a neighbourly gesture to help Duke and Cletis with their screenplay. Though stoned, Pluto manages to distract the two killers and free himself. Cletis and Duke's script is ironically realised in front of their faces, complete with the thickest-sounding *thwock* from a falling knife and the messiest death-cough of blood they could imagine.

Although Pluto is finally redeemed, earning a Hero Cop headline for himself, he is too close to Juan and his family to see Maribel's complicity. And when the truth finally dawns on him DiCillo's hero makes a choice to just let it go.

Double Whammy is at heart a gritty, slightly surreal tale of redemption. In protagonist Ray Pluto we have not only a flawed detective, but a flawed man. Nonetheless, as in DiCillo's other films, Pluto's flaws are what make him human. So human in fact that at the end of the film, even in his moment of triumph, his back goes out again and he has to place himself in Anne's supporting arms to make it home.

In many ways *Double Whammy* is not really a cop movie at all. It uses the well-known forms and structures of the genre to create something more complex and difficult to define. The crime and criminal aspects of it are extremely detailed. One never doubts for a second that Jojo and Ping Pong are real killers. The blood they shed is real and when they turn on Maribel herself the terror she feels is palpable.

Double Whammy is an expansion of ideas and interests already established in DiCillo's previous work: questions of identity, familial relations and the world of media. *Living in Oblivion* and *Double Whammy* respectively offer ruminations on independent filmmaking pre- and post-*Pulp Fiction* but *Double Whammy* more specifically explores the culture's fascination with violence. "When I wrote *Double Whammy* the world was in its most orgiastic response to Tarantino," DiCillo recalls. "You couldn't go to a movie theatre without seeing a 'quirky, darkly hilarious' film about goateed hipsters shooting people through the scrotum. Don't get me wrong; I have a lot of respect for Tarantino. He brought an amazing intensity back to independent film right when it needed it. Nothing can compare to the cool, manic insanity of *Reservoir Dogs*. I'm only talking about the blind ferocity with which he was not only embraced but copied – even by himself.

DiCillo continues: "But there was such a manic hysteria about his films that it started to feel to me like a whole new 'genre' had been formed: Pseudo Neo-Nihilism. The emulation became so absurd that I decided to incorporate it into *Double Whammy*. I'm confounded by the obsession with violence," DiCillo admits; "the use of it as a joke; as a kind of hip, disaffected cool. 'Hahaha, that old woman looked at me funny so I shot her. And then I set her on fire and pissed on her to put it out, hahaha.' I think violence is a necessary and crucial element in art and cinema. But I don't think in and of itself it is cool. And I certainly don't think it is funny and cool. Duke and Cletis act as if they're into violence but in reality they are the homogenised counterparts to the real gangsters that Maribel hires, JoJo and Ping Pong; they've never seen real violence."

DiCillo's commentary on the media exaltation of violence extends to the hilarious subplot of little Ricky Lapinsky, the freckled, red-headed hero who single-handedly brings down a deranged gun nut and becomes the hero of New York City. The child is hoisted upon the nation's shoulders in valour with appearances on TV talk shows and is front-page news, receiving plaudits from the Mayor – "If I had twenty more like him I could wipe out crime in this city!" All of this intensifies Pluto's humiliation.

"I like the title *Double Whammy*," DiCillo explains. "Usually in films something bad happens and then that's that. But in life, when the piano falls on your head and you somehow survive and stumble to your feet, usually right then is when the bus comes by and runs you over."

DiCillo experienced some of this recurrent mayhem in funding the movie. Lakeshore Entertainment started out financing *Double Whammy* but bailed out after DiCillo's resistance to their dictum of pumping the film full of A-list stars again. And so, after a relationship that spanned five years and two films DiCillo found himself unmoored once more. His search for financing would take him four years, three different financiers and one potentially devastating lawsuit.

"One financier never responded after months of waiting," DiCillo recalls. "Finally I called him. He was the Acquisitions Exec at a large indie studio. He was annoyed I was calling him. He couldn't understand why I sent him the script. 'We don't do cop movies', he sniffed. I tried to explain that *Double Whammy* was as much a crime movie as Godard's *Alphaville*, or Altman's *The Long Goodbye*, but he'd already hung up."

In 1999, four years later, DiCillo finally made a deal with Gold Circle Films who agreed to let him cast his top choices, which included Denis Leary, Steve Buscemi and Chris Noth. They also agreed to let him reach out to Elizabeth Hurley for the part of Anne Beamer.

The sparkling sexual chemistry between Det. Pluto and Dr. Beamer spurs a crucial arc of the film; Pluto's post-traumatic reconnection to his life and career. Dr. Beamer advises a series of spine adjustments to ease Pluto's back pain. These physically intimate therapeutic sessions ignite a spark of potent attraction between the two. Just as the moment seems to be leading toward sexual consummation, Dr. Beamer pulls back. "Now wait just a goddamned minute! I like you, Detective, but if you think I'm going to screw you on this table...!"

"It struck me what an intimate moment that is when you're getting an adjustment on a chiropractor's table," DiCillo says, "especially when it's a man who's alone and it's a woman who's missing somebody, and it's a very physical thing that's happening. I like the fact that it's not just lust, it's more like what would really happen if two people just took a chance in that moment."

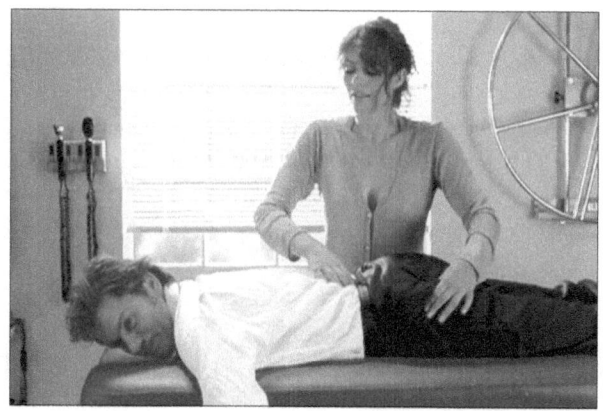

Dr. Ann Beamer (Elizabeth Hurley) adjusts Pluto's spine

Nightmare Headline: Pluto is haunted by ghosts of the past and career anxieties

A key moment in Beamer and Pluto's relationship occurs in his apartment after the two make love for the first time. As Pluto drifts off asleep the film takes us into a dream sequence which explains the demise of his family. The detective's guilty conscience plays upon him after having sex with Beamer; Pluto's first intimate moment since his bereavement. With this scene DiCillo creates a surreal distortion of the senses, with a hauntingly desolate diner and a nightmarish newspaper headline presenting Pluto with a faceless image of himself. He is wrenched back into reality by the horror of Juan's attempted murder taking place only a floor beneath him.

"I looked at how Buñuel designed dream sequences," DiCillo admits. "He could take you in and out of a dream without you even knowing it. When you're in the middle of a dream it is so real it can terrify you or bring you to tears; you feel as if it's actually happening. To me this dictates a kind of reality, a necessity to have things in the dream that are real and normal but are also there as signposts that get you into the dream and then get you out of it; the newspaper for example. I needed Pluto to look at something so normal he would take it for granted. Then the picture of himself he sees has no face and he gets his first inkling that something isn't quite right. That was partly influenced by Magritte, whose paintings are so surreal; full of haunting reality and beauty."

The conception of this dream sequence is only one of a number of elements DiCillo introduces to subvert the well-defined genre tropes of a typical crime film. Another significant one is DiCillo's sensitive treatment of Det. Jerry Cubbins' confused sexual identity.

Originally written as a "large, beefy cop", DiCillo altered Cubbins' physical attributes to accommodate the casting of Buscemi, whose lean and slight presence brings the character a much-needed vulnerability. "Getting Steve Buscemi to play the role altered my initial idea for the character's physical appearance," DiCillo affirms. "Steve is neither large nor beefy. But he brings something incredible to a cop who suddenly finds himself looking at other men's asses. I took the name from Dr. Seuss' *The 500 Hats of Bartholomew Cubbins*. It's about a boy who is ordered to take his hat off before the King and every time he does another one appears on his head. It helped bring a similar frustration to Jerry."

The police world Cubbins works in is charged with testosterone-fuelled masculinity. For him to reveal even a hint of attraction to another man is an admission of catastrophic proportions. Even his best friend, Pluto, despite his immediate acceptance, shows a bit of unease at Cubbins' revelation.

"Most men have real difficulty experiencing deep affection for one another," DiCillo ventures. "They seem to think the only logical next step for such strong feeling is sex. Women can share very deep and intimate relationships without even a hint of sexuality. For most men this is impossible. Again, I find this humorous and tragic in equal proportions. I thought there could be some strange humour in the fact that Pluto's best advice, and I believe he is being as supportive and honest as he can be, is for Cubbins not to worry about it because '…deep down inside everybody's gay.' As heartfelt as this advice is, it is definitely the last thing Cubbins wants to hear."

The role of Jerry Cubbins was not the first time Buscemi portrayed a character of alternative sexuality. In an early film role, Buscemi appeared in Bill Sherwood's acclaimed look at homosexual life in the 1980s, *Parting Glances* (1984). However, playing a symbol of potent manliness – an NYPD detective – *Double Whammy* afforded the veteran actor the opportunity to play with the conventions of a stock genre character.

"It was fun for me to play a detective. It's something that I had never done before," Buscemi recalls. "And not only a detective but one who is struggling with his sexuality in a very macho environment. Being partnered with Pluto he feels he has a friend who he can trust; there's chemistry between them. I like playing characters that have complications, and this character was definitely struggling to understand himself, looking for guidance, looking for affirmation, and looking for support. He was a character with a lot of heart and a lot of humour, and a lot of deep feelings."

DiCillo apparently set out to intentionally to tweak the traditional buddy-cop relationships inherent in so many police films. "I thought it would be more dramatically interesting," the director admits. "Cubbins is Pluto's only friend. He's his link to the world. In fact, without him there is a sense that Pluto would be completely alone in the universe. Cubbins is definitely an odd bird but it is clear the affection the two men have for each other is real. And the odder he is the more interesting it makes the relationship. He's the only cop in the whole station who would want to be Pluto's

Cubbins embraces Pluto while a passerby takes offense with the public display of intimacy

friend, and whom Pluto allows to be his friend. I like the way Pluto just simply accepts him."

The director continues: "Cubbins' sexuality went into the script quite early. I love characters who are struggling with things, who don't know all the answers, people who are genuinely confused and yet somehow keep going. I hate characters that know no real confusion. They are boring and useless to any human story."

Buscemi not only brings the pathos of a man going through such an enormous identity crisis, but also a sense of absurd humour that DiCillo excels in encouraging from his actors. A key scene has Pluto opening his heart to Cubbins about his anguish and guilt over the death of his wife and daughter. There is a rush of emotion in Buscemi's eyes as he comforts Pluto and declares, "I love you, man. Okay? I mean it!" Just as they embrace a nearby truck driver yells out, "Hey, faggot! Why don't you just fuckin' kiss him?" Buscemi explodes into seething yet hilarious anger. "What'd you say, asshole?!" he screams while jamming his gun in the guy's face, "You greasy, fucking, fat pig!"

Pluto smokes dope to escape from his tortured career and personal demons. After toking up one night he gets a call from Cubbins, who casually asks him what he's doing. "Oh, just sitting around smoking some hash," Pluto candidly informs his partner. Cubbins' knee-jerk response to Pluto's frankness is to laugh and jokingly retort, "Yeah, me too! I just did a whole bucket of crack." Cubbins' guileless devotion to Pluto as a friend and colleague blind him to Pluto's candid admission to a misdemeanour. Buscemi performs the scene with such naivety and innocence he makes you believe he really thought Pluto was kidding.

While Ray Pluto is undoubtedly the focus of the film, it is his nemesis, Det. Chick Dimitri (Chris Noth) who turns out to be the most perceptive detective in the story. Dimitri's innate intelligence is crucial to the unfolding of the narrative. He is presented as sly and cunning but also as a smooth, confident and quietly alert detective, a coiled professional in opposition to Pluto's natural sloppiness.

Having been close friends since the late-1970s, when they worked for the same catering company while studying acting together, *Double Whammy* brought Chris Noth and Tom DiCillo together professionally once again; this time minus the hors d'oeuvres.

A veteran of police procedurals, Noth brings considerable credibility to the character, informing him with qualities that would traditionally be assigned to a film's hero. Noth renders Dimitri as polished yet rugged, taciturn but intuitive – the elements that make up the most memorable film noir anti-heroes. Dimitri's superior detecting skills repeatedly undermine Pluto's, providing a twist in the hero's journey, another surprising subversion of the genre. With his extensive repertoire of cop roles, Noth relished the opportunity to rework the stereotype with his keen interpretation of Dimitri.

"I gave myself into Tom's hands," Noth admits. "With a cop like Dimitri, you don't want to portray him like one of these TV detectives – including those on *Law and Order* – you want to bring something else to it, because it's a different world, really.

You don't want to fall into the mundane, prosaic TV-detective world, and that's not what Tom wrote anyway."

"I love what Chris brought to Chick Dimitri," DiCillo applauds. "He is definitely drawn from some of the slick, oily detectives out of a Sam Fuller movie. But the choice to have him be more astute than my hero Pluto was really showing my interest in the underside of the genre. Dimitri is Pluto's nemesis in the police squad room, but he's also the only one who figures out that it was Maribel who set up the attempted murder of her father."

"Dimitri is very much like a hard-boiled 1940s detective," Noth affirms. "He's tough, but he's well-groomed. He definitely reminded me of some detectives who are obsessed by their appearance, their clothing, their attire. Some of them wear a lot of big rings, or wear a lot of flash, and I think Dimitri is one of them. The flash is important; it sets him apart from other gumshoes. It was a focus that Tom bestowed upon the character too, because Dimitri isn't full of dialogue, he is full of thoughts; you never quite know what he's thinking. So there was a certain mystery that I wanted to hang on to with that character."

"I could have cast Chris as Pluto. I'm not sure why I didn't," DiCillo admits with an element of regret. "But at the time he was not as 'bankable' as Denis Leary."

Amplifying DiCillo's distortion of the traditionally gritty tenets of the crime genre, the film is imbued with rich colour and strong frames. The dynamic visual aesthetic of *Double Whammy* is one of the most immediate elements of the film. The eye-popping primary-coloured civilian world jolts forth in contrast with the dull silver and greys of the halls of justice that demoralise Pluto. From the verdant green tones of Pluto's tenement to the luminous matching red suits of filmmaker-wannabes Cletis and Duke, DiCillo's playful use of colour explodes off the screen to hit the viewer with a pop art palette that buoys the absurdist humour and off-beat narrative.

"I feel that every film should have its own particular look," DiCillo explains, "inspired by what the film is and what makes it unique. Cinematographer Bob Yeoman and I talked about giving *Double Whammy* a hyper-realistic feel. We wanted the colour to be rich and very saturated, so if something was sky blue then it was almost surreal in its intensity. Bob was great at that. For example, I like the way Cletis and Duke's red suits pop against the blue walls of their apartment. Everything looks just a little tweaked, slightly exaggerated – it lifts the film above the dull expectedness of 'reality'."

This tone is set immediately in the whimsically absurd opening credits sequence. A plastic eyeball, like a voodoo eye, playfully rolls back and forth across the screen as if trying to elude capture. It is the same eyeball DiCillo gives Dimitri as a hand prop; his eye is the one that sees all.

"I found the eyeball in a head shop on the Lower East Side," DiCillo explains. "The inside of it is floating in liquid so that when it rolls the iris stays straight up. I had the idea to use it rolling across the screen for the credits but I didn't know how to control its movements. We ended up having two guys with air hoses just off-camera, and they blew the eyeball back and forth. But if you look at the sequence you see these two technicians were really into it. One would send it across and the other would hold it in the centre of the frame with a stronger push of air and then let it dart up and out of the frame. I gave them credit as 'Eyeball Wranglers'."

Another striking aspect of *Double Whammy* is the fresh talent who share the screen with the more seasoned cast members. Melonie Diaz, Donald Faison and Keith Nobbs are superbly cast in early roles of their respective careers. For one in particular, it would prove to be her big break.

"*Double Whammy* has a very special place in my heart," Melonie Diaz confesses. "At the time I was studying to be an actor at the Professional Performing Arts High School but it was more like a hobby. There was an open call for young girls to play the daughter of Luis Guzman, so I was like, 'Sure!' It was my first audition ever. *Double Whammy* kind of dictated my journey as a serious actress. To be around professional people like that on my first film, it really changed my life."

DiCillo recalls the moment that change occurred. "Melonie brought such a beautiful innocence and reality to her audition I decided on the spot she was Maribel. She broke down in tears. What struck me the most was that she couldn't wait to tell her mother." In addition to her acting capabilities, the director noticed something he could assign to a character that the audience at once sympathises with and reviles. "In her audition Melonie was wearing braces on her teeth. I loved the personal, human element this added. She called me a week before shooting, very excited. After two years she was getting her braces off – just in time for her first film. I congratulated her and then carefully asked if she would consider keeping the braces on for another month so we could film her with them on. To my amazement she said yes."

A first film could prove daunting for anyone, especially with a role as demanding as Maribel. In one emotionally complex moment she visits her father Juan in hospital as he lies semi-conscious, recovering from his multiple stab wounds. Here, Pluto returns Juan's "Papi" necklace, a gift from his daughter that was stolen during the botched murder attempt. Seeing the necklace, Maribel breaks down, unable to carry the guilt of what she tried to do to her father.

"That hospital scene was really hard for me," Diaz recalls. "It was very emotional and I had to dig deep and I remember Tom closed the set for me. I was glad to have someone like Tom protect me in that environment so I could focus on the work. Even at that age I knew that if he I needed to ask him a question he would be available. A lot of Maribel was really me," she continues. "I was uncomfortable, I was weird, I was awkward … I was all of those things. That's what the director does, they hire the right person and Tom knew I would be able to channel the light and the dark of Maribel – I still do! I think that is why Tom has such a good sense of actors and gets who he wants to be in his movies."

For Diaz, *Double Whammy* proved to be a vital training ground, utilising her experience of working with DiCillo as a litmus test when it comes to considering future collaborations with other directors. "After working with Tom I have a certain level of expectation from the people I work with," she explains. "But I have come to realise it's not always going to be that good all of the time. With *Double Whammy* being my first film it set that high standard. Tom films at a different pace and I can see that when I walk onto another set. I've worked on episodic TV and on other movies but it was

Double Whammy that helped show me how a director can tell a story efficiently. Tom is such a bad-ass; he dares to be different whereas a lot of people won't. I always want to be on set with someone who is a visionary and a non-conformist like him.

Seeing the finished film for the first time was an amazing experience," Diaz recalls. "Seeing it cut together made me love the filmmaking process so much more because I realised how hard it is and yet how easy Tom makes it look. I was really proud of the movie. It certainly changed me a lot. It was the film that really made me want to be an actress and to take it seriously. It made me realise that this is what I want to do with my life."

Maribel's paradox is her inherent innocence working in contrast to the desperate nature of her actions. Retaining an audience's sympathy for a character can be a delicate balance. We've become so attuned to the conventions of commercial narrative storytelling that we expect our heroes and villains to be drawn in broad, easily-recognisable colours of "Good" and "Bad".

"The line between good and bad is very complex," DiCillo offers. "I hate the simplistic ideology of most Hollywood movies where everyone is either all good or all bad. If you look at the characters in my films most of them move back and forth along that moral boundary line."

This is something that particularly resonates with Buscemi, who acknowledges the fact that DiCillo writes protagonists devoid of judgement, leaving it up to viewers to work out the characters' complexities and intricacies for themselves. "Part of Tom's talent is that he creates these complex characters that are likeable. Sometimes they are just people with problems, people who have delusions, but Tom is always interested in their heart and soul, and that's evident in every character that he writes. He's not just interested in presenting a character one certain way, he honours each character."

Diaz explains how she came to terms with her character's aberrations; "I justified it as a girl who just really wants to fit in and who wants to belong and to be cool," Diaz admits. "She just wants desperately to belong to someone or something … anything. I just thought of it as a person wanting something so bad and being influenced wrongly; she makes a bad decision, an evil decision."

While on the surface the story presents the casual ease with which Maribel hires two killers to murder her father over something as inconsequential as a tattoo, the film ultimately reveals something disturbingly human behind her actions.

"We are always shocked by the horror and brutality of these kinds of acts," DiCillo elaborates. "But it seems to me that underlying them all are very basic human impulses. Maribel is alone; she deeply longs to be accepted. As horrific as her plan is I felt it needed to have a tiny flicker of understanding. To me this helps make Maribel a real human being instead of just a monster. I was interested in this one child's desperation and the consequences of it."

Completed in 2001, *Double Whammy* touched upon several hot topics in American society at large; mass murder, media hype, the dysfunctional family, dysfunctional cops and sexy violence in cinema.

"I had high hopes for it," DiCillo reveals. "I thought it had really come together well. I do see it as an expansion of some themes I've developed in earlier films. But to be sure it is a departure. There is something built-in about a crime movie. It has a tension, a thrill that can drive a story forward in ways that more conventional films do not. But I wanted to do it in my own way. My cop is the last guy to figure out the crime. There is a kind of Kafkaesque quality to it that excited me."

What was even more Kafkaesque for DiCillo was how the film ended up never being released theatrically. Through a series of double, triple and quadruple whammies, the film was picked up at Sundance by Lionsgate but languished there for almost a year. Executives who'd championed the film came and went, which resulted in *Double Whammy* suffering a fate every filmmaker abhors: it was released straight to video.

Chris Noth believes the film fell afoul of a greater cultural apathy. "I don't think people really understand what Tom's work is actually about," the actor observes. "It would take a really imaginative company to release *Double Whammy* properly." Noth elaborates on what he believes the distributor missed by dumping the film straight to the home video market: "There are a lot of laughs, and a lot of interesting relationships and a different take on things in *Double Whammy*. Tom always likes to explore the idea of what you think is normal. He takes that which we unquestionably accept as reality and get used to, which is actually, from a certain height, just absurd and he's able to reflect that often. I think that's the core of his writing and his vision."

"For me it is always unfortunate when a good film doesn't get the exposure that it should," Buscemi says. "I've seen this time and time again. I do take comfort in the fact that the films I've made with Tom and with other filmmakers who, for whatever reason, have not got the respect they deserve, I feel that in time they will get their due."

DiCillo looks back at the film with an element of resigned acceptance. "It is an odd film," he admits. "In some ways it might reflect a personal conflict between being drawn to tense, realistic drama and whacky, surreal comedy. I love them both. However, I think the sudden shifts in tone created a problem for audiences. But it has been done before. Fellini did it in *Nights of Cabiria*; Schlesinger with *Midnight Cowboy*. However, it takes great skill and requires really versatile and compelling actors. For some reason I thought I could try it."

And thankfully, try it he did. *Double Whammy* is a wryly observed satire with a playful postmodernist take on the crime genre. An ambitious melding of police drama, thriller, romance and comedy, the film also echoes a recurring subtext inherent throughout DiCillo's work: an exploration of man's search for identity and value in a milieu defined by external forces. Pluto's blinding, misplaced faith in Maribel, and Cubbins' sexual crisis are symptomatic of men who don't conform to society's standards; both are stymied by neuroses that men don't often exhibit in front of their peers.

Parallel to that is a devastating look at familial dynamics and the sense of abandonment one feels when those basic connections are lost. Pluto and Maribel share an unspoken bond informed by their feelings of isolation. Pluto has lost his family through fate and circumstance, and Maribel has nearly annihilated hers through choice. The optimism of DiCillo's narrative allows Maribel to repair a connection that was literally severed, while Pluto can redeem himself and allay his personal feelings of guilt by finally bringing the true villains to justice.

With *Double Whammy* DiCillo elicits wonderfully ebullient performances from the cast of fresh faces, as well as offering the likes of Leary, Hurley, Buscemi and Noth the opportunity to work within a realm not normally afforded to them. With its edgy, surreal humor and sharp visual style the film is an aesthetically accomplished picture, absolutely deserving a release on the big screen. It may not contain the sheer immediacy of *Living in Oblivion* or *Delirious*, but the film remains an underrated and deeply misunderstood piece of work.

"I've actually thought every one of my films had commercial potential," DiCillo confesses. "But that has never been what has motivated me. It always comes down to the idea, does it excite me? Does it thrill me to the point that I'm willing to commit myself to years of trying to get it made? With *Double Whammy* it did, so, in that light the film is a success for me, if simply for the fact that I got it made."

* * *

Wayne Byrne: *Tell me about the genesis of* Double Whammy. *What informed the development of the story and characters?*

Tom DiCillo: I'd been toying with the idea of a crime story with a detective who could not figure out the crime. I was mainly interested in the fact that the hero (Pluto) is the last one to figure it out. The script took many forms. Originally it was going to be a bit more like *Alphaville*. In fact, in the original drafts Pluto dies in the end, killed by his gun going off accidentally. You should have heard the financier scream on that. But the first intent was something a bit more absurd and existential. So in feeling pressure to move away from that I focused more on the crime aspects but in my own way. That is, by making all the characters as human as possible, with weaknesses, foibles, idiosyncrasies, fears etc.

How did the rest of the screenplay evolve?

I'd read a story in the newspaper that disturbed me. A young girl hired two friends to kill her father because he wouldn't let her go to a party. The cold desperation of it really shook me. I took this basic idea and created the plot thread of Maribel hiring someone to kill her father for not letting her get a tattoo. It became the crime that never gets solved.

Detective Pluto is your first cop as a lead character. He's not only an anti-hero but he's so unlike his colleagues he's like an anti-cop.

I wanted my cop to be an outsider. That's why I named him Pluto; the furthest planet from the sun. Ray Pluto is smart but he's also got a compulsive irony and bitterness that keep him just barely in the cop solar system. I was interested in the idea of him knowing and not knowing. His trauma about the death of his wife and daughter make him so sympathetic to Maribel that he can't see what she has done.

He's flawed both emotionally and physically. I also gave him a bad back. Most cop films have their heroes leaping around like week-old monkeys. I thought it would be interesting to have mine plagued by a back that would go out on him right at the worst possible moment. It made him more human to me. I was interested in seeing how real people respond to real violence.

So, why doesn't he die at the end?

Because he wants to keep having sex with Elizabeth Hurley. By the time the script fully emerged it had become much different than the cold, existential concept that prompted it. Pluto was more of a human being than an idea and it felt dramatically wrong to snuff him out at the end.

Double Whammy *took over four years to get into production. What took so long?*

It's always hard to pinpoint. Certainly it had something to do with the way *The Real Blonde* was received. But people were still looking for my next *Living in Oblivion*. I was actually getting offers from directors in Europe who wanted to remake *Oblivion* in their own language; some offering a lot of money.

What stopped you from taking them?

Stupidity, I guess. Maybe I just felt that it was such a personal film to me that I didn't want any little half-brothers and -sisters following it around in perpetuity.

So investors didn't get Double Whammy?

Some financiers were interested but only if I cast name actors in all the parts. I tried that for a while; which took over a year or two. One actor I really liked and thought would be amazing in the part told his agent he didn't want to play a guy with a bad back. Another told his agent he didn't want to play a guy that was old enough to have a daughter, even though the fictional daughter was dead and was three-years old when she died.

So I eventually found myself back in no-man's-land. This means you are essentially adrift and looking under every rock for the money. You talk to strangers on the subway, you meet well-meaning supporters whom you find out are only capable of investing $150, total. I have to give my producer, Marcus Viscidi, a lot of credit. Marcus had been with me since *Living in Oblivion*. We did four films together: *Living in Oblivion, Box of Moonlight, The Real Blonde* and *Double Whammy*. I think it was *Whammy* that did him in. It's what made him get out of independent producing.

But he stuck with me during this very scary time. We ended up making a deal with two guys who were going to raise eight million dollars. One of the guys was a convicted drug felon living here illegally and unable to return to Britain. The other was an inventor living in a van in a parking lot on Santa Monica beach. His invention was a foam rubber device that men could place over their penises for maximising pleasure during masturbation. Neither of them had a dime.

I learned this from the inventor's ex-wife. She'd called me in the middle of the night with this valuable information which enabled me to free myself from these two producers who sued me the moment their option expired. A year later we ended up in a deal with Gold Circle Films, a company that has since gone out of business. I don't remember how we convinced them to finance the film.

The film comes across as the voice of an artist who is frustrated and disillusioned by the level of violence that underlies American pop culture. The violence in Double Whammy *is often swift and brutal, but executed with a satirical edge; did you find that the media's fascination with death and destruction is something that needed to be addressed?*

I'm not sure it needed to be addressed. More I felt bewildered by it on a deeper personal level. People have always been fascinated by death and destruction. It's why we still have day-long traffic jams caused by people rubbernecking at an accident. This is such a great word; it implies an unavoidable instinct that pulls the head around on the neck.

I've never really understood horror films but I can see why some people love them; the same way people watch science fiction or pornography. Again, though, I've never understood why it is illegal to see a man making love to a woman while it is legal to see him cutting her head off with an outboard motor.

Aspiring screenwriters Cletis (left, Donald Faison) and Duke (right, Keith Nobbs), planning a scene of ultra-violence for their film

Knife's edge: Pluto struggles with murderous thug, JoJo (Maurice Compte)

I wanted the violence in *Double Whammy* to be as shocking as real violence. The two screenwriters concoct a fictitious torture scene where someone gets a dart thrown into his eyeball. They act it out with a store dummy tied to a chair. It works for them. Later, Pluto gets one of those darts thrown into his leg where it sinks in to the hilt. It makes him scream in agony. And that's just his leg.

I think people's fascination with violence has changed as technology's ability to depict it has gotten more realistic. If you look at some of the earliest "extreme" gangster films like *White Heat* or *Little Caesar*, you don't see a drop of blood even when someone gets shot point-blank in the chest. If you did that today, audiences would laugh. They want to see what they've come to expect from a close-range bullet wound: impact, shirt blown open, blood spray, blood spurt, open body cavity and the finale: the splatter of blood and human material against the nearest white wall.

I was interested in how this fascination with the graphic details of violence seems to coincide with an increasingly numb emotional response to it.

In Living in Oblivion *you commented on the nature of independent cinema. You do it again here but this time from a post-*Pulp Fiction *perspective. By 2000 independent cinema had been consumed and adopted by the mainstream and had become a commercial industry in itself, with a particular brand of cynical humour and extreme violence as the order of the day. Cletis and Duke represent aspiring young filmmakers eager to cash in on this phenomenon. Is this an indictment of what independent cinema became at some point in the mid- to late 1990s?*

Lawyers and priests make indictments. I was just having some fun. And whatever comment I was trying to make was completely lost on people because a) no journalist ever mentioned it and, b) no one saw the movie. All I was trying to do was hold a kind of funhouse mirror up to this reverence for disaffected violence.

And the neo-violent genre did become very profitable. *Stranger Than Paradise* and *sex, lies and videotape* used to be the markers for a solid independent success. I remember investors were very impressed when *Stranger Than Paradise* grossed $2 million. Well, *Pulp Fiction* grossed $500 million. To me, that was the beginning of the end of independent film. No producer or distributor would ever again be satisfied with a film that grossed $2 million.

Double Whammy *alludes to and pays homage to a history of detective films, a genre which rely on the strengths of the hero – or anti-hero – and the femme fatale/love interest; what was it about Denis Leary and Liz Hurley that informed their casting as the jaded, tortured detective and the woman who could sooth his soul?*

I think the part of Det. Pluto is a pretty juicy role for an actor. He's sharp, he's funny and he's an outsider fighting against a clogged and soulless system. Plus he's got some emotional vulnerability. I was really surprised at the number of actors who turned it down. Finally, it struck me one day – perhaps in the fourth year of trying to get it made – that Denis Leary would be great in the part. I'd worked with him on *The Real*

Blonde and really liked him. Denis has a slightly unsettling edge about him that makes him very hard to categorise or put in a box. I think that's a great thing for an actor.

I felt that he could bring out some of the spiky undercurrents of Pluto; the anger, the sarcasm, the instinctive willingness to ridicule everything. My producers were not so convinced. They finally agreed to let me cast him but insisted I get a bigger name for Dr. Beamer. Again, I'd offered this part to many actresses whom I thought could have a blast with it. Then I happened to see Liz Hurley in *Austin Powers* and in the much grittier *Permanent Midnight*. It impressed me that she could do both.

These were decisions I made; partly out of real interest and partly because years had gone by and I wanted to make the movie so badly.

Buscemi is uniformly excellent in the film, but what is a particular standout for me is the young actors you worked with. Donald Faison and Keith Nobbs provide the funniest moments in the film as the screen-violence-obsessed screenwriting duo Cletis and Duke, while Melonie Diaz carries the film's most daring role. How did you find working with these younger actors while on the same film with Vic Argo, Chris Noth, Luis Guzman and stars like Denis Leary, Liz Hurley and Steve Buscemi?

There are three things that excite me in an actor; commitment, willingness and imagination. If an actor is firing on all three cylinders then creative miracles can happen. In my experience I've found that younger, lesser known actors are more open and eager. I mentioned this before; something happens when an actor becomes famous. I'm not saying that stars are not talented. There are many who are and I'd work with them in a second.

But with younger actors I find there is more flexibility, more enthusiasm to explore and discover. This is a way of working that I am drawn to – no bullshit, no protection, no fear of looking foolish. And that is what I loved about Donald, Keith and Melonie. I felt I could say anything to them and they would try it. And maybe because I cared for them all so deeply they trusted me and sensed that my direction was always to help them find the most pleasure and enjoyment in the moments. Maybe they wanted to please me; I don't know. All I know is every scene with them was a delight for me. And it pains me to say that was not the case with some of the other actors on the film.

A few of the more experienced actors were less willing?

Some of them. I don't think Denis or Elizabeth ever felt comfortable in my world. At the US Premiere in Sundance, with a sold-out audience of about 1,000 people, they both got up and walked out during the closing credits. During the customary Q&A I had all of my actors on stage with me except my two leads. This never happened to me before, or since. When *Living in Oblivion* screened at Sundance every actor in the film was up there with me, and many of them had paid their own way to get there. It was a huge family love-fest. But, Leary and Hurley just disappeared. Still kind of infuriates me. They weren't part of the team and there is some sense of that in the film itself.

On the other hand, some of the other stars were amazing. Chris Noth brought a great sense of play and a real intelligence to his character. Victor Argo, who was tremendous in a number of Scorcese films, came in, did his work and was a joy to work with. I'm deeply grateful to him.

Was it then that you wished you'd cast Catherine Keener?

I don't know. I look back on it now and wonder what I was thinking. Some people did question my casting of Liz Hurley. They thought, "What the fuck is Tom doing casting a model-celebrity in this role?" Liz took the part very seriously and worked hard on it. Ultimately, she wasn't quite believable as a chiropractor. It's not her fault. She's just too glamorous.

Why did you cast her?

I wanted to get the movie made. *Box of Moonlight* was a bomb. *The Real Blonde* was a bomb. You start to believe that casting celebrities or stars is how you make a movie that more than twenty people see. You start to believe you need to make a movie that makes enough money so you can make another one without spending five years crawling on your knees.

But it didn't work. And it never has, for me at least. Yeah, maybe I should have cast Catherine. She would've brought something amazing and real to the part. Some of it was even written for her; the insecurity, the compulsive honesty. She would've really kept Leary on his toes.

You mentioned that you'd grown apart. Was it anything in particular?

It's funny; when we were just starting *The Real Blonde* Catherine came in for a costume fitting. It had been a while since I'd seen her. As we were choosing her clothes and discussing possibilities for her hairstyle I remember a very subtle tension between us. It really threw me because by this point we'd done three films together. And suddenly the costume designer looked at us both and laughed and said, "You two are like an ex-married couple."

Why? Were you were fighting?

No. More like a very real connection we'd had was somehow slipping away.

She didn't want to do the film?

She wanted to do it. But we tangled about things that we hadn't before.

Things beyond costumes and hairstyles?

One incident came during the scene where she beats up Denis Leary in the film. He plays this pompous martial arts instructor teaching women how to defend themselves but ultimately demeaning them. If anybody deserved to get the shit kicked out of him it was him.

What was her objection to the scene?

Catherine is a very strong-minded person and this is a large part of what I really admire about her. She has very specific views on what is right and wrong in the world. In this case she brought her own aversion to violence to the scene. She personally felt physical violence was wrong, which I totally agree with. I tried to explain to her that in this case it was so absurd it was absolutely justified. There's a biting, ironic comedy to it. It's not literal. I had to close the set for two hours one night as we kept arguing about it.

What did you want that you weren't getting?

I felt there could be a greater sense of joy; a real pleasurable release. It was an acting moment to be savoured and enjoyed. It was an extremely rare moment; when does a woman ever get a chance to knee some fatuous prick in the balls? But Catherine was drawing on a tense, hesitant resentment that deflated the scene. I wanted her to soar with it. Ultimately, we got it. She knew it was important to me so she tried very hard. At the end of the night she was covered in black and blue marks and I felt terrible; like it was me who had beaten her up.

None of this is apparent in the film.

No, and that's a great tribute to Catherine. She committed 100% to the part like she always does.

Was she aware of how hard you'd fought for her? Did she know of the trainer and the make-up artist that Lakeshore had foisted upon you?

No. She was getting attention from a lot of very well-respected directors and perhaps she was simply looking to move on.

Were you not thinking the same about other actresses? I mean, certainly with your reputation you would also have the opportunity to work with other talented actors.

You're right; there are many talented women I'd like to work with. Cate Blanchett is unbelievable. Kate Winslet. Robin Wright. Amy Adams. But there was something personal already established with me and Catherine. She was like one of those great friends you have as a kid, where each of you provides something missing for the other. Each of you is the other's most delightful inspiration, prompting you to do things you'd never do by yourself. So together there is this force that is exhilarating and unstoppable.

For a few years that's what Catherine and I had. Even though we lived on different coasts we talked all the time. I shared script ideas with her as I was writing. I talked to her about every minute change and development in the progress of the films, from all the incarnations of *Box of Moonlight* through *Living in Oblivion* and *The Real Blonde*. She always listened, she was always supportive and she always helped me feel that I wasn't fighting the world completely alone.

But maybe that all got tiresome to her. I can see how it would; all the ups and downs, the possible good things, the crashing disasters. As I mentioned earlier, this is not a business where anyone wants to feel hemmed in or restricted. Everyone wants to feel free to move instantly toward the most fruitful opportunity.

Do you feel she moved and you didn't?

Well, that's a heavy question. She has certainly achieved great success with other directors. I've made the films I've wanted to make but I haven't had the kind of success that leads to more films. I know that when *Double Whammy* came around there was a mutual feeling we needed a break from each other. There wasn't a sense that one of us was leaving the other. But that didn't make the separation any easier.

It still pains you?

It's like any strong connection; the loss of it leaves a wound. It eventually heals over but you always feel the scar. I think real friends, particularly in this business, are very rare. There's too much at stake. But we were friends for a while on quite a deep level though perhaps much of that came from me.

You don't think the artistic and personal connection was mutual?

Absolutely it was. I'm just saying I brought something to it. Over the years I've had a number of dreams in which she appears. They're all the same; just as we're about to reconnect on some profound dream-level she vanishes, leaving this ache that would stagger me for days. In the dreams she represented something magical, exciting and full of possibility. It took me years to understand these were all parts of myself that I'd been taught to believe did not exist in me.

Like Les Gallantine?

Let's just say I knew Les very well.

Double Whammy had perhaps the most tortured release of all of your films. After a bitter struggle with your distributor it went straight-to-video, a marketplace usually reserved for the cheap, the tacky and the Steven Seagal. What happened?

Well, I can tell you that never in my wildest nightmares did I think I'd ever make a film that did not get released theatrically. The film was financed by Gold Circle whose CEO was a real champion. We got accepted to Sundance with it in 2000 and quickly made a sale there to Lionsgate, a well-respected mini-major distributor. The Lionsgate executive who bought the film had previously run the publicity company I hired for *Living in Oblivion*. We were good friends and he too was a real champion of the film. The sale was announced in all the trade papers, each stating Lionsgate's enthusiasm for a fall 2001 theatrical release. I felt the film was in great hands.

Three things happened, in this order. The Gold Circle CEO got fired. Three weeks later my friend at Lionsgate got fired. This left the film essentially orphaned. I tried establishing a connection with their successors but they clearly felt at best no obligation to the film and at worst, a kind of resentment of it, like it was a distasteful remnant forced on them by their departed predecessors. Then, a month later, two planes crashed into the World Trade Center.

This had a devastating effect on the film business; especially independent film. No one was interested in anything remotely risky. When Lionsgate stopped returning phone calls and emails I knew something bad was coming. Finally, the silence was broken by their announcement that they were not going to honour their contract and instead were going to release the film only on video.

Was that legal? You said you had a contract.

No, it was not legal. But nothing means anything in this business. Lionsgate didn't want to release the film theatrically so they didn't. I fought them with everything I had, which wasn't too much. My own lawyer conceded to them after only a day or two, telling me with distinct annoyance that this was the way things worked and there was nothing I could do about it.

Lionsgate then denied they'd ever agreed to a theatrical release. I sent them their own press release from several papers in which they were quoted as saying how excited they were about "a fall theatrical release". But the end result was simple and brutal. They dumped the film to video.

The film received several nominations from the DVD Premiere Awards, at which you won Best Original Screenplay. Did you see this as some kind of recognition that the film was at least worthy in the eyes of some people, however small or under the radar, or was this the death knell for the film as far as you were concerned?

Oh, it was definitely a knell. That awards ceremony was so bizarre. Robbie Robertson from The Band got up and said, "Is it just me or does this evening feel like an episode of *The Twilight Zone*?" I accepted my award and said, "Thank you. I sincerely hope this is the last award like this I will ever get." Today the DVD Premiere Awards no longer exist. I kept the award but pried the text plate off and replaced it with one that I made myself: "Best Film Made Without Committing Homicide or Suicide." It's in the back of a closet now.

But the reality was that I was so shaken by what had happened to the film I was very close to both of those extremes.

Despite the obstacles the film had to endure, do you look back on the film as something you are happy with?

Absolutely. I was pleased with it as a crime drama, especially the edgy, unstable combination of pathos and humour that came out of it. I think the intersecting stories and interwoven plots lock into place and my goal of creating a very real drama and tension was successful. There are many scenes that still affect me strongly. One of my favourite moments is when one of the hired killers puts a Sundance bag over his head to see if it will work as an efficient blindfold for one of their intended victims.

CHAPTER SEVEN

Delirious

'Rule # 1 – Friends is friends.'
— Toby Grace

'A friend is somebody just waiting for a chance to talk about themselves.'
— Les Galantine

By 2006 the momentum of Tom DiCillo's career had for all practical purposes come to a complete stop. The recognition and accolades won from *Johnny Suede, Living in Oblivion* and *Box of Moonlight* were seemingly irrelevant. According to the film business dictum, "You're only as good as your last picture", and DiCillo's *Double Whammy* went virtually unseen.

"Everything in the film business is based upon perception," DiCillo admits. "How your film is perceived, how you are perceived, how your future is perceived. A film going straight-to-video pretty much takes all those perceptions and flushes them down the toilet."

Yet five years later, DiCillo would return triumphant with one of the most vital works of his career, his sixth feature film, *Delirious*. From the opening frames to the closing credits *Delirious* has the immediate spirit and urgency of a filmmaker embracing his love of the medium. It's a film of great passion and seemingly effortless artistic resolve, a renewal of the director's distinguished creative credentials. But the truth of its realisation from script to screen is that it was born out of the despair of seeing several of his films falter on their paths to distribution.

"I recharged all the motivations I had for getting involved in filmmaking in the first place," DiCillo recalls. "I said to myself, 'Write something that genuinely excites you. Write something that you can't wait to direct,' because when all the shit goes down, that is the only thing that is left. Perhaps this is the lesson I learned from *Double Whammy*. Make the film you are dying to make. Anything less will never survive."

An artful contemplation upon male companionship and the emotional vulnerability we submit to in forming connections with others, *Delirious* is an edgy dramatic comedy as well as a scathing satire on celebrity exaltation. The film tells the tale of Toby Grace (Michael Pitt), a young homeless man who skillfully ingratiates himself into the lonely world of Les Galantine, an emotionally unstable, middle-aged photojournalist with a damaged sense of self-worth. Les (performed, inhabited and consumed by Steve Buscemi) hopes to someday become a photographer of note, but for the time being takes pride chasing down photo ops of the rich and famous. A denizen of the lowest rung of the media fraternity, Les is a paparazzo. As master of all he surveys, Les maintains a strict adherence to his own set of ultimatums that dictate to anyone who enters his world the terms and conditions of life in Les's presence. It is always Rule #1, there is no such thing as a Rule #2, so one better obey…

The World According to Les Galantine
Rule #1 – The bigger the ass, the bigger the asshole.
Rule #1 – There are players and there are peons. I'm a player.
Rule #1 – Never let a hooker slip you the tongue.

Toby befriends Les by offering to work for free. Wary of Toby's intentions and the forced intimacy his presence brings, Les is nonetheless thrilled at the bargain and despite his suspicions the two men form a deep bond of friendship. This bond is tested to its limits when Toby falls in love with pop star, K'harma Leeds (Alison Lohman), and is effortlessly accepted into her exclusive inner circle of celebrity – the kind of elusive world that Les has been yearning to enter for years. Further strain is put on their friendship when Toby is taken in by a smart and attractive casting director, Dana (Gina Gershon). Dana gets Toby the lead role in a faux-reality television series called "Slice of Life", in which he stars as a "sexy serial killer" who is very good with a knife. This leads to all-out Tobymania in the media. Burned by what he sees as Toby's betrayal for leaving him behind, Les plans a devastating revenge. But what he really seeks is a re-connection to the one person who truly values and appreciates him as a human being. For the first time in his life Les has experienced compassion and affection from Toby and, like us all, desperately wants to cling to the comfort and reassurance this human contact offers.

Stardom is a major theme of *Delirious*. The question of what makes someone a star has intrigued DiCillo for years. He has witnessed the meteoric rise of several actors after casting them in key early roles before emerging as household names, such as Brad Pitt, Catherine Keener, Sam Rockwell, Peter Dinklage and Michael Pitt.

"What makes someone a star?" DiCillo asks. "I didn't want to ridicule or satirise this concept because the idea of the star is one that I believe in. I feel, as everyone who goes to the movies does, that some people have a certain magic in them that makes them supremely interesting to watch. I began trying to determine just what it is in our greatest stars that touch us so deeply. Most of them ironically open themselves to us so completely that we feel for a moment in the darkened theatre that we're being granted that rarest privilege of looking into their souls; beyond the sex appeal or the good looks is an unshakeable honesty. That was one idea that I worked into the script. Another theme developed after Princess Diana died trying to escape a horde of paparazzi; their obsession with photographing her ultimately led to her death."

To get inside the mind of the paparazzo, DiCillo spent time hanging around with a real one; someone with whom he'd had some tense encounters before. "I've dealt with paparazzi throughout my career," DiCillo explains, "and have never felt completely comfortable with the profession. I don't believe that celebrity makes someone an open target with no limits on violating their privacy. This made me start thinking: 'What inspires someone to become a paparazzi? How do they justify what they do?'"

The director continues: "I immediately thought of this one paparazzo that I'd thrown off several of my sets. He was astounded and pretty nervous when I called him. But once I got him calmed down I ended up spending about three months with him, going to events, driving around in his car, going to his apartment and seeing how he lived. In doing this I managed to get a glimpse into his persona, something that really touched me. For all his vehemence in justifying why it was his right to intrude into the lives of celebrities, there was a deep undercurrent of self-loathing. Underneath his bluster he felt keenly inferior to the people he was stalking. This gave me a great hook into the character that became Les Galantine."

For DiCillo, there would only be one man for the job of playing Les: Steve Buscemi. "The deeper I got into the character of Les the more fascinated with him

DiCillo directs Buscemi on the set of *Delirious*

I became," DiCillo reveals. "Despite all his conniving and maneuvering Les is really brutally honest. He may not see it in himself but he's incapable of camouflaging his feelings. They're all right there on the surface: his fear, his rage, his jealousy, his loneliness, his self-doubt."

DiCillo had been left a little wary after his last experience working with stars. This time around he made a conscious decision to write a lead part for an actor he would relish seeing on the set every day. "I wrote it for Steve," DiCillo reveals, "even before he knew it. It coincided with my realisation that making a movie doesn't have to be accompanied only by angst and disappointment. Fellini said once that the crucial ingredient in making a film is a willingness from people; actors especially. He explained that every option should be open and available to solve a problem. This requires a general letting go of ego from everyone. It doesn't mean that you don't fight strongly for something. It means that everyone is aware of the larger scope of the film. And so, all solutions work toward the film, not the isolated bubble of each person's private needs. This applies to crew members as well. Steve Buscemi is one of the most willing actors I've ever worked with. Maybe it's because he trusts me. Maybe it's because he knows how much I trust him and respect his gift. But contrary to everything you hear about how painful it is to gain a great performance, our work together is absolutely effortless. And enjoyable."

The director details why this is so unusual. "I don't mean that Steve does whatever I ask him to. Steve always has very clear, specific ideas as to what he wants to do. If he doesn't like an idea he lets me know and we try something else. But if I make a suggestion his first impulse is to consider it. And many times that's all it takes, just a suggestion. I'll whisper something to him and I'll see his eyes light up. I keep these suggestions private because it helps create a sense of surprise for the other actor. Then I step back and watch him fly.

The amazing thing about Steve's gift is that he can easily do what is written on the page and fill it with a world of meaning. When you start to improvise and give him room to run he always has a sense of not only what the scene requires but also how everything he's making up will fit into the film as a whole. This is such a rare talent. And I think it comes directly from who Steve is as a person. He's one of the most generous and gracious people I've ever met.

And like Catherine, I feel a little possessive of him. I feel like I see things in Steve that most people don't even consider. He's not just a whack-job. He's not just 'the goofy-looking guy' as a waitress describes him in *Fargo*. I think he's got a combination of *all* the Marx Brothers in him. He can make you weep with laughter, and weep with pain. Somehow even in his most disturbing moments he manages to find the character's humanity which opens the window for an unexpected and enlightening touch of comedy."

Which is why, after four months of writing *Delirious* specifically for Buscemi, DiCillo was stunned when the actor turned him down. The actor felt there was something missing from the character whose dark nature and tortured inner demons at times made him wary.

"I don't want to go into something where I'm judging the character and therefore can't do the job that's required," Buscemi reveals. "I needed to have empathy for Les. I don't have to like the character but I do have to have some kind of understanding of him."

The director now faced the daunting task of re-casting the role. He considered many esteemed character actors but ultimately realised he'd written himself into a box. It was clear to him there was only one actor who could play the part. After months of little contact with Buscemi, DiCillo decided a real, face-to-face meeting was the only hope of re-interesting him.

"So the first thing I did was lie to him," DiCillo admits. "I told him I needed to come out to Brooklyn to pick up something from my wife's sister. I suggested I drop by and just have a cup of coffee with him. Steve said OK and we met in a coffee shop on the bleakest, coldest day in February."

The two talked about the script. At one point Buscemi recited some of Les's lines, startling the director by bringing the character unexpectedly to life right in front of him.

"I could barely speak from excitement and longing," DiCillo confesses. "Afterwards we walked back to his place. Just before we said goodbye I asked him, 'So Steve, what do you think? Do you want to play this part?' The ensuing silence lasted for more than five minutes. He looked at me; I looked at him. He looked away. A bitter wind scraped some dead leaves along the icy gutter. Another minute of silence went by. He never answered. Finally I just said, 'OK, Steve. I'll see you later.' And I drove home. The whole ride back, the only thought I had was, well, at least he didn't say no."

"Tom just badgered me." Buscemi wryly admits, "He wouldn't give up. He talked to me about Les and who he is and where that pathology comes from. Perhaps I thought at the time that I had played dark characters like that before and I wasn't interested in exploring that stuff any further. Tom really helped me see that Les did have this artistic, sensitive side to him; that he wasn't just this superficially brash guy filled with anger. He definitely has a lot of anger in him but Tom helped me to see where it all comes from, and helped me to see who the real Les is underneath all of that anger. There was something in the theme of family that resonated with me, Les's relationship with his parents and how they see him and his reaction to that; it gave me a real place to work from."

DiCillo was able to tap into something personally relevant to his leading man, a move that afforded Buscemi the opportunity of a searing performance that went beyond dark and eccentric and into something devastatingly honest and all-consuming. A pivotal moment of illumination came for Buscemi at a script reading. DiCillo recalls: "After I'd done some more work on the script I set up a staged reading. And it was here that Steve and a group of actors read the whole script out loud for the first time. The entire room was electrified; all the other actors could feel it too. We could actually see Steve bringing Les to life right in front of us. This was what finally convinced him to commit to the film. Afterwards, he pulled me aside and thanked me for being so persistent and having such faith in him."

It was apparently an emotional moment for both men. "I thought I saw tears in his eyes," DiCillo says. "I know there were some in mine. I never felt such a sense of relief in my life."

By far the next most crucial part was that of Toby Grace, the young homeless kid Les takes in and who eventually leaves him when he becomes a star. DiCillo talks

Alison Lohman as successful but troubled pop star, K'harma Leeds

about the critical casting choice this required. "Toby is a very tricky part. I needed an actor who could be believable as someone living on the streets and then be just as believable walking up the red carpet toward his pending stardom. Again, the producers were pushing me to hire a 'name'. A bunch of them came up, strangely all from the *Lord of the Rings* franchise. Again, I persevered and convinced the producers that the part required more than anything the depth and skill of a great actor. I preferred someone who was relatively unknown and was really thrilled to discover Michael Pitt. He brings a great soul and credibility to the part. It came at a great price but ultimately it was worth it."

By time of production on *Delirious* Alison Lohman had made a splash with *Big Fish* (Tim Burton, 2003) and rivalled Nicolas Cage and Sam Rockwell with her commanding and energetic screen presence in *Matchstick Men* (Ridley Scott, 2003). It was this opportunity to bring a modest human quality to a much-maligned cultural stereotype – the pop starlet – that intrigued the young actress to pursue the role so doggedly.

"I really liked the idea of playing this Britney Spears-type pop princess but with the view to bringing some dimension to her," Lohman enthuses. "K'harma isn't just a vapid blonde dancing on the screen. I wanted to explore the vulnerable side of her and to show that she's a real person just like any girl having to deal with family, boyfriends, work. So I wanted to bring some layers to a type of person that is never afforded that kind of depth in the media. K'harma is a supporting character, the movie isn't just about her, but I loved that Tom paid so much attention to portraying her as such a fully realised character."

Once again, star-centric financiers almost derailed DiCillo's choice of Lohman for the role. "Since K'harma was a pop star the producers felt we should try to land a real pop star," DiCillo reveals. "So at several points over the course of the five years it took to raise the money I actually wrote letters to people like Britney Spears and Christina Aguilera expressing my 'desire' for them to star in the film. This is part of the uncomfortable compromise that comes with the film business. I wanted Buscemi. I knew no one else could do the role. The financiers were letting me cast him so I tried to appease their demands for casting big stars. Perhaps I even convinced myself that having Britney Spears in my film would be a good thing. All I can say is thank god she never responded. I finally came to my senses and convinced the financiers that the part was too complex to be played by anyone less than a real actor."

"I had seen *The Real Blonde* and I was really attracted to the quirkiness of Tom's style on that film," Lohman reveals. "Tom sees the world differently from most, he has a different slant on life and his humour is so unique. His films are this mixture of being quite heavy and but also light at the same time, and it is how he balances that that makes them so interesting. I really fought for my part in *Delirious*. I loved Tom, he is just a really normal guy, nothing pretentious or unapproachable about him, but yet he has this really idiosyncratic and very precise style, he knows what he wants to say and how to get it on to the screen."

DiCillo gave another strong female role to Gina Gershon. Her character, Dana, ushers Toby into the world of red carpets and flashing bulbs. Dana immediately recognises a star quality in Toby; of course, she also sees a good-looking young man she's sexually attracted to, but she is also instinctively aware of his marketability.

"Tom was someone I had really wanted to work with for a long time," Gershon recalls. "For me it's always about the director. I will take a smaller part, if I really want to work with that director, and hopefully it can evolve into something more significant. But here it came down to the fact of it being a really great script to start with, the brilliant idea of having this weird paparazzi guy as the main character and trying understand who he really is. I thought that Tom had an interesting take on this whole world."

An intensely alluring and daring actress, Gershon's is a career marked with profoundly provocative roles in controversial films such as Paul Verhoeven's *Showgirls*, the Wachowskis' *Bound* and William Friedkin's *Killer Joe*. She has a marked ability to inform her characters with a vigorous intensity and fiery individualism, qualities that DiCillo elicits here for Dana, along with a level of emotional depth and vulnerability.

"Gina is very smart," DiCillo says. "Plus she has a wonderful sense of humour; sharp and delightful. She also has a great soul and I believe it is that, in combination with her talent, intelligence and humour that makes her so special. Like Buscemi, she is a very willing actor. She is game for anything."

Dana is one of the three central characters to be hypnotised by Toby's charms, whether he is fulfilling something void in their lives, or merely embracing them for who they are. All three relationships are mutually beneficial, emotionally and otherwise. For Dana in particular, Toby appeals to and satisfies both of her seemingly dominant appetites: work and pleasure.

Seductive casting agent Dana (Gina Gershon) grooms Toby (Michael Pitt) for stardom, and bedroom

"First of all, it was her job to find talent," Gershon elaborates, "and she did that in coming across Toby, she found someone she could mold into a star. She sees him and thinks, 'I know what to do with this kid', and then she ends up sleeping with him. Why not? He's cute!" Gershon proclaims. "I don't think she was sleeping with him in order to get him to become who he does, she was just attracted to him."

"Gina brings a real humanity to Dana," DiCillo remarks. "There is no one on the planet that does not feel pain from rejection. The fact that she lets it show gives us a glimpse beneath the surface of this woman who has seen it all and yet who is hoping against all odds that somehow things could work out with her and Toby. The intention with the writing of Toby's character was that he had a natural innocence and charm. He could make people instantly feel like they were important and they had value, not only to him but to themselves. He brought a sense of hope to everyone's life he touched. Plus, being young and good-looking, he offered a strong attraction for Dana. The age difference probably made it even more exciting for her. But we do get the sense he admired her and liked her as well. However, Toby is equally a manipulator. He knew that by moving in that direction with Dana it would help him. He didn't take advantage of her or lie to her; he simply walked through the door she opened for him. One senses Dana's attraction went a bit deeper than his."

Both Dana and K'harma are illustrative of a character that DiCillo has excelled in crafting over the course of his career: the powerful, independent, and strong-willed woman who often succeeds in life where his male protagonists do not. From Johnny Suede to Nick Reve, and from Al Fountain to Joe Finnegan and Ray Pluto, each leading male of DiCillo's previous films has sought refuge in the solid grounding of the women in their lives. The females of DiCillo's narratives are often financially responsible emotional bedrocks whose empathy for their men's emotional paralysis and lack of development is stretched to breaking point. For these men there is usually an impetuous temptation to stray from such steadfast support. DiCillo's men take for granted the loyalty of those closest to them, but when the tables are turned all the male fears and insecurities come crashing down with the force of an avalanche. DiCillo empowers his women with the ability to flourish without reliance upon men. Dana and K'harma already made it in the worlds on the outside of which Les and Toby are both merely spectators. It is only that Toby is useful to both women he eventually succeeds in scaling the fence.

"Women are strong in real life," Lohman explains, "and Tom is able to get that on the page and onto the screen, whereas they aren't portrayed that way in a lot of films. Tom is clearly not politically correct, he just tells it how it is, which means that his portrayal of women is different from most other directors who feel that women have to be shown a certain way. I think it's getting a bit better for women these days with TV shows like *Girls*, but it's not always like that in cinema. Tom's female characters are always dynamic."

Gershon similarly acknowledges that, "Tom has a huge respect for women and he writes bright, strong female characters and that attracts people to his roles. He creates a world that you really want to play in."

"Tom is always fair and sympathetic to his characters," Lohman concurs, "even those less-favourable ones. I'm sure that has something to do with his choice of actors; they are able to bring a level of depth to them that goes beyond simple 'good' or 'bad' and makes you think of their humanity. Tom never moralises or offers us easy answers; the characters are always deeply three-dimensional. Unfortunately, some people want their art to be drawn in broad strokes. Working with Tom, you see that he is incredibly specific."

With *Delirious*, DiCillo has crafted perhaps the deepest examination of male companionship of recent decades. Recalling such seminal works of the New Hollywood era as *Midnight Cowboy*, *The Last Detail* and *Thunderbolt and Lightfoot*, the central relationship of the film between Les and Toby is one which goes beyond the mere bonhomie of two male pals. It underscores the genuine affection and tender, deep-seated bond that can surface between two men under the weight of intense experience and volatile circumstance. DiCillo previously laid waste to a caricatured and generic cinema of masculinity with *Double Whammy*. Here, DiCillo once again satirises notions of misguided intimacy among men, but executes it far more dramatically and with a greater degree of empathy. Toby's sexuality is put under scrutiny by both Les and his parents, and if there is a bubbling undercurrent of homosexual tension throughout the film (Toby is literally put into the closet at one stage by Les) it is motivated more by Les's inability to respond to genuine emotion. His natural reaction is to be suspicious of another man being so openly and physically affectionate towards him.

Several exchanges in the film astutely underscore the tension of intimacy. One in particular occurs after Toby's first job as Les's assistant. With Toby's help, Les snaps a photo of famous TV celebrity, Chuck Sirloin, emerging from a penile surgeon's office. Later, as Les and Toby celebrate the sale of Les's photograph of "The Beef" for $700,

Les Gallantine (Steve Buscemi) puts Toby Grace (Michael Pitt) in the closet

Les thanks his assistant with the promise of taking his headshots and sending them to casting agents, to which Toby responds with a spontaneous and enthusiastic hug. Les is almost crippled by the physical intimacy of the moment, responding only with a defensive resort to humour, "All right, take it easy, I thought you said you weren't gay."

"I do think Les falls in love with Toby," DiCillo admits. "It's like a first-love infatuation. His sarcastic remarks to Toby about being gay are more an illustration of his nervousness and uneasiness in the face of Toby's simple, honest affection. Les has never had anything like that. The intimacy of it makes him very uncomfortable and so he jokes about it, trying to deflect his own inability to simply be real and connect with people."

"Les just wants to be accepted," Buscemi says, "and Toby accepts him for who he is. It took Toby to find Les's openness, and I think he does have an open heart but it has been stepped on so many times that it has made him become very protective. Because of that he turns it into a defense mechanism driven by his anger and that could be really dangerous. That's one of the things that I came to admire about Les," the actor reveals, "that he has this incredible inferiority complex and at the same time he can muster this courage to just say, 'I belong in this world and I deserve to be noticed!' It's a character that's so full of contradictions and it's wonderful for an actor to play that kind of role because you just know you're going to be on a really interesting journey along the way."

"Toby instinctively accepts Les as an equal, as a human being," DiCillo continues. "And Les cherishes the affection so much he wants more and more of it. And then, when Toby becomes a star it pushes Les's dependence into obsession. I was interested in the idea that Les has literally no contact with people, let alone sexual relations with women. This is more a result of his self-image than a sexual preference. He doesn't know how to be intimate with anybody. He is so afraid of being rejected, so convinced that no one could ever find him attractive or loveable, that he has completely shut himself off from any physical contact with other human beings. Les can't believe someone actually likes him. This makes him very dependent on Toby."

What leads Les and Toby to share such an intimate co-dependency is an emotional void stemming from their respective familial dysfunction. This emotional reliance has less to do with climbing the ladder of fame and success, and more to do with the demons they share due to years of physical and psychological abuse at the hands of their parents.

DiCillo admits that the notion of this shared history of family conflict was one of the crucial motivations of the film: "That was an idea that I structured in, to have both of them be severely damaged. But the amazing thing is that Toby has been able to reconcile with it in a major way. When he says to Les, 'you can't depend upon your parents' approval for your own identity,' it's a rather massive statement for someone so young. For Les, having someone able to see so deeply into his soul, it startles him."

There is an emotionally wrenching scene at the heart of the film that suggests Les is the way he is because of the fractured relationship with his elderly parents. When he takes Toby home for dinner we see that the domestic situation of the Galantine household is a bleak one. As Les tries to connect with his parents they blatantly disparage him and his profession.

"I have a feeling that no matter what profession Les chose or whatever he did with his life, his parents would still devalue him," DiCillo says. "He's like this hungry baby bird that is just squawking, 'Mom! Dad!' Because he's starving, so frail and such a needy person his parents are incapable of dealing with him."

Les's mother, Lois (Doris Belack), is an obsessive-compulsive who demands that Les wash his hands repeatedly. His father, Carl (Tom Aldredge), is a gruff military buff who collects and restores old weaponry. Both parents are disgusted at their son's candid snap of Chuck Sirloin with bandaged-enhanced penis in full view. "Get it out of here; I don't want the fucking thing in the house!" Carl angrily shouts at his son before dumping all copies of the magazine in the trash.

"I'm fascinated by the destruction that family can cause, whether willfully or blindly," DiCillo admits. "We place enormous weight on how our brothers, sisters, mothers and fathers see us or value us. Many of us suffer the guilt trips, the judgements and the jealousies for our whole lives, as if they were all pre-ordained and somehow unavoidable. Les wants his parents to acknowledge him and to see him as worthy of their love and respect. But, tragically, their limitations make this impossible. Les can't see this. He can only see their judgement of him and he accepts it as true. He always sees himself through their eyes and through them he is worthless, and worse: unlovable. There is nothing more destructive to one's sense of self."

This scene is one of the most pointed examples in all of DiCillo's work of how the director juxtaposes weighty themes such as family and one's place in it – or outside of it – with his searing sense of humour and satirical edge. This balancing act is such a tricky manoeuvre that in the wrong hands could easily undermine the gravity and pathos of the high emotions fuelling the scene. DiCillo manages to be achingly truthful and honest while maintaining the comedy that is the essential backbone of the film.

Though powerfully acted by everyone, it is Buscemi's brilliance that drives the scene. In one particular moment Les attempts to impress his father with his published photo. Without saying a word Buscemi brings a longing and hunger in his face and body language that suggests deep wounds from years of emotional distancing and non-acceptance from his family.

"Tom has met my parents," Buscemi candidly recalls. "And he is very intuitive and very sensitive and I think he probably found something to say to me in that moment that related to my direct experience with my parents that was able to trigger something I could use. It made the scene more emotionally charged."

The actor continues: "There was something to that theme where he tries to show his parents his work – and I totally understand his parents' reaction – that made me understand that to Les this was his work, it was his art, and he puts a lot of time into it and is proud of it. No matter what anybody thinks, this is what Les has chosen to do and he's actually pretty good at it. It's frustrating to him that it's not recognised, and especially so by his parents. That gave me a window into Les's heart, and what a damaged heart that is."

DiCillo elaborates: "What's so compelling about Les is that even though he's been slapped down a hundred times, when he goes back again he has the same expectation that somehow his father will finally see and acknowledge him. I think I may have said to Steve in that moment that this might be the time when his father finally says, 'Hey, that's great, Les.' That's what is brilliant about Steve as an actor, he is able to immerse himself into all the positive possibilities of an acting moment, and that's the most human thing, to reveal a hope, to expose this desperate sort of longing. The scene felt like it was this real thing that was happening all by itself, but at the same time I was right there in the middle of it."

DiCillo continues: "Tom Aldredge, playing Les's father, had left the scene and was standing behind me just watching Les and his mother finish the scripted dialogue. All of a sudden Tom walks back into the room and joins in again. I just let the camera roll. The end of the scene was completely improvised by all of them with a jolt of spontaneity I never could have written."

"I do remember Tom let us improvise that scene," Buscemi fondly recalls. "Sometimes he wouldn't cut the scene, he might just tell us to start again with a minor adjustment or throw in something totally different, while we're rolling, just to see what he could get. Each filmmaker has their own personality and I think Tom just has a real love for what he does and a real love for the people that do it with him. He brings a different kind of energy to the set. Tom really lets actors explore their roles and just reminds them not to take their parts for granted, to take chances and to experiment. He will suggest ways that maybe the actor hasn't thought of. He is very open to actors' ideas and he's very free with his own ideas. Tom has a playful attitude in him and in his direction. It's that playfulness that allows the actors to take risks and you can see it really pay off in the film."

Delirious is DiCillo's most direct and brutally honest expression of his unease at the institution of family and the question of obligation to it. Look beneath the surface of his dark satire one will find broken familial bonds informing the pathology of much of DiCillo's protagonists. "We take abuse from family members we wouldn't take from our closest friends," DiCillo candidly admits. "There are times when I see a mother and a father interacting with their kids and I feel a real ache for some of the things I missed out on. It enforces my belief that a healthy family relationship can exist on some level. I'm even adjusting my expectations so that I can see what value exists in my own family, as small as it is. With my parents, anything that is emotionally real, anything that deals with what's going on with people on the inside, makes them very uncomfortable."

DiCillo continues: "There is a certain code in my family that is never broken, and that is to say that any questioning of the self is seen as not manly; not masculine. I know that it always made my father uneasy when he perceived that I was going through these conflicts that any artist or any human being goes through. But if you look at my films they are all about this kind of introspection, they are about an inner struggle that comes before any crucial step forward.

I was interested in showing how Les keeps going back to his family, his father particularly, to continually seek what he never got from them. Les's father throws his son's photos into the garbage. He is in essence saying Les is garbage. My point with that scene was to suggest something of Les's psychological make-up. People don't turn out like him out of nothing. To me it made Les's decision to become a paparazzo more complex and interesting."

Les's fringe association with celebrity is a perfect vehicle for his damaged sense of self-worth and confidence. He constantly reassures Toby that celebrities are "just people; we're all equal", yet when Les is actually confronted with a celebrity his facade crumbles and his fierce sense of insignificance comes to the fore. When Toby is invited to K'harma's birthday party Les guilt-trips Toby into bringing him as a plus-one. All goes well until Les finds himself face-to-face with a celebrity he genuinely admires: Elvis Costello.

"Since Les has no foundation for belief in himself, the moment he comes into contact with someone who is recognised as a genuine star, in this case, Elvis Costello, all of his fears and insecurities rush to the surface," DiCillo says. "This paralyses Les to the degree he becomes incoherent when he finally meets Costello. His crippled sense of self literally renders him speechless."

It's an intense moment of truth for Les. Even more devastating, Toby has now seen him crumble. As his neuroses get the better of him, Les reflexively resorts to snapping photographs of Costello with K'harma. Costello evidently makes more sense to Les when viewed through his camera lens; to Les there is a distance implied when behind his camera where he doesn't have to ingratiate himself to the celebrity. With camera in hand Les is in a professional and powerful capacity, a position of worth. As Les is snapping pictures he feels equal to the celebrity, he sees the relationship between paparazzo and celebrity as mutually dependent, and for that moment when he is behind the camera lens he is not the peon that his parents have raised him to believe he is.

If there is one single image which sums up Les Galantine it is his computer screensaver, a self-portrait that is both brilliantly funny and intrinsically sad. In the image, Les affects a serious, self-satisfied attitude with an assertive grin that is effectively saying "This is me!" to the world. The sheer austerity of this photo provides one of the funniest moments of the film. Practically no one sees the image other than him. This picture is Les's mirror, how he likes to imagine himself: the master of his universe.

Buscemi amusingly acknowledges the effectiveness of the portrait. "Tom knew what he was trying to say by Les having this image as his screensaver and why he would want to. I think Les has to be his own champion; he has to promote himself because nobody else does. The image is how Les presents himself: tough and indomitable; but it masks all of these misgivings he has of the outside world."

With *Delirious* DiCillo deconstructs the world of fame in a brutal but deftly absurdist manner. Apparently everything can be packaged and sold in the age of social media. Toby declares his love for K'harma in a promo for "Slice of Life", which instantly goes viral and melts the hearts of his female fan base. This is romance as business. Witness the military-precision timing of the red carpet walk in the final scene, with Dana and K'harma's manager Gabi at war over whose talent emerges from the limousine first. The scene is played straight, and while the cut-throat manoeuvring over an inch of carpet space seems comically preposterous, such is the nature of the business that some see it as not that far-fetched.

Gershon iterates the verisimilitude within DiCillo's work, one that operates in tandem with his equally anarchic and absurdist takes on pop culture institutions. "There is a lot of truth to *Delirious*. When I did *The Player*, Robert Altman just said, 'Play it straight, it will be funnier because it will reveal that these people are ridiculous'. I mean there are definitely paparazzi guys who are genuinely like Les, they cross the line, and there are people like Dana and Gabi. I don't consider *Delirious* to be entirely satirical, because there's so much truth in it. The depiction of these types of people is so realistic that you end up recognising them all."

For those who know DiCillo best, *Delirious* was an obvious labour of love as well as a cathartic release. Actor Kevin Corrigan, a friend and collaborator of DiCillo's for over two decades, plays one of Les's paparazzo cohorts, Ricco. As he does with everyone, Les keeps Ricco at arm's length, despite the amiable colleague's best efforts to form a friendship. Corrigan witnessed the intensity that both actor and director went though in realising the tortured malaise of Les Galantine.

"I'm thinking of that scene where Steve and I are playing cards and he gets really pissed off with me because I compliment this kid Toby that he hates and so he kicks me out of the apartment," Corrigan recalls. "I remember when we worked on that it was the last scene on the call-sheet. We didn't spend a lot of time on that scene; I think we got it in an hour. Tom was pretty hands-on, not just with me but with Steve too.

Paparazzi at play:
Les (Steve Buscemi) and
Ricco (Kevin Corrigan)

I remember how there was this deep sense of tension; Steve seemed to be carrying a heavy heart that night. He seemed a little preoccupied, maybe he was just in character, I don't know, but when we were doing that scene I was a little afraid of him, actually, during that bit where he gets angry at me. I think it goes back to a feeling of Tom and Steve being like my older brothers. I love watching that scene. Someone put it on YouTube and once in a while I watch it, and thinking about it now it really emphasises how Tom likes to walk that balance between humour and pathos."

The gallows humour of *Delirious* is something Buscemi believes is vital to the DiCillo aesthetic. "I think Tom's films are funny," Buscemi enthuses, "but I wouldn't necessarily call them comedies because to me they are so much more than that. It's some of the funniest stuff because the humour is just coming out of something that people can relate to, something real."

"It is for real!" Corrigan agrees. "I remember reading the script for *Delirious* and it is so specifically rendered and detailed; I knew Tom would put so much effort getting it to work as he sees it in his head. It's like the inner workings of a clock, all aiming towards telling the story of a man's pain and frustration, which I imagine Tom knows something about; I'm sure he knows something of those emotions. Tom is a very serious man; it's the intensity of a true artist. For me the line between Tom the Artist and Tom the Person – that guy I have a personal relationship with – can get a little blurred. Tom is a staunch craftsman; he's like a master when he's on the set."

Corrigan elaborates: "There were times on *Delirious* where I felt like I was coming up short. There was tension with one of the other actors in the movie and it was really throwing me off. It was one of those paparazzi scenes where we're all standing outside the club and there was something I just couldn't get right. Tom was really insistent on helping me get it and kept coming up to me after every take; and it was really frustrating for me that I couldn't get it. I was just not happy that night. There is a sense of privilege to have that kind of creative tension with a director. With Tom it's like he cared enough to be that pushy with me, that he trusted me enough that I would get it. Our relationship is like that; if he didn't care or didn't trust me maybe he wouldn't be so hands-on and the work would reflect that."

"Tom is right there with you," Buscemi states. "He's a great supporter of what actors do, so much so that he's like a cheerleader, and he gets excited when he sees something that is surprising or that is well done. It's like having an audience member on set with you. Having been a DP and having studied acting I'm sure helps inform his directing also. He likes for everybody to be as committed as he is. With Tom and me, there's a kind of shorthand. It's something that can develop even from the first time you work together with someone."

Gershon draws upon DiCillo's background in the independent New York City film scene of the late 1970s and early 1980s, as well as his training in acting, as a source of influence in creating the unique body of work that he has.

"It's Tom's vision," Gershon states, "and this is how he sees the world. He's got this quirky sensibility mixed with a very strong point of view that comes from having been both in front of and behind the camera. He is an observer and a performer. I love that he has so much input in his films, writing and directing and also doing some of the music. Tom gets an idea and he puts it out there." Gershon continues: "He has that guerrilla sensibility and he came from that world, that idea of 'let's just go out and do it!' I really admire that in him. Tom trained as an actor himself years ago, and so I think this plays a part in how he relates to actors and how he helps craft his scenes with his performers. He likes to be part of the team – he is not one of the 'Other'. Some directors can be very dictatorial, as in this is their way and you have to conform. On Tom's set it is very collaborative. It feels like we're all in this together, he's one of you; he feels more like your buddy than your director, which isn't always the case with filmmakers."

"Tom was a part of the important early work of that New York independent scene that I was in thrall of," Corrigan states. "I always felt I was in the shadow of that whole scene, but I feel fortunate to have breathed that air. There was a time when nobody really knew what was going on below 14th Street. The only way to find out was to be daring enough to go down there and experience it. You had the art world, the gay world, the punk scene ... it was transgressive. Tom worked on *Permanent Vacation* and *Stranger than Paradise*; he was like a caterpillar waiting to morph and blossom into his own career as a director, as an auteur."

Alison Lohman saliently sums up the experience felt by those who worked on the film. "Whenever people ask me 'what movie of yours should I see?' I always say, '*Delirious!*'"

Delirious is DiCillo's longest film, and yet it feels like his shortest, perhaps because each scene is informed with a pulsing aesthetic vitality. Accompanied by the searing lead performance of Buscemi, the director achieves a restless, almost manic sense of immediacy in his editing and camerawork. The film has the intensity and buoyant morale of a debut filmmaker itching to announce his arrival, but the truth is it's the sixth film of a director in his third decade of the film business, and as such the film carries the discipline of an artist who knows exactly what they want and how to achieve it.

Delirious reaches many aesthetic highs for DiCillo. It is branded with the director's idiosyncratic blend of the absurd and the dramatic, bound with a narrative sleight of hand that blindsides the audience with surprise and revelation. Moments have you. By the time Les is air-dusting his clandestine camera/gun with Toby firmly in his sights there is no doubt in our minds that Les is truly in the realm of the psychotic. But just as the film seems to be taking a severe turn towards devastation, DiCillo jolts us into poignant reality with one of the most moving moments of the film. Toby spies Les in the screaming throng and instinctively gives him a simple glance of recognition. Amidst the controlled chaos of a film premiere Les and Toby finally acknowledge each other without skepticism or cynicism. Les gets a shot that will be heard around the world, Toby has become a star, and the two men reiterate their love of one another. There is an immense sincerity to DiCillo's films, and the dramatic crux of this final scene is one of the most indelible and satisfying endings of the director's entire work. Instead of fading to black we fade to white, illuminated as Toby leaves Les to enter the blinding light of his strange new world.

The subtle absurdist comedy of DiCillo's work serves to build his world and its inhabitants. The director never makes arbitrary jests for the sake of a cheap laugh;

"Shot heard around the world": Les takes aim with his camera-gun

Les witnesses his protégé become a Star on the red carpet

he parlays visual gags into intricately rendered character development. God is in the details. DiCillo brings his economy of exposition and visual information sharply to bear in Les's apartment, where the surroundings say as much about Les as any verbal communication could relate. The cramped rooms reflect his life of hunting and stalking as a paparazzo: witness the faux nature backdrop wallpaper, the taxidermies of various animals, and the cheap, rather small imitation heads on the wall. "Collectors' items", Les would call them. Les is a trapper, of a different kind of wildlife; he is an urban hunter of celebrity, his trophies: photos of Goldie Hawn eating lunch, Elvis Costello without his hat; "shots heard around the world".

The production design of his lead character's abode illustrates DiCillo's deft use of visual comedy to Inform character psychology. Few other directors could move an audience to tears as Buscemi delivers an overwhelming moment of pathos while affording them a sly chuckle at the delightfully preposterous surroundings. It is that delicate balancing of the dramatic and the absurd which DiCillo executes from film to film with flair and originality that makes him singular as an American auteur filmmaker.

Underscoring the film's fractured fairy tale aesthetic is a densely layered discourse on themes DiCillo clearly relished bringing to life; themes that are relevant to every member of the audience: our relationship with our parents, with our friends, with our partners and, most of all, with ourselves.

"I put my soul into every frame of *Delirious* and it showed me that is the basic requirement for every film that I make," DiCillo affirms. "I can never give anything less. I can see that result in the film. It is looser in some ways than my previous films, but in other ways it is much more specific and focused. I think it has a richer emotional depth as well as some sharp, unexpected humour. Some of the themes are very personal to me but I think the film finds a way to express those ideas in a way that is universal to other people.

Something amazing happened in the scene after Les and Toby come back from the disastrous dinner at Les's parent's house," DiCillo continues. "As he's talking with Toby about his father, Les breaks down. I had whispered something to Steve just before that take, sensing he was close to something regarding his own father. And when those tears came I felt so blessed, so fortunate to have Steve playing this part. Then, months later, Steve came to one of the early rough cuts. He pulled me aside and said, 'Tom, you can't use that take of me crying. Please find another one.' I think it was the depth of the emotion that bothered him. It's not something he usually reveals on film. I took him by the shoulders very gently and said, 'Steve, that moment is the reason why I made this film. Please trust me. I'm going to leave it in.'

This film could have gone off the rails so many times, in so many unpredictable ways, and yet, somehow, either by luck or my force of will, I managed to keep it on track. It is up there for me as one of my most satisfying films."

* * *

Wayne Byrne: *After the premature demise of* Double Whammy, *with its release only to home video, how did you find the will and the passion to not only continue making films but to follow up with such a strikingly immediate picture?*

Tom DiCillo: I was utterly unprepared for what happened with *Double Whammy*. I never imagined I'd make a film that did not get released. Some very close friends whispered to me that they doubted I'd ever make another film. The damage from an unreleased film is intense. It sends a signal out into the industry that your product is unwanted and unsellable; in any form. There is no escaping it. You can't hide from it. You can't pretend it didn't happen.

How did you keep going?

Perhaps it was blind naiveté. I knew *Double Whammy* was as good as any number of films that were released in 2001. Something in that conviction just pushed me forward. I didn't think of the damage; of course I knew it was there. But I just focused on a new idea. There are things in *Double Whammy* that I love. But in writing *Delirious*, I reconnected with the addictive lust I had for movie making. It has to be lust or the film never comes to life.

How hard was it to find financing for this film after having your previous one go straight-to-video? How does that affect the value of a filmmaker's name and reputation?

It was very difficult to find the financing. I started on the normal journey with the script. I went to all the US independent distributors who all passed. I then went to all the US independent producers. They all passed. I tried European sources. They all passed. And so very quickly I found myself once again treading water in the middle of the ocean looking for a piece of debris to latch on to.

A friend of mine from NYU film school surfaced after several desperate years and made a phone call to someone who made a phone call and miraculously there was a company willing to finance the film. One important factor to remember is that I'd written the script for Steve Buscemi. I knew I was never going to cast anyone else in that part. This was 2005, before *Boardwalk Empire*. As thrilled as I was that Steve was going to be in the film, I knew I would have a very hard time financing it with him. And of course, that's the first thing all the investors said, "Get us someone beside Buscemi and we'll make your film."

Let's talk a little about Michael Pitt. What was the impression he made on you to cast him? I don't believe he had many lead roles prior to Delirious.

My casting director introduced me to Michael Pitt, whom I'd seen in John Cameron Mitchell's *Hedwig and the Angry Inch*. I knew from the moment I saw him he was Toby. I also knew that in order to get the performance I needed I'd probably have to cut my arm off.

How do you mean?

There is an amazing purity to Michael's acting. He is intensely real and believable on screen. He also has a great heart and I knew this would bring another crucial dimension to his relationship with Les. He sees him for who he is and does not judge him. This actually blows Les's mind. No one has ever treated him this way. Michael brought this quality to the character effortlessly. He also brought a real-life emotional confusion that was very difficult to fathom at times. When we worked well together the experience was exhilarating; just as exciting as when working with Steve. Michael would bring rich, unexpected colours to the scenes and was really adept in improvising with Steve.

On the other hand, there would be times where our communication just disintegrated. I still don't know why. I literally gave him everything I had; including one of my favorite shirts. It pains me to this day that the experience had such violent extremes.

I'm still confused about the image you used of "cutting your arm off".

I knew when I met Michael there was no one else who could play Toby. He had a depth and complexity that was exactly right for the character. I also saw that part of that complexity was beyond his control and far beyond mine. I knew there would

DiCillo directs Michael Pitt on set of *Delirious*

come a time during the making of the film that I would be forced to deal with it and that it was going to hurt.

You or him?

Me. I'd allowed many crucial moments on previous films to slip away from me due to my own insecurity, or hesitancy in confronting stubborn people; or my fear of upsetting someone, getting them angry. I knew exactly what this film needed and at this point in my career I had nothing to lose.

Michael was resisting you?

He was resisting himself. I think I brought something out of him he had been reluctant to explore in his previous films; a kind of joy and spontaneous delight. Many actors dismiss that quality as "not serious" or "not having the real weight of acting," which is bullshit and severely limiting. Listen, I think Michael is brilliant in the film. He brought some amazing ideas that I never would have thought of. It was his idea to open the film with Toby crawling out of a dumpster. You get those kinds of ideas from actors and there is nothing to describe the joy that brings to a director. But in a split second he would shut down completely.

Why?

I don't know. I never figured it out. You have to understand, this was a very tricky part. It wasn't just some generic role that anybody could have played. I put everything I had into writing it. I had to invest everything with Michael; not only to help him but to make sure he fulfilled everything the script required of Toby. It was an extremely risky and delicate endeavour. The stakes were very high, even higher than *Johnny Suede*. If Toby wasn't believable then the whole film fell apart.

But, he was believable.

He was. There's a scene where he spends the night for the first time with K'harma in her hotel. They take a jacuzzi together and as K'harma falls asleep in her bed Toby walks into her room and tucks her in. I'd written it for him to be wearing a white, terry-cloth robe; something from the hotel, like he was for one tiny moment enjoying the luxury benefits of a spa. Later in the script, K'harma's self-serving boyfriend wears the same bathrobe in a shot designed to mirror the earlier one with Toby. It was intended to be a visual reminder of Toby and suggest K'harma's longing for him at this point of loneliness and despair for her.

Right before we started to shoot the scene, Michael told me that he wasn't going to wear the robe. He wanted instead to wear his street clothes. He felt that wearing the robe meant that he was buying into K'harma's luxury lifestyle. I listened to him. I considered his point and then I presented mine. He refused to consider it. The discussion turned into a disagreement, then a quarrel, then an argument and finally an all-out war.

Judging by what ended up in the film, you won the battle.

No babe in the woods: cunning Toby works his way into a life of luxury and into the heart of K'harma

Yeah, but it did not feel good. It was about halfway through the film and the thought of finishing it with the air poisoned by animosity or resentment, from either of us, really depressed me. Over the weekend I happened to see this book on my desk called *Directing Actors* by Judith Weston. I'd read it before but I picked it up and it fell open to a page that startled me. Weston was talking about working with resistant actors. She wrote: "Whatever actors do, love them anyway, the way a mother loves her children, even the difficult ones. Give them unconditional love. When there is a problem, let them understand that you are ready to reach into your own chest and hold out your heart" [1999: 277]. As frustrated as I was with Michael these words made complete sense to me on a deeply profound level. It was the exact opposite of anything I'd experienced in my own childhood. The next day I wrapped up this favourite shirt of mine that Michael had admired, and went into his little dressing room and gave it to him. I told him how much I respected him, cared for him and appreciated everything he was investing in the film.

A half-hour later we filmed one of the most amazing scenes of the whole shoot. Toby is leaving K'harma's hotel early the next morning and on his own Michael stops, goes back and gives the startled doorman a genuine, euphoric hug. It's an absolutely amazing moment.

So, it worked – unconditional love.

It worked for about a week. Then the dysfunction returned. Things fell apart completely once the film was finished. Apparently Michael was upset that he wasn't involved in the score even though nothing was ever mentioned about him being involved and I already had a composer. Ultimately, he decided to not do any press for the film, or support it in any way.

That is incomprehensible to me. The film is wonderful and his work in it is spectacular.

It's not only incomprehensible; it's kind of tragic. There was a great sense of delight and accomplishment from everyone who worked on the film. This business is tough and brutal. The rewards are so rare and fleeting. It was incredibly distressing to see Michael unable to enjoy it. It was also hard for me not to take it personally. I was having a tough time with my incompetent producers and the steady cold shoulders from distributors. But still I could deal with that on a certain level. But to be abandoned by one of my lead actors took something out of my soul. I'd cast him at great risk. I had to fight the producers to convince them he'd be better for the film than Frodo or Legolas. I was fighting against a system where truth and talent mean absolutely nothing. It's not that I expected gratitude. I just thought he was an ally. Instead, he was like one of those soldiers who fires on his own troops.

How do you explain it?

Listen, I think Judith Weston's words about working with actors are absolutely true and I will always honour them. But in some cases I think you have to accept there are things going on with people that are completely out of your control.

The notion of fame and celebrity is obviously something that intrigues you. What was it about this theme that fascinates you?

Fame has become an intensely complex concept. How does anyone survive in a world where all personal value and self-worth are weighed against the attention and interest lavished upon those deemed to be celebrities? What does this say about us? Why has the planet become so obsessed with celebrity? What does it do to one's sense of personal value and worth when someone as staggeringly unremarkable as Kim Kardashian becomes interesting to so many people? Those were questions I wanted to consider.

We get to see how a star like K'harma is manipulated by the celebrity machine, particularly by her manager and PR people. Her personal life is in emotional upheaval yet she is pressured into stepping out and putting on a happy image for Access Hollywood *who will be covering the "after-after party". Is this absurd neurosis of those who turn the wheels of the celebrity machine something that you have been itching to address since being exposed to this industry?*

It's almost impossible to be in this business and not be astonished by some of the things that go on behind the scenes. Some of it is laughable. Some of it is repulsive. But this whole concept of the manager as the professional "life/business coach" is new to show business. Elvis didn't have anything like it. Jim Morrison didn't. To me it creates a buffer; a kind of insular fantasy world where the star is treated like a helpless, precious infant. Everything is done to create a world where nothing goes wrong, nothing disturbs them and everyone loves them.

K'harma's character was based somewhat on a real person, a pop singer who was going through some tough times. That's why I loved what Alison brought to the character. She showed the real person underneath the facade. It's what keeps the role and the film from simply falling into satire.

The film is a world of contrasts. Les and Toby exist on the gritty fringes of the celebrity world until Toby is discovered. Throughout the film you take us from Les's grubby apartment to K'harma's luxury hotel. How strongly does New York City itself influence your decision to set your story here?

I've lived here in NYC now for almost thirty-five years. It can be a brutal place but for me it is the most exciting and stimulating city in America. You are right, on these streets the haves and have-nots jostle each other constantly. The polarity exists and is visible to everyone.

I find that interesting both personally and artistically. The fact that the city is actually a very small island condenses everything into an extremely dense mass of humanity. Most people walk here. All kinds of interactions take place in public. You can have someone living in a decrepit basement apartment with only one window that looks out onto the entrance to Madonna's gleaming penthouse. I love that about the city. You literally bump into people. You smell them, you feel their sweat.

Why brutal?

Because all the time there is this pounding, like some giant animal pursuing you. You know you have to stay at least ten feet ahead of it or it will crush you. By that I mean that your means of survival are life and death. You've got to have a place to live so you have to be able to pay the rent. You've got to eat so you need money for food. And there's something about the city with all its concrete, glass and steel that can make it seem like a relentless machine, utterly indifferent to your struggles. And unless you are intentionally blinding yourself you see the ones who did not survive on the streets every day.

What's it like to shoot here?

Like riding a motorcycle full throttle along the edge of a cliff. It is equally thrilling and terrifying. At one point halfway through pre-production, the financiers decided we had to move to Toronto to avoid dealing with the expensive NYC unions. I was so depressed I couldn't even talk to people. I knew the film would never come to life if I did not shoot it in NY.

So when we finally found a way to keep the film here I embraced shooting on the streets like a lovesick lunatic. We shot the entire film here in twenty-five days. That meant we had to move so fast there was no time for any disasters. Even the loss of half a day would have killed us. We were so lucky I still can't believe it. Just to be safe we saved the sequences of Toby sneaking onto the subway until after all the main shooting.

Why did you wait?

The NYC Transit Authority charges over fifty thousand dollars to shoot legally on the subway. There was no way we could afford that. But if we'd "stolen" the shots while we were still in production the city could have shut us down. So one night me, the cameraman, his assistant and Michael Pitt snuck onto the train around 1am. We shot with a 35mm movie camera until 5am and no one even looked at us twice. We actually shot Michael leaping over the turnstile in front of a token booth clerk and jumping onto a train. It was pretty exciting; a great mixture of cinema vérité and juvenile delinquency.

You dabbled in digital imagery for the first time on this film. There is the wonderful fantasy sequence in which Toby steps into the puddle that is reflecting a billboard image of K'harma. Did working in this digital arena help you aesthetically in terms of expression and narrative economy?

I'm glad you mentioned that scene. I'm rather proud to say it is not digital at all.

Really? There is such an amazing clarity and tonal quality to what I imagined would have been a very hard shot to capture physically; I assumed that it was digitally manipulated.

None of this was done digitally. The DP, Frank DeMarco, came up with a way that we could do it right in-camera. That was a real puddle with a large transparency of K'harma suspended over it with light shining through it. We positioned it so it reflected into the puddle and Toby actually stepped into the puddle causing the image to dissipate.

The inspiration actually came from Gene Kelly's famous scene from *Singin' in the Rain* where he's splashing through puddles. There is great joy in that sequence because Kelly has just fallen in love. The same is true for Toby. While remaining true to the urban grit of his world I wanted him to have a moment of blissful delirium. So this image is part of a sequence that has him standing in a snowstorm of pink, falling rose petals. It was all achieved in-camera, on set.

So where did you use digital effects?

Only in the final colour-correction for the film. We made a deal with an editing facility that included what is called a digital intermediate. I had never been able to afford one before. This is where they take the entire original film negative of your film and upload it into a high-resolution digital format. This enables you to then manipulate every element of the frame, just like Photoshop but with motion.

Because of our tight budget and limited time I kept things very simple but I was able to add a slightly exaggerated sense of colour and atmosphere to the film. I used *Midnight Cowboy* as a model. In particular there is a great use of turquoise blue in *Midnight Cowboy* on the walls of diners or the condemned building Ratso and Joe Buck hole up in. Frank Demarco did a fantastic job lighting the film but this digital intermediate gave me the chance to layer in a rich, mysterious mood that would have taken months to achieve in shooting.

Delirious *contains what feels to me like your most accomplished musical score to date. It is emotive and expressive but also integral to the plot. Instead of your regular composer Jim Farmer you used Anton Sanko. Why the change of personnel and what attracted you to Sanko's aesthetic?*

In the five years since *Double Whammy* Jim had moved into playwriting and producing his own plays. By the time I got the money for *Delirious* I think we both felt it was the most natural thing to move on. Something struck me about Anton's music immediately. It didn't sound like a hundred other "scores". There was a great use of instruments in unexpected ways. It had a sense of play as well as an edge and emotion.

Hiring Anton was like a dream. He is a complete musician. He understood the concept of themes and unity. Music in film is like the flesh and tissue that holds the film together. It is usually over-used and so generic it sounds like the same composer scores every film. Anton shared my belief that every film should have its own particular sound as well as its own look.

Why was this so unusual for you?

Most film composers become very possessive of their music. They write the music they think should be in the film. If you offer a different suggestion then they become offended and frequently all collaboration ceases. With Anton, if I made a suggestion he listened. If he disagreed we talked about it. If he agreed he jumped into the idea with no reservation. If he really disagreed then we went with his idea. The end result is a score that is absolutely his; it has his intricacy, his detail and his intuition. And for me, it adds that crucial layer to the film. It doesn't tell you what to think or feel – it offers possibilities. It ignites what is already there in the film and makes it blossom in richer, deeper ways.

You use the musical score not just to suggest mood and tone but also as a narrative tool. In the emotionally charged scene where Les and Toby drive home from the Galantines' house the score shifts seamlessly into the next scene and becomes the song that K'harma is writing on her keyboard. This later becomes the melody of K'harma's track, 'You Can Take Your Love and Shove It'.

Not many people noticed that. Yeah, I put quite a bit of work into that transition. Actually the score there is something I wrote. Since I also wrote 'Shove It' I knew the basic chords and it seemed like it could be an interesting transition for me to experiment with. Again, to Anton's credit, he did not mind at all and actively encouraged me to drop in little music cues of my own.

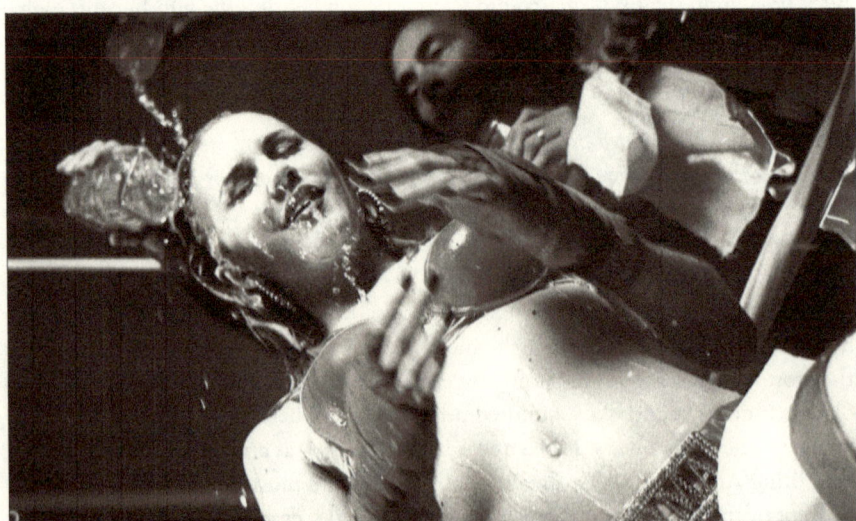

K'harma gets wet in the music video for her single, "Shove It"

You wrote 'Shove It?'

Yes. I needed a track for K'harma that was a little silly and exaggerated and yet wasn't so stupid you couldn't believe it. I'm rather proud of how successfully the song balances between the semi-believable and the idiotic. But Alison really sings it. We went into a recording studio with the instrument tracks and she just dove into it. She loves to sing and she put her heart into it.

The film received some of the best reviews of your career. Yet despite praise and critical plaudits coming from the most important trade and newspapers, the film disappeared. You have an approachable movie, a career-best Steve Buscemi, a hot soundtrack, a young, beautiful cast, and a director at the top of his game. What happened?

I could lay it out for you in all the excruciating detail but after a few minutes your eyes would glaze over. By the time it was released I had put five years of work into it. I had practically willed the film into being. I had fought for the cast I wanted and whom I knew would be brilliant in the film. Forget the film; I think Buscemi should have been nominated for an Academy Award. His performance is unbelievably compelling. He didn't even get a nomination from the Spirit Awards, which is theoretically the bastion of support here for American independent film.

Some of problems with the film's release had to do with the financiers. They were novices. Don't get me wrong; it was because they were novices that they took a chance on me and financed the film. But after the film won Best Director and Best Screenplay at the San Sebastian Film Festival in Spain, their plan to secure US distribution was merely to send DVD copies to all the major US independent distributors.

They didn't set up screenings?

No. The best way to see a film is on a screen with an audience. The worst way to see it is on a DVD in some empty office or on some junior executive's computer while he's checking his email and playing solitaire. And sure enough, all the major independent distributors passed on the film.

Did they say why?

They never do. But even given the uninspired way the film was presented to them I was still pretty astonished that they *all* passed. This left us only one option; take the film to Sundance and hope a strong showing there would rekindle interest in the film.

The financiers, who had never been to Sundance, hired an expert named Karl Mulloch to help them navigate the tricky waters of negotiation. It's a very fickle and rapidly changing environment there. You have to have a plan. You have to move fast. I warned them this was our last chance and that they could not leave anything to accident. We had big audiences at our first two screenings but not a single distributor showed up. Mulloch flew in late after our third screening which again, no distributors attended. I called an emergency meeting on a rainy, dreary afternoon. Mulloch was instantly belligerent and defensive. He was about sixty-five, an ex-VHS manufacturer from NYC. He looked like a shorter, fatter Fred Flintstone with much less hair. After I told him no distributors had come to any of our screenings he announced his strategy with condescending annoyance, "We'll just get some distributors to come to the next screening."

I leapt out of my chair and screamed at him in the middle of the room, "There are no other screenings!!"

The expert himself had missed all the screenings?

Yeah. But of course they all looked at me like I was insane. Which I was I guess, seeing the film and five years of my life just going down the drain.

Were you not able to get any distributors to see the film at Sundance?

No. That was it. I can't describe to you the feeling of seeing without question that your film is heading to a crash and burn. I've had the questionable ability to foresee this on a number of films. It brings no consolation. When it starts to go down there is nothing you can do to stop it. It's like witnessing a plane crash with your own children on board. You think of all the years of work that went into it; the writing, the casting, trying to raise the money – everything that led to the truly miraculous achievement of actually getting it made.

Didn't Mulloch or the financiers have any emergency plans?

Yeah, they decided they would release the film themselves. They allocated a total budget of $350,000, which was to cover all prints, advertising and the publicist's fee. Anything left over would pay the salary of the guy they hired to play the part of "distributor". So he had very little incentive to spend any of that money on promotion.

There was no advertising, no TV, no radio. No posters; no premiere and barely even a day of press in NYC. The tiny newspaper ads started on a Friday and were pulled completely on Monday, never to appear again. So despite some fairly strong reviews no one even knew the film existed. It was gone in a week.

Delirious *had a champion in Roger Ebert; he was one of the prominent critics to really admire the film. He gave the film a great review and even screened it at his annual Ebertfest in Champaign, Illinois. You wrote to Ebert detailing the dismay you felt by the failed release of the film. Did Ebert's response offer any hope to you?*

I was so moved by his review in the face of all the indifference coming from the financiers that it prompted me to contact Roger and let him know how much his support meant to me. I'd even asked the "distributor" to take out another ad with a quote from Ebert's review on it. He and Mulloch refused, furious that I was interfering.

To my amazement though, Roger Ebert wrote me back. He identified two factors. One, the fate of independent films is so tenuous. I don't think people really know the kind of faith and courage it takes to release a film. Most distributors give a film one shot and if it doesn't take off immediately they dump it. In my case the film never had a chance. The financiers spent nothing to promote the film and then complained, "The opening weekend was less than we expected so we're pulling the film."

The other thing Ebert touched upon was that independent film has changed. The market has become much more competitive. Films with stars or a "high" concept are more likely to get promoted and pushed into distribution. Smaller films like *Delirious* have no place in the market now. This is very different from the way things were even five years ago. "I liked the film a lot; I gave it 3.5 out of 4 stars. My concern is that an entertaining film with a superb Buscemi performance has disappeared, and that it never had a chance. Indie films will rarely have big opening weekends because they don't have the publicity machines to grind out press junkets, talk-show guest shots, celeb magazine profiles, big ad campaigns, and fast-food tie-ins. They need a chance to find an audience. Indie films are labors of love that their makers had to make" Ebert (2007: 1).[1]

You made several hilarious promotional videos for the viral campaign of the film, in which we see your frustration in selling the film. Were they based on the lack of support from your distributor?

I met a young filmmaker after one screening in NYC. He asked me about the publicity plans and when I told him there were none he started talking about ways to promote the film on the web for very little money. His name was Chioke Nasoor. His idea was to shoot some fake encounters with me pressuring the actors to do publicity for the film. I wrote the sketches with him. A basic idea was laid out but then we all just kind of riffed and improvised.

How did it feel for you to be acting again?

It was a thrill, especially all the improvisation. We got Steve Buscemi to let us crash his real press day for his own film *Interview*. Some crazy stuff happened between us but he just rolled with it. So many people wrote into YouTube complaining about how poor Steve was being abused by this "intrusive director" that Chioke had to close the comments page – even after other people explained that it was all set up.

How did you get Gina Gershon to do a sketch about doing a sex tape to help publicise the film?

I just asked her. That is one of the things I admire and respect so deeply about Gina. She is talented, beautiful and game for anything. And we really got into some intense stuff in the sketch. Again we had to close the comments because people really thought she was doing a sex tape. That one has over two million hits. I'm not sure if these short films affected the distribution at all. They probably didn't. But they were a blast to make and they helped me channel my frustration at the wretched release into something more cathartic.

Do you feel that while financial success eluded the film you nevertheless made a personal aesthetic achievement with Delirious?

I do. But as proud as I am of the film I know now that is not enough. What happened to *Delirious* had a very real effect on my ability to make another film. I know I'm not the only director this has happened to and I'm not bemoaning my fate. What I'm saying is that the business side of filmmaking is very serious shit. Every misstep, every lost opportunity, every executive who loses his nerve, every financier who takes the safe way out to cover his ass, every critic who doesn't take the time to really see the film – it all takes a toll.

That's the game. And if you want to play it you have to know that. Artistic satisfaction is only half the battle. It's been over six years now since I made *Delirious*. I have spent every day of that time trying to raise the money for three feature scripts that I've written. At this moment I can't honestly say I'm any closer to making one of them than I was five years ago.

What do you see as a possible way forward for you?

I keep resisting it but I'm closer now than I ever have been to simply making a film for nothing. I'm going to write something that can be shot in three weeks, in two rooms. Just go back to the way I made *Living in Oblivion*. I was in complete limbo then. No one would give me a dime. So I made a film for less than a dime. And that's what I have to do now.

CHAPTER EIGHT

When You're Strange: A Film About The Doors

'I think that these days, especially in the States, you have to be a politician or an assassin to really be a superstar.'

– Jim Morrison

With six feature films under his belt, all thematically personal and aesthetically daring works, it would have come as a surprise to anyone following Tom DiCillo's career that his seventh feature film would be a music documentary. The subject of the film is The Doors, the legendary rock band consisting of singer Jim Morrison, guitarist Robby Krieger, keyboardist Ray Manzarek and drummer John Densmore.

Casual music fans may be familiar with the basic narrative of The Doors' career. The band released six influential albums between 1967 and 1971, each running the gamut of psychedelic blues rock infused with an idiosyncratic carnivalesque quality that marked them as counterculture icons. In the eyes of the media, Jim Morrison was the focal point of the band; an enigmatic and controversial rock n' roll star who shone so brightly only to burn out quickly like so many of his musical contemporaries. By age twenty-seven, after five intense and often troubled years as one of the most acclaimed and revered of popular musical artists, Morrison was dead, leaving behind a legacy that has been championed and analyzed for decades. Further, the group's history has been repeatedly documented in books such as Jerry Hopkins' *No One Gets Out Alive*, James Riordan and Jerry Prochnicky's *Break on Through: The Life and Death of Jim Morrison*, as well as several autobiographies, including Manzarek's *Light My Fire* and Densmore's *Riders on the Storm*. But with a story as dramatic and illustrious as theirs it was only a matter of time before Hollywood came knocking on The Doors.

In 1991 Oliver Stone made *The Doors*, a bloated discourse on the mythology of Morrison (channeled by a career-best Val Kilmer), with particular focus paid to the mysticism and oracular personality of the singer. Densmore, Krieger and Manzarek are relegated to peripheral supporting characters. Stone is predominantly fascinated by the culture of excess that plagues and inspires Morrison, as if the singer's dark muse was informed by the lifestyle of rock n' roll hedonism rather than something more personal and deeply troubling. The Doors flourished and made their most profound impact upon culture while Stone was a young grunt serving in Vietnam and his film reflects the spellbinding effect the group had on disaffected music fans of the 1960s. But what is missing from Stone's film is equal attention to the band as four distinct musicians and personalities that each contributed to the magic that is The Doors. There is no denying the cultural impact of Morrison as a revered rock icon, but behind the universal legend of the voracious drinker, womaniser, drug user and tortured rock star is a son, a brother, a friend, a lover and a band mate whose personal demons perhaps lay deeper than the pressures of fame may suggest.

How did a director whose narrative films specialise in penetrating the myths of celebrity become the person to oversee this monumental re-visitation? "I got a phone call," DiCillo recalls. "I had been coaxed into directing my first *Law and Order: Criminal Intent* by my friend Chris Noth, who was then starring in it. I went in a bit reluctantly, considering my independent background. But, to my surprise, when I directed an episode the producers allowed me a large amount of freedom and creative input, which is unusual in TV. I'm not suggesting these shows were as creatively stimulating or as challenging as my own films but as a way to keep in practice and to pay the rent, it was not so bad."

The episode apparently turned out well. A few months later DiCillo received a call from Dick Wolf and Peter Jankowski, the show's producers. They'd just acquired the rights to The Doors' entire archive. They were looking for a director who could put together the first feature-length documentary about The Doors. DiCillo said yes immediately.

"I knew The Doors had made some powerful and original music," DiCillo explains. "I also knew the music was a little strange. It had an uneasy dramatic edge to it. It felt like it was made for people who were on the outside, people who saw the world differently. I knew that Morrison led the band to amazing heights before he plummeted to the ground. The story had all the classic elements of cinema. It had great promise and great tragedy. It's like a contemporary myth; a distinctly American one."

When You're Strange begins on an ominous note. A foreboding synthesiser chord reverberates while the haunting sound of Native American children singing ushers in the opening shot of the film: a scorching ember sun rising behind a pillow of dark clouds which then gives way to a bearded and disheveled Jim Morrison emerging from a car half-buried in a sand dune. This footage is excerpted from outtakes of *HWY: An American Pastoral*, an experimental film made by Morrison and cinematographer Paul Ferrara in 1969. The images portray Morrison as a wanderer adrift in the desert. A car stops to pick him up and the scene quickly transitions to Morrison driving the car just as the radio news broadcast announces the death of Jim Morrison in a Paris apartment.

'Mr Mojo Risin'': the striking opening image of *When You're Strange*

And so the story of The Doors begins. Kicking off in 1963, the year that American innocence and optimism was forever changed, DiCillo immediately sets the mood with the tremolo guitar notes of the Lively Ones' 'Surf Rider'. But the director juxtaposes the sunny twang of surf music and idyllic beach revelry with the most devastating political moment in modern American history: the assassination of President John F. Kennedy. Thus follows key socio-political touchstones of the era: the Civil Rights Movement, the raging Vietnam War, Kennedy-successor Lyndon B. Johnson cracking down on anti-war protestors, the emergence of the youth movement which signals the decline of the conservative patriarchal values of the 1950s. The counter-culture has arrived and clamours to be heard.

With *When You're Strange* DiCillo ties in the story of The Doors' spectacular ascent and subsequent fall to the eruption and implosion of the youth movement under the weight of disenchantment and faded idealism. In charting the career of The Doors, *When You're Strange* inextricably works as a document of a tumultuous period in history as succinctly as it does work as a document of a seminal rock band.

"The film was a constantly developing concept," DiCillo explains. "I never explicitly said to myself or to the members of the band that I'm going to investigate your place in the 1960s and see how you affected this, this and this. The 1960s was just like this world that existed around them and the band were a part of it."

Indeed, the 1960s were a time of extreme change in America. For the first time the hierarchy of old ideas and authorities were being seriously challenged. There was great interest in expanding consciousness and not just with drugs. The Women's Liberation Movement came into focus during that time; so did a heightened awareness of racial tolerance. The Youth Movement was convinced that love was the answer. And they were more than willing to fight for it.

"It still blows my mind," DiCillo confesses, "that college students were regularly making the nightly news for protesting the Vietnam War. They were getting arrested and beaten up. That's how passionately they felt about it. I can't imagine something like that happening on college campuses today. But there was the innocence to it as well. Young people really did believe they could change the world. And it was in this rich, chaotic time that The Doors came into being. It is interesting to me that they never really were hippies. They were always just on the periphery; connected to it but

Doors guitarist Robby Krieger

not driven by it. And I felt that their development could take on a larger meaning if it was presented against this time of turbulence and potential."

For the surviving members of The Doors, *When You're Strange* was an opportunity to set the record straight once and for all on the factual narrative of the band.

"Most important for me was that the dynamics between the four members of the band needed to be explored," Robby Krieger admits. "With the Oliver Stone film it was more about Jim Morrison and all his craziness; it never really attempted to understand or explore how the music was made, nor did it examine any real relationships within the band."

"Oliver Stone is the anti-Doors," Ray Manzarek proclaims. "His movie makes Jim out to be an alcoholic, drunk weirdo; a strange poet totally out of control and you never see the intellectual side of Jim Morrison. You never see the wit, the charm, the elegance. You never get a sense of the real poet ... Now this, *When You're Strange,* is the antidote to the poison Oliver Stone spewed out twenty years ago.[2] We talked to Tom, and his ideas were terrific, especially his framing it with Jim Morrison being dead and yet driving that car – that reference to shamanism, or the shaman being able to work beyond space and time. In essence, Jim being alive kind of flip-flops the idea of death and makes it a different experience entirely".[3]

John Densmore sees DiCillo's film as an extension of the groundwork laid down in Stone's ultimately ambiguous and rambling epic – a film in which Densmore appears as the recording engineer of Morrison's spoken-word album, *An American Prayer*. "Although I thought Oliver's film was very good, I had wished it would have focused more on the 1960s," the drummer says. "The period we were living in while writing those songs is so important to the story. Tom intercut the era beautifully, showing what was going on politically and socially, and what influenced us in that context."

"I didn't know too much about Tom before the film," Krieger admits. "But I then met with him and he seemed to know exactly what he wanted to do with the film, and that was important to me. My thing was to just let them run with it and see what happened. I don't like to get too involved in stuff about The Doors anymore. On the Oliver Stone film I was present as a kind of technical advisor, I was there when they were shooting all of the live concert stuff to make sure they recreated it as close as

Doors drummer John Densmore

possible to the way it happened. With Tom, I just wanted to see what he could come up with."

"When I first met Tom I found him immensely amusing because of the way he flipped his hair back all the time," Densmore wryly recalls. "I went and watched *Living in Oblivion* and immediately realised that he was a very talented filmmaker. That encouraged me to go and watch another one of his films and after that I just spoke to him about his vision and I realised that he was the guy for *When You're Strange*. Having come up through the independent film scene he brings with him an alternative, outsider mentality, which plays a part in his attitude and approach to the material. That cinematic history definitely made him the perfect director for *When You're Strange*."

Densmore and Krieger differ somewhat in how they respectively regard the cultural context of the 1960s and the measure into which The Doors were relative. Densmore acclaims DiCillo's narrative subtext of the political and social trajectory of the 1960s as a thematic backdrop to the film; conversely, Krieger doesn't consider the political ethos of the counter-culture as particularly pertinent in reporting the story of The Doors.

"I don't think the politics of the era is something that is all that necessary to go too deep into when it comes to the history of our band," Krieger says. "Jim never thought of himself as political, he considered himself more of a mirror of society, so in which case it would certainly be relevant to have that parallel with the social climate of the 1960s, but I think you can run the risk overanalysing it in that regard. We weren't trying to change the world."

Densmore considers the depiction of the socio-political spirit of the era to be a key ingredient in the story of The Doors; a portrait of the band as four men buoyed by the mass disillusionment and cry for change voiced by the youth movement. "We cared!" the drummer proclaims. "We cared about our generation, about not buying the bullshit that was given to us. Every generation gets bullshit, but the Vietnam generation got truckloads. Of course, if society had fully learned the lessons of Vietnam, we wouldn't be in Iraq, Afghanistan, etc. There is so much crap shoveled down kids' throats, so it's refreshing when some art comes along and cuts through and points out what's real and what's bullshit. Jim's rebel spirit had a very low tolerance for lies. That weight is part of what took him down. Tom's film gets this exactly right."

"I think I probably shared more of Robby's idea," DiCillo elaborates, "which is that I don't think that artists or people who create moments that affect a generation are always aware of it. If anything it is most effective when they are not aware of it; it's real and it's coming out of them at that moment. And so that was the path I took with the film, which was that these guys were just doing what excited them."

Indeed, *When You're Strange* shines a fascinating light on how much of the power of The Doors' music came out of an accidental confluence of elements: Jim's fevered chaos, Ray's all-encompassing musicianship, Robby's world-influenced guitar and John's intensely fluid jazz beats. If it is true that everything happens for a reason then there was also a tremendous amount of luck and good fortune that brought these four particular musicians together.

DiCillo further offers a glimpse into the background of the precocious young Jim Morrison, the introspective son of Navy officer, Admiral George Morrison. A ravenous reader of poetry and philosophy, an independent intellectual but a truculent student, Morrison unsuccessfully goes through several schools before settling on a UCLA film programme, another course that he fails to graduate, but where he will form perhaps the most important friendship of his life. Ray Manzarek is a fellow film student and prodigious blues and classical piano player. Impressed by Morrison's poetry and writing, Manzarek is struck by his words for a composition entitled 'Moonlight Drive', which would eventually develop into the song of that title on the band's second album, *Strange Days*. The two form a band, the name of which would come from the William Blake poem, *The Marriage of Heaven and Hell*. Blake wrote: "If The Doors of perception were cleansed everything would appear to man as it is: infinite."

DiCillo charts the creation of 'Light My Fire', written by Robby Krieger – the first song he'd ever written. The Doors' subsequent residency as the house band at the Whiskey-A-Go-Go leads to their signing to Elektra Records by Jac Holzman. Jim's erratic behaviour is shown from early on: from missing shows to infuriating management of the Whiskey by screaming the lyrics of 'The End', "Mother, I want to fuck you!" in front of hundreds of astonished patrons. A key moment in the band's ascension was their appearance on *The Ed Sullivan Show*. Sullivan wanted the word "higher" taken out of 'Light My Fire' because of all its corruptive drug implications. Morrison refused and sang the song exactly as written. DiCillo suggests that this national television exposure was the catalyst for the previously hesitant singer stepping forward and becoming the mercurial showman and performer that has become legend. From here on the film follows the success of the group; that of massive arena shows, increasingly intense fan worship and pivotal album releases. Throughout it all celebrity follows; stalking Morrison in particular.

In the film's third act DiCillo chronicles the band's most devastating moment, the ill-fated Miami concert at the Dinner Key Auditorium on 1 March 1969. It is here that Morrison allegedly simulated oral copulation and masturbation, and apparently exposed himself on stage. The concert would prove to be the zenith of the band's rise. The Doors were hauled in front of judge and jury and Morrison was convicted on a felony charge of lewd and lascivious behaviour and sentenced to real jail time. A clear message was sent: the retaliation from the establishment against the wild excesses of the counter-culture youth. While appealing the charges against him Morrison recorded one more album with The Doors, the beloved *L.A. Woman*. He then moved to Paris, where on 1 July 1971, he died under circumstances that were mysterious at the very least.

When You're Strange functions within the context of DiCillo's body of work by continuing a theme which has informed much of the director's narratives as far back as *Johnny Suede*: the allure of idolatry and one's struggle with identity in the pursuit of fame.

In Jim Morrison, DiCillo was faced with a character who represented the fears and anxieties of his previous fictional protagonists but who had achieved what Johnny Suede *et al* had not: real fame and acceptance. However, the embrace that Morrison craved most may have been one we take for granted: the love of the family. While we get to see Morrison in the throes of rock stardom throughout the film, DiCillo reveals the man behind the public persona and what we get is a contrasting personality. For all of Morrison's provocative onstage antics and pop star posturing, the singer is portrayed as demure and coquettish with backstage guests and fans; he is a man fully and playfully aware of the personality he is portraying to the media.

But in several instances throughout the film we see Morrison at ease when not under the glare of stage lights: his gleeful delight at a little girl tousling his leonine mane, or him gently caressing the wound of an injured female fan backstage. While making it look like a simple act of concern, Morrison seems also to know what his intimate touch meant and looked like to that fan in that moment. As Johnny Depp dictates from DiCillo's narration, "Jim relishes the attention; he seems to be born instantly ready for fame. Everything he does seems either brilliant or brilliantly calculated for effect."

"I was definitely fascinated by Jim's struggle with the celebrity beast," DiCillo confesses. "The amazing thing about Morrison was that for a moment he controlled it completely. His intuitive intelligence enabled him to sculpt and create his own celebrity image. And it was perfect. It had sex, danger, art, beauty, passion and complete irreverence. I think he knew this combination of elements had never existed before. And it worked. It worked so well it ultimately consumed him."

Jim Morrison shows his playful side backstage

Krieger elaborates: "Fame is something that really affected Jim more than the rest of us; he certainly bit off more than he could chew. This theme of celebrity and how it can affect people is something that is definitely relevant in telling the story of the band."

DiCillo continues: "Jim seriously tried to quit the band several times. He knew he was turning into a cartoon of himself. He really wanted to be an artist. He put a lot of work into his poetry but he also was seriously interested in film. And here he was increasingly singing to audiences that only wanted to hear 'Light My Fire' and to see him do something crazy. I think when he moved to Paris with Pam he really was trying to focus on his poetry. He was doing a lot of other things over there too; alcohol, coke and very likely heroin. But I think it was the fame high that he really craved. Here was a guy that had thousands and thousands of people screaming his name and now he was sitting alone in some French hotel room scribbling in his notebooks. No amount of mental methadone can help you through that kind of withdrawal."

In stitching the film together it became apparent to DiCillo that he needed a structural element to help bridge the gaps in the archival footage of the band's chronology. He began to write a narration. A major coup for the film came with the hiring of Johnny Depp to speak it. Depp's delivery augments the film with a layer of admiration and deep appreciation for The Doors. In the timbre of his voice you feel that this is a subject of which he is in awe. As a media personality, an icon himself, and as a musician, Depp chronicles the band's story with gravitas and lyricism, much more than a mere disembodied omniscient voice relating narrative information.

"I knew the narrator needed to be someone who really believed what they were saying," DiCillo admits, "not just a voice that gave a fake depth to the words. When I wrote them and spoke them, they were for me words of truth. I put some time and thought into the way I read them but the sole purpose of my originally doing the narration was to simply have something to work with when in the editing room."

DiCillo originally recorded the narration himself as his written text was changing daily. In the morning he would record what he'd written the night before but by the afternoon the work with the visuals required rerecording the words. If a paid narrator had been engaged DiCillo and his editors would have had to wait days for revisions. When the film was accepted to Sundance it still did not have an official narrator. DiCillo kept pushing the producers to hire one but a suitable choice could not be made in time. The reaction to this tactical decision had dire consequences.

"Press response was almost violent," the director admits. "I'm still not sure I quite understand the level of vehemence directed at me personally. There were too many words," DiCillo continues. "I knew that right away. But it was my first documentary and I was learning as I was going along. The good thing was that it opened the producers' eyes and prompted them to get serious about a narrator."

Upon DiCillo's insistence the producers made an offer to Johnny Depp who accepted immediately after seeing the film. "I was thrilled," DiCillo confesses. "Johnny's a very gifted actor. He's also a very personal actor. Every role he does, no matter how exaggerated, he invests a huge part of himself. I knew that if he connected to the film he could bring that crucial level of intimacy to it. He was also the right age. I did not want the voice of the film to be coming from the past. I don't see it as a nostalgic film – 'Golden Oldies for Stoners'. Depp brought the perspective of a whole new generation to the music. He made it seem modern; which to me it always was."

"Johnny's narration meant everything to the film," Krieger acknowledges. "He just brought an intangible quality to it. Neither I, nor John, nor Ray knew him prior to doing this. Tom's a great director, but perhaps not as good a narrator. But I will emphasise this:" the guitarist continues, "Tom's writing of the narration was absolutely excellent. His writing is really one of the truly great things about *When You're Strange*."

"Johnny understands fame," Densmore proclaims, "and he is also a musician; he knows what it's like to be a part of that world. Just as Tom was the perfect director to tell our story, Johnny was the perfect narrator." Manzarek concurs: "Johnny's got that subtle, understated quality about him that lends itself to the narrating this whole Doors story. It's not sensational and yet it's very decisive."[4] "Johnny made a few small changes but he basically said the words as I had written them," DiCillo recalls. "He did it for very little money. All he asked was to have time to record the narration on his own."

So DiCillo left the actor alone. And one-by-one Depp started sending him CDs. What impressed DiCillo most was the thought and personal investment Depp brought to the whole process. Instead of just grinding non-stop through a recording the actor would stop and give different meanings and readings to specific lines. He never indicated which he had a preference for. He merely recorded them all and let DiCillo decide which he felt were best for the film. Depp's readings and DiCillo's placement of them create a narrator whose voice is so engrained in the film it's almost like he's the fifth member of the band. Some of the most powerful moments are when the actor actually assumes Jim Morrison's persona and speaks directly in his voice.

And Depp clearly valued the collaboration. "DiCillo's *When You're Strange* is a meticulously crafted, exhilarating ode to one of music's greatest, most exciting ensembles: The Doors," the actor writes. "Watching the hypnotic, hitherto unreleased footage of Jim, John, Ray and Robby, both on and off the stage, I felt like I was there, with them, living and experiencing what they were experiencing, seeing it all through their eyes. Ultimately, Jim has been resurrected here to remind us that he is to this very day, one of the most significant frontmen/poets/shaman to ever grace a stage and that the band behind him kept the music alive every step of the way, adding fuel to an already raging fire, all along their wild and electrifying ride into history. The raw material entrances throughout. In terms of a rock n' roll documentary, or any kind of documentary for that matter, it simply doesn't get any better than this. What an honour to have been involved. I am as proud of this as anything I have ever done."[5]

With *When You're Strange* DiCillo found himself working for the first time with factual material and characters rather than those crafted from his own unique fictional constructs. This presented the challenge of maintaining his aesthetic ideas while simultaneously keeping the film always rooted in truth.

"Actually, it was kind of a relief to have these 'characters' – Jim, Ray, John and Robby – all complete and formed," DiCillo reveals. "And the more I learned about them the more I wanted to simply present them in the most truthful way possible.

After researching the band's rise and fall I was convinced that nothing about it needed to be manipulated. But there were many things that I manipulated visually: the choice of archival footage from the time period, slowing down the footage, speeding it up. There is a long montage set to 'Riders on the Storm' that is all Vietnam War footage I cut together. It just struck me as a rich metaphor for the war."

The director continues: "But I still had to find the dramatic arc of the film. It needed to have a clear structure and direction. I can build this into one of my scripts just by sitting alone and hammering out four or five drafts. With this documentary, all the hammering came while editing the film. And it was a long process of trial and error that took place in public. You'd never know if a section was going to work until you put all that together and screened it. Then I'd go back, re-edit and keep inching forward."

For DiCillo, this involved the mammoth task of trawling through the dense archive of The Doors' visual documents. But when he first started the pressure was immediate. The producers wanted to know exactly what his 'concept' was. "I understood their concern," the director admits. "There are a million ways this film could have gone and I found out later they'd actually tried a few with some other directors. But I told them I could not honestly present my concept until I'd seen every frame of footage in The Doors archive."

DiCillo felt he needed to know what his storytelling foundation was before even considering of a way to put it all together. So for the first three weeks he did nothing but look at footage ten hours a day. This made his producers exceedingly nervous. Every few days they would knock on the editing room door and enquire again, 'Do you have a concept yet?' And truth was even after three weeks the director had still not found a way into the story.

DiCillo offers some insight into what he felt was holding him back. "I needed something that was real to me: a hook, an emotional connection that would drive me – and guide me – all the way through. And it got pretty intense. I couldn't sleep. I'd lay awake in this little apartment they put me in, asking myself what the hell I was doing out here in LA even thinking I could make this documentary."

At one point the pressure got so bad DiCillo got out of bed at 4am and seriously considered packing his suitcase and driving to the airport. While sitting alone in the darkness the director suddenly remembered some silent footage he'd seen that day of Morrison wandering through the California desert. In particular he recalled a shot where Jim pries open the door of a car buried in the sand and staggers out of it. Further images welled up again; shots of Morrison driving a car, a fragment of him turning the dial of the radio – again, all silent. DiCillo's first revelation that night was to consider using those shots in the film accompanied by some archival audio to put on the radio, perhaps a period commercial or news bulletin about the Vietnam War.

"But something in Morrison's face struck me," the director recalls. "There was something haunted in it. The image of him getting out of the sunken car suggested something of the tomb – like he was rising out of the ashes. And for some reason it struck me that it could be the announcement of his own death that Morrison hears on the radio, like he's the spirit of Jim come back to find out what happened – to him, to

The End: Morrison hears of his own death on the radio

the band and to the time that was so particular to them. And that, miraculously, gave me the first real building block of my concept. These images of the bearded Morrison wandering through the desert could help structure the whole film as a journey."

Revelations like this make it evident that *When You're Strange* is more than an average music documentary; it is a strikingly original take on non-fiction filmmaking. DiCillo utilises authentic material and documentation but manipulates them to an astoundingly deep effect. The director duly interweaves outtakes from Morrison's film *HWY: An American Pastoral* into the trajectory of The Doors' career, giving *When You're Strange* a dense sub-text and concurrent alternative narrative that parallels the real-life story of the band. It also layers the film with an ethereal, often surreal quality, not something often seen in documentary cinema. Whenever the film cuts to the *HWY* footage the tone of the piece changes to a metaphysical, otherworldly ambience that briefly takes us out of the chaos of The Doors' fierce career momentum, as well as the socio-political turbulence of the 1960s.

The images are striking: the nomadic character from *HWY* drifting through the lonesome highways of America and hearing of his own death on the car radio, the implication of him being the wandering soul of Morrison himself, creating an eerie, alternative realm instilled with a meditative quality. DiCillo even finds footage from *HWY* that prompts Morrison into a moment of deep contemplation upon hearing of his own death, which is the catalyst for the film that unfolds before us.

"It wasn't until I had that nightmare/epiphany that something dramatic, and cinematic, began to excite me," DiCillo admits. "I don't think I intentionally set out to subvert the documentary form; I was only going off of an energy that came from the original footage. All that real footage of The Doors had such power and authenticity to it that it felt like a rich vein of gold. Even in its most relaxed moments it had something a million times more vital than some music celebrity sitting around talking about how Jim Morrison changed their life. It was real. I knew that it was the strongest way to tell the story."

To be sure, the use of the *HWY* footage in *When You're Strange* adds a great sense of mystery and surprise; as well as a refreshing break from the chronology. It enables DiCillo to step outside the confines of events for a moment and then start his story again from a slightly different perspective; rendering the narrative more circular

Morrison walks among fans during The Who's supporting set at the Singer Bowl

motion than linear. The footage from Morrison's film is visually different yet it is just as real and authentic as the performance footage. Both are from the same period in time. This actually helps support DiCillo's artistic suggestion that there were two Morrisons: the one who lived and died and another one who is still with us, still wandering and seeking the meaning of the whole experience just as we are.

The music of the *HWY* passages was scored by DiCillo himself, instilling in the picture a tranquil but brooding respite from the intensity of The Doors' music and the often shocking imagery that accompanies it. In addition to the *HWY* footage, DiCillo scored other scenes, giving additional weight to moments which show Morrison offstage, as when mobbed while wandering through the crowd during The Who's performance at the Singer Bowl, and when dancing with the tattered children of picnickers in the desert. DiCillo's music instills the film with an eerie, transcendent quality; contrasting exquisitely with the scorching rock n' roll of The Doors.

"I was out there in Los Angeles for five months. On weekends I had a lot of time on my hands," DiCillo recalls. "I'd brought my guitar and my laptop and one Sunday I started messing with a transitional scene that wasn't quite working in the editing room. I said, fuck it; let's see if a little odd ambient music will help it. I hooked up my keyboard and laid down a tone bed and then played some simple guitar lines over it. It was intended to be temporary, just something to help us in the editing room."

But the editors liked it so much the next weekend DiCillo sketched in a few more. The producers heard his music and liked it as well. Then Ray Manzarek heard it at the next screening and to DiCillo's complete astonishment, said it should stay in the film. The director ended up writing and recording about twenty-three minutes of music, one piece ending up as the score for the opening credits.

Densmore concurs with Manzarek's assessment: "Tom is a very musical person; he is multi-talented and so this was a plus to the film. We benefitted from having this director who could bring so much to the film, and his ambient score is one of those things that made it work even more."

A lack of both music theory knowledge and prodigious technical precision has never discouraged DiCillo from working on sound and music of his films. "I can't read music and I can barely play three chords on the guitar. But the stuff I wrote was very simple. And it needed to be. I used a hell of a lot of Doors songs in the film, most of them in their entirety. I didn't want to cut their music into little familiar sound bites.

So their music in the film, plus the story itself, is pretty dense and intense. My music is like the audio palate cleanser in-between intensity courses. There is something fragile and emotional about it that brings out those same qualities in Jim."

For the past half-century The Doors have become as legendary as The Rolling Stones, The Beatles, The Who, Jimi Hendrix and Led Zeppelin. Any historian or documentarian must approach the depiction of these idols with great sensitivity lest the wrath of fans and critics be unleashed upon them. DiCillo has not escaped the indignation of those who worship at the altar of Morrison and who felt infuriated about perceived slights against their rock god. There were wild accusations that DiCillo had "faked" the scenes from *HWY*. Fans can be quite damning and vocal when they perceive that a work impedes on a legacy as beloved as The Doors. There is an element of ownership among their most devoted disciples. Robby Krieger ponders the precious and personal thing that his music has become to fans.

"Doors fans are on a different plane altogether," Krieger admits. "They are extremely passionate and they want to keep it for themselves, there's a sense of ownership. They think they are the ones who discovered it. I've always said that I think of The Doors as an underground band, even though there have been Hollywood movies made about us it still feels like we are this underground band and people think of themselves as owning the right to tell other people about The Doors."

DiCillo concurs: "Fans that truly embraced the spirit of The Doors were very open to the film and many told me they were deeply moved by it. They appreciated the honesty and the intimacy. Others felt I'd pissed in the dust of their private shrines. The icon of Jim Morrison is incredibly seductive to many people. They see him as a kind of tortured god who said 'fuck you' to the world. People love this image. It's a really cool persona to slip on. They go to his grave at Pere Lachaise with bottles of Jack Daniel's and they get wasted in his honour. But I don't think this was Jim Morrison at all."

It is possible the Morrison DiCillo presented in *When You're Strange*, although closer to the real man, may have created a threat to some of these fans. In any event DiCillo was clearly taken by surprise by the intensity of some fans reactions to his film. "I knew I couldn't bullshit, especially with this band," the director confesses. "But it wasn't until after the film was released that I realised what I was up against. What makes The Doors so powerful is that their music speaks personally to every listener. And indeed, if their music is for the different, the uninvited or un-included, then the personal attachment to the music and the band becomes very intense. People become very possessive of that connection and it affects how they see anything that is even slightly different from it. I wanted to make a film about the band that was not a myth; one that was based solely on the truth about every one of them. Jim was not a god, nor was he a demon. He was a human being. And that's what made him interesting to me."

DiCillo's concern for validity kept him constantly returning to the original footage. There could be no questioning of what was right before your eyes he felt. But to his great distress early viewers expressed doubt about the legitimacy of the footage from *HWY*. To dispel any confusion he even added a subtitled explanation at the beginning of the film, identifying exactly where all the footage came from. But feeling that it started the mysterious journey of his film on too much of a clinical note he removed

Morrison in a scene from the film *HWY*

it. He took solace in assuming that even if there were a few people puzzled by some of the extraordinary footage from Morrison's own film that journalists and keen Doors fans would quickly emerge to explain it. But that didn't happen.

"To my amazement, even major critics panned the film accusing me of using a stunt double for Morrison and shooting re-enactments," DiCillo relates. "Morrison's film has been around since 1969. Excerpts from it have been on the web for over twenty years. It is probably one of the most bewildering reactions to one of my films that I've ever experienced. No one attempted to simply identify the source of the footage. When we took the film to Sundance a distributor walked out of the theatre after the first five minutes. I ran out after him because I'd really wanted him to distribute the film. When I asked why he was leaving he whirled on me and said, 'I can't believe you used a stunt double for Jim Morrison!'

I said, 'It's not a double! It's Morrison. It's from a film he made and acted in called *HWY*. I can show it to you.' And he just stared at me in this twitching, flustered rage, as if I'd just played an even sneakier trick on him. He never saw the remainder of the film."

It is indeed baffling to comprehend where the stiffness of this resistance came from. A small clue may lie in the pristine quality of the footage DiCillo excerpted from Morrison's film. Just before the final edit was locked the production gained access from the Morrison estate to the original negative of *HWY*. Morrison had been very impressed by Dennis Hopper's *Easy Rider* and insisted that his film be shot on 35mm. Upon viewing this original negative, which remains stunningly clear and beautiful, DiCillo decided to just leave it in its intended state even though it stands in heavy contrast to the rest of the archival footage which was considerably grainy and scratched.

A further clue may lie in the fact that even most die-hard Doors fans retain an image of Jim Morrison as clean-shaven, wearing a white shirt open to his waist and looking like Adonis. In truth Jim had a heavy beard which he allowed to grow out frequently. He is fully bearded at the ill-fated Miami concert and throughout the entire court proceedings. And thus he was bearded while acting in his own film but apparently to many viewers this conflicted with the image of the Jim Morrison they thought they knew.

Further, out of respect for Morrison and his film DiCillo did not use any edited sequences from *HWY*. He worked only with outtakes, meticulously piecing them together into scenes of their own, which he then with nearly invisible precision worked into his own film. Some of the most disturbing shots taken directly from *HWY* were of a coyote that has been hit by a car. It is here the accusations of re-enactment take on an absurdity verging on the macabre. DiCillo ruminates on this with deep puzzlement and dismay: "The coyote is clearly dying. Did people really think I'd actually run over a coyote just to get a shot of it?"

Krieger is particularly satisfied with the way DiCillo integrated the footage from Morrison's film. "I especially admired the way Tom used that movie *HWY*, even though a lot of people had the impression that that stuff was recreated and acted; people thought we used a fake Jim!" Krieger states incredulously. "The image was so clean that people really didn't believe that it was Jim driving the car. I had initially doubted whether Tom would get the use of the film from the Morrison estate, but Tom's powers of persuasion are pretty good."

Densmore considers DiCillo's use of *HWY* to be essential to the spirit of *When You're Strange*. "The way in which Tom weaves *HWY* into the film is so unique that I think it is better here than in its original form. It was destined to be in this film. The lonely Jim wandering through the film looking for its heart is brilliant. At Sundance, a potential buyer for the film ran out during the first few minutes and Tom chased after him. I love hearing this story! The Doors have always been unusual, and this concept of using the footage of Jim as the hitchhiker, wandering his way through the film looking for the centre and then becoming the centre fit The Doors aesthetic perfectly."

DiCillo's unique approach to documentary filmmaking also extends to the fact that he chose to eschew contemporary talking head interviews and recollections, relying instead only on genuine original footage of the band on and off stage to tell their story. "That's a good example of why Tom's vision for the film and his ideas were so great," Densmore enthuses. "I was against a 'talking heads' type flick even before I met Tom. I was worried that a standard film documentary with old farts reminiscing about the past would not serve the film well because The Doors seem to light the fire of each new generation on how to break the umbilical cord."

"I thought it was really great the way the narration delivers the story," Krieger states, "rather than having the three of us talking away in the background forty years later. I particularly love the fact that the narration tells the story in the present: Robby 'says' this, and Robby 'does' that, it wasn't past tense, it puts you right there with the

The Doors performing on stage. Left to right: Jim Morrison, Ray Manzarek, Robby Krieger, John Densmore

band, in the moment. Tom keeps you within the period for the whole film. I thought that was a brilliant thing to do."

"Most of the archival footage had no sound," DiCillo discloses. "At first it was frustrating and annoying. We're all accustomed to hearing sound when we watch something. It fills in the vacuum. It provides a comforting sense of familiarity and connection. But once I got used to it I found myself seeing the footage in a rare mental state. It was just me and The Doors; in silence. It was like going back in time but the footage was so detailed it was like all these people with strange clothes and funny haircuts just stepped out of a door down the hall. It was like a time capsule but utterly devoid of nostalgia. That's when I decided I'd try to tell the whole story just using this real footage. Don't cut to the band members today. Don't cut to other musical celebrities offering their opinions. Let The Doors talk just as they were. They said some pretty amazing things. And watching them perform was more revealing than anyone talking about them."

DiCillo recalls the diplomacy it took convincing The Doors that the way forward for the film would mean excluding their present selves from the finished product. When he first presented this idea to The Doors they were alarmed and skeptical; particularly Ray Manzarek. He questioned how DiCillo could consider telling the story of The Doors without hearing from The Doors. Then the director showed him the first fifteen minutes of the film beginning with Jim Morrison hearing the announcement of his own death and then chronicling the birth of the band, using only the archival footage.

"From that moment on Ray was on my side," DiCillo states. "The same was true for John and Robby. I think they saw that my intent was truthful and that using the footage in this way would almost in effect enable them to tell their own story. At one stage Robby wanted me to put in more information about his current life but I suggested that would diffuse the story and he was cool with that. The band and the music speak for themselves. Plus, they never get old in the film. We only see them in their prime."

DiCillo has a point. Set within this specific time period the film actually serves to immortalise The Doors. However, as the film approached a final cut, some conflicts resurfaced. First, DiCillo had a bit of an issue with Densmore when the drummer tried to change the opening credits a week before the film opened. That issue was

Doors keyboardist
Ray Manzarek

resolved with the credits staying the way the director had originally done them. The trickiest battle developed with Ray Manzarek. The keyboardist had gotten his degree in Filmmaking from UCLA and DiCillo actually respected his cinematic sense. But a real disagreement came over the ending. DiCillo knew early on he wanted to end the film on the line of narration: 'And as of this date, none of The Doors music has been used in a car commercial.' Manzarek resisted this idea with a vehemence that revealed some much deeper internal conflicts with the band. In fact the whole issue of Morrison refusing to let Buick use 'Light My Fire' in the car commercial was very complicated for The Doors. Manzarek and Morrison fought bitterly about it. Morrison abhorred the idea thinking it was nothing but a crass sell-out to commercialism. Manzarek on the other hand felt it was just a stupid commercial and saw nothing wrong with everyone making a few bucks.

DiCillo elaborates: "This issue was still very sensitive among Ray, John and Robby at the time I was making the film. In fact, they were suing each other over the right to use The Doors' music in commercials. So when Ray saw that line in my final cut he was pretty incensed. He told me I had to take it out. We ended up talking it over for about an hour. I told him I understood his point of view but suggested that to most of their fans this belief in The Doors not selling out was a deeply ingrained part of their devotion. And I think he heard me. Ray gave me his blessing to use it and to proceed and that meant so much to me. John and Robby later told me it was their favourite part of the film."

As with much of the director's work, the theme of family also finds its way into *When You're Strange*. Throughout the research and production of the film, DiCillo uncovered some startlingly similar parallels between Morrison's life and his own. They both have a brother and sister apiece and both grew up in fiercely demoralising households under the thumb of dominant patriarchs. Both of their fathers were career authoritarians with high-ranking positions respectively in the Marine Corps and the Navy. Besides the rigidity of discipline this forced upon them both it also meant a peripatetic life on the road as their families moved from base to base. DiCillo and Morrison discovered an artistic outlet in opposition to their fathers' expectations.

"One of the most surprising revelations was Jim's relationship to his father," DiCillo states. "It almost mirrored exactly my own. When you're a child, when someone tells you to do something your natural instinct is to say 'why?' But, when the response is 'because I said so' it creates an instant mistrust of authority. Morrison almost immediately took steps to get away from it; he left home when he was seventeen and he never went back. This whole idea of family to him was an extreme version of what I have said before in relation to *Delirious*: that family does not own or define you. I believe we all have a personal obligation to define our own selves, even if it means leaving the family a million miles behind."

And Morrison did define himself, not just to his family but to millions of people all across the world. Yet DiCillo carefully suggests that the void created by his father's indifference was a crucial and constant motivation for the superstar. "I can't speak for Jim Morrison," the director readily admits. "I can only speak for myself and I know my father's perceived indifference created strong, conflicted emotional turbulence in me. I think Morrison had similar conflicts. It made me wonder if every step he took out into the void was an attempt to find, in his own crazy way, some sanity, because the other side is insanity. A father saying, 'I don't like the very essence of who you are', that is insane."

"Listen, I'm not suggesting in any way there are artistic similarities between me and Jim Morrison," DiCillo concludes, "but, this unexpected glimpse into a shared family experience helped me enormously to see him as not a drunk, not a frenzied acid-freak, not as a demonic legend with a death wish; but simply as a human being. It is what gave me the key to opening the personal door which made it possible for me to tell this story."

DiCillo's journey through The Doors has enabled him to deliver an artistic declaration as profoundly personal as one is likely to find in non-fiction filmmaking. Morrison, as the film's central figure, not only affords further discourse on themes which have been examined throughout DiCillo's career, but the singer's own personality embodies the spirit of DiCillo's aesthetic: poetic, witty, rebellious, distinguished and a little absurd. In that sense *When You're Strange* sits appropriately alongside DiCillo's original narrative features, exploring as it does his continued fascination with the question of identity, whether on the world's stage or in our parents' living room, where one can be devastatingly rebuked by his own next of kin. DiCillo examines the destructive pressures imposed upon those whose path is dictated by the expectations of the Other. Morrison represented different things to many different people. To his family: a son and a brother. To his band mates: a friend, an artist and a colleague. To the conservative establishment: an enemy. To the world: a legend. To himself: one can never truly know. Only those closest to him can offer a glimpse into the true nature of Morrison.

"Jim was great to work with," Manzarek admits. "The Doors laughed all the time. It was a joyous time in the 1960s! I mean, sure Jim got drunk. When he got drunk, he was a nasty fellow. But that wasn't *all* the time. That was some of the time. He was great to *laugh* with. A great guy to drink with at the bar and tell stories. Very loquacious, very verbose and a real pleasure to know. That's *my* Jim Morrison. And I think you get a sense of that Jim Morrison in *When You're Strange*."[6]

"I remember the time when Tom and I had a blast doing interviews in Europe promoting the film," Densmore recalls fondly, "and we did an amusing photo shoot where we got the idea to pretend we were pissing on opposite walls in a cobblestone alley. Later, when the U.S. distributor didn't promote the film as well as they did in Europe, I put this photo on my website with the caption that we were pissing on the distributor. *When You're Strange* is a film that has such depth that I think it might take some people a couple of viewings to fully understand and appreciate it. It has all this familiar material but yet it is put together with Tom's unique vision. I was pleased that the three 'side' musicians got their due. I consider *When You're Strange* as a companion piece to Oliver Stone's film, adding humour and a feel for the period, that of the 1960s. It completes the full picture of Jim. There are things that are missing in Oliver's movie, such as the fact that before Jim's addiction took over he was very funny and very playful at times. Tom explored that and we see it in the film, what we see is the Jim I knew. Obviously, I miss him."

"*When You're Strange* is my favourite visual document on The Doors," Krieger enthuses. "I think it's the best film of The Doors ever made, because it has a certain mood to it that seems right for The Doors. I love the reality of it, I love that it's all genuine footage, put together exceptionally well, and with no bullshit. You can't top that. In the beginning of it we just thought it couldn't hurt to try to at least get it right. And with *When You're Strange* we got it right."

Manzarek applauds the film: "This, *When You're Strange*, is the true story of The Doors."[7] "Tom did a brilliant job, I must say. He cut the heck out of this movie ... It's a very exciting documentary for people who both know The Doors and as a great introduction to The Doors."[8] The keyboardist continues: "I liked seeing Jim Morrison alive ... That's my buddy. That was my pal. I haven't seen him alive since 1971, and he was alive in the film as he could be in this stage of our existence. It was great seeing us as young, vibrant, vital men seeking our musical destiny."[9]

"So much has been written and said about The Doors by people more learned and informed than me," DiCillo says. "I knew I had to make a film that was more than just a rehash of their rise and fall. I had to find something that struck me on a personal level." DiCillo reflects for a moment, and then continues. "I put as much of myself into this film, and worked as hard on it, as any film I've made. At the end of the day it feels like one of my own. And there is no feeling more satisfying than that."

When You're Strange won the Grammy Award for Best Documentary in 2010.

* * *

Wayne Byrne: When You're Strange *was a massive departure for you. Were you a huge Doors fan?*

Tom DiCillo: A fan but not a fanatic. I had only a basic knowledge of their music and their story. But what I did know instantly got me excited. Plus, for the first time in my career, I was being offered a film that was fully financed and ready to go, which is kind of funny when you think about it. Over the last few years I've gotten shit from journalists who've been somewhat dismissive about the fact I've done some TV work. I'm not sure what people think I'm living on. I get lauded in some circles for sticking to my guns and not selling out but few people seem to consider the financial toll that comes with that. And the irony is that this rare opportunity to make one of my most personal films, even though it is a documentary about a rock band from the 1960s, came directly from my connection to television.

As a filmmaker who has solely directed pictures that were conceived and written entirely by yourself, how did it feel to be approaching material that was already set in stone regarding historical fact and existing footage?

I was actually looking forward to trying a documentary. I'm a big fan of Errol Morris and the documentaries of Werner Herzog. Both of them have an amazing gift for presenting reality in a way that it becomes almost mystical and surreal – like the hint of a drop of pure acid as they take you on the trip. I was excited to try that.

What did you bring to the film in terms of your acquaintance and familiarity with the music of The Doors?

I was fourteen when 'Light My Fire' hit number one. My musical sensibilities were pretty unformed. I didn't have any money so I wasn't buying records. My source for music was the radio. Somehow I scraped up the money to buy The Doors' first album. Something about the music spoke to me. It was different. It was a little odd and spooky. It was outside the norm and clearly at odds with authority. One night, there was a dance in my high school gym. Something prompted me to empty a small shampoo bottle and fill it with my father's scotch. I drank it at the dance while the long version of 'Light My Fire' played. My first thrill of rebellion was The Doors with an alcohol buzz laced with the reek of shampoo.

But there was so much I didn't know about them. I really learned about The Doors as I made the film. And my whole perception changed with every passing week.

What were some of the more surprising things you learned?

Something as simple as the fact that Robby Krieger wrote 'Light My Fire'. I know that sounds mundane but you'd be surprised how many Doors fans don't know this. Morrison tweaked it a little bit but it was Robby's song – and the first song he'd ever written. Robby wrote many other songs, including a large number of their Top Ten hits. But what was most interesting to learn was how intricately the band was connected. Each of them brought something absolutely crucial. It wasn't just Jim; and in fact Jim could probably never have felt comfortable going off like he did if he didn't sense Ray, John and Robby were always there musically and artistically to guide him back to Earth.

You said that you worked on the film as a developing concept, you discovered as you endeavored. At what point did Jim as a protagonist, become a 'DiCillo character', if you know what I mean?

That's a very good question. I mentioned to you before that I went into this film with a few naive and stupid prejudices; for example I liked The Doors' music but Morrison being so excessive kind of bugged me. I thought, "Did he really have to destroy himself to make music?" And that mentality kept me at a distance from him for quite a while.

The key moment came for me when I had dinner with Jim's sister, Anne. We were talking about the family and what it was like living with the Admiral and I said, "So, where do you think Jim's drinking came from?" At that point one of Anne's sons just erupted at me. He said, "Jim was an alcoholic! An alcoholic doesn't choose to be an alcoholic, it's a disease!" Even though the guy was kind of an asshole I realised he was right, and that prompted me to see Morrison in a completely different light. Jim wasn't just going out and getting drunk for the thrill of it. He was clinically an alcoholic, and it's true; it is a disease. Then you have his conflict with his father and the man's relentless refusal to connect emotionally with his son. You put those two factors together and suddenly you've got a really interesting character. It's not that you have to forgive him or condone him but you can understand him and your heart goes out to him because you see what a struggle it was for him. Throughout my films the characters are all struggling with something similar. It made Jim human for me; as human as Johnny Suede or Les Galantine.

How did that shift in perception change the tone and aesthetic of the film?

It gave me a lot more empathy for Jim. To be honest, I never saw the film as a "documentary". It was always like a narrative film to me. And as such, I came to realise Jim was my main character, my hero actually. So I needed to be able to see him as clearly as possible. More importantly, I needed not to judge him in any way. I think he was a severely tormented soul and the demons he was fighting were incredibly powerful.

The film doesn't romanticise him nor does it criticise him. It doesn't condemn him but neither does it shy away from showing the parts of him that were destructive and how that behaviour affected the band; how it literally led to everything falling apart. This enabled me to bring a more emotional narrative approach to the film.

The way you used the HWY *footage makes for an extremely distinctive form of documentary filmmaking.*

The way it happened was completely accidental. The producers began shipping me boxes of DVDs of footage labeled only "Doors: Archival Footage". So I would sit through each DVD, all of which were about ninety minutes long containing random footage of the band in no form or order. Suddenly here's a shot of Morrison with a beard crawling out of a car half submerged in sand. I had no idea what that was; I thought it might have been from a music video that they did or something. It took me a while to find out that it came from a short feature Jim made. The first thing I did was put a note on it saying, "We're using this somewhere!" At that point I had no idea where.

The film shows many scenes where Jim seems to be at bliss: amongst his fans, amongst children, amongst people who are enjoying his free spirit. This is quite the opposite from the Oliver Stone image of Morrison as a morose, tortured artist and self-destructive wild child.

That footage was there. There were scenes of Jim laughing, clowning around like a sixteen-year-old juvenile delinquent. There are scenes of him being courteous and wittily diplomatic to complete strangers. Scenes of him loose, relaxed and enjoying himself – like any other human being. But I think these scenes reveal something hidden or almost willfully ignored by people; particularly the scene from *HWY* where he's dancing with the children by the side of the road.

I know from talking to some people who worked on that film that this was a completely spontaneous moment. They'd come upon this family camping out in the desert. The kids started dancing and Morrison just joined in. There is a look of genuine delight and euphoria on his face.

And this was a part of him; just as all the drinking, the drugs and the tormented self-destruction were a part of him. I felt it was crucial to show it. One of the main reasons I found the Oliver Stone film unsatisfying was because he focused so much on the obsession and self-destruction that at best only half a man appeared.

I was amazed by the frequency and power of Morrison's smile.

I was too. Some other fascinating pieces came from listening to the hours and hours of un-labeled audio tapes that were also shipped to me. One was of him and John right after a concert. They were in the limo trying to get a guy on the street to buy them some beer. You feel like you're right in the car with them. Another sound snippet was of Jim walking into a club. He goes up to the bouncer and you can hear him say very clearly, "Any groovy pussy in this joint?" The bouncer laughs; Jim laughs. I found it so spontaneous and human I put it in the film.

John Densmore and Ray Manzarek in the studio with producer Paul Rothchild (far right)

Jim Morrison recording vocals in the studio

The point is, Jim Morrison was all of these things. He had all the complexity of a living, breathing human being. I felt I would do him a tremendous disservice if I didn't show as much of who he was as possible.

Your treatment of Jim Morrison is no more reverential than the way you treat Robby, Ray and John. Was it important to you that the band as a unit receive equal veneration rather than focusing solely on Jim?

When I first started the film I believed like a lot of people, including some hardcore Doors fans, that Jim was the key artist and creator. I soon discovered that was not true at all. Of course Jim had something tremendously powerful and unique but Ray was the one who first started putting his lyrics to music. Ray had extensive training in piano. He knew Bach and he knew Coltrane; he also knew Kurt Weil as well as the blues and rock n' roll.

You can hear it in The Doors' music, especially in songs like 'People Are Strange', which has a kind of woozy, surreal carnival vibe to it. I wanted to try and identify what The Doors' sound actually was. Robby started on classical guitar then moved on to Middle Eastern and Flamenco. John was heavily into free form jazz. I listened to all of their songs trying to get a sense of what made them different and unique. And I think it comes down to a combination of classical, jazz, rock n roll and a raw, powerful simplicity. You add Morrison's manic, uncensored intensity to that and you've got a band with more than just a sound.

All three of these guys really knew how to play. And they knew how to change and adapt to Morrison's unpredictable excursions into unknown territory. I came to realise that the sound was completely dependent on the four of them, not just Jim. I felt it was time to shake the dust off that part of the myth.

You don't go into any speculation about Morrison's death.

It's a very murky and somewhat creepy subject so I decided to leave it alone. It's not that I don't think it's important. How and why Jim died is very significant but so much of it is clouded in hearsay, superstition and psychic heavy breathing. The fact is Jim is gone. And when he died it was the end of The Doors. Ray, John and Robby all acknowledge this. The band known as The Doors consisted of the four of them. Without any one of them they were not The Doors.

And, the film is not "The Life and Death of Jim Morrison." It is the story of The Doors.

The film was invited to the Sundance Film Festival. How did the screening go?

Audience reaction was very strong but we got a pretty chilly reception there from the press and distributors. Maybe it was because the film still had my narration; maybe it was a review in *Variety* where the critic suggested, "This film should never be distributed," which I thought was a little extreme. I mean, the whole reason you take a film to Sundance is to get distribution. Without it your film is doomed. I grant everybody the right to like or dislike the film. But to publicly pronounce at the most important US film festival that no one should ever see the film? First, it is completely unjustified and second, it's like journalistic terrorism. Where was this guy when *The Flintstones* got distributed? Or *Meet The Fokkers*?

Ray, John and Robby accompanied you to the festival. How did people respond to seeing them?

Sundance is a very young crowd so not everyone really knew who they were. The people that did were ecstatic and in awe. One day I was doing some interviews with Ray and Robby in a store that sold musical equipment. During a break Ray walked over to a keyboard and started the opening riff to 'Riders on the Storm'. Without a word Robby picked up a guitar and started playing with him. Someone in the room sat down at the drums and someone else picked up a bass. It was incredible. People were just standing there, mesmerised, especially me. It was my one and only experience seeing even some fragment of The Doors playing live. What amazed me was how completely immersed in the music both Ray and Robby were. They were playing the song like it was the first time. That was the highlight of the festival for me.

Another unforgettable moment came after the first screening. Robby came up to me and quietly said, "Thank you." I said, "For what?" He said, "For letting people know I wrote 'Light My Fire.'" I was really unprepared for how moved he was.

How was distribution of the film handled?

Like a team of drunken plumbers trying to do a heart transplant. Believe it or not, the producers hired the same "distributor" who'd handled *Delirious*. And the exact same scenario played out. No money was spent on advertising. There were no posters, no TV ads; nothing. They saw no theatrical potential for this film. They minimised everything about it instead of thinking *big*. This was the first documentary on The Doors, one of this country's most influential rock groups. It is a film where the music and the imagery are so vivid that they deserve to be seen and heard in a big theatre with a great sound system. It should have been a big screen theatrical event.

What was the critical reception like?

Frankly, the reviews were mixed. Some loved it; some hated it. Again, I think some of it had to do with how personally people relate to The Doors and their music. Even though every word in it came from my conversations with Ray, John and Robby many people felt their own personal version of their story was more important. A number of reviews expressed outrage that I had used a "double" and "recreated" footage. There was no double, there was no recreated footage but no one even bothered to investigate. Like I said, if they'd even done the most basic fact-checking they would have seen all the "questionable" footage came directly from Morrison's own film *HWY*. I'm still amazed that no one even thought of asking me.

The film was screened at various film festivals around the world, some of which you attended with John, Robby and Ray. How was the reaction and reception to the film in these other countries?

It was very strong. The Doors still have a huge international fan base. Sales were made to countries all around the world. The film did particularly well in France. The distributor was very excited about it and committed to showing the film on seventy screens, which is pretty amazing. They came up with a fantastic poster which they put up all over the Paris Metro. I couldn't believe it when I saw it. It made the film bigger than life; which is what the band was. Many, many more people saw the film in France than in the US.

I went to Paris with John Densmore for the premiere and press. We hung out together for over a week. I was still having the moments where I was shaking my head going, "is this really me sitting here getting drunk with John Densmore?" He told me

DiCillo in Paris during the promotional campaign for *When You're Strange*

this amazing story about how Jim showed up at his house one afternoon kind of down and depressed, but no one paid him much attention. So Jim went alone out into the hills for a couple of hours. When he came back he said he'd written a new song. He sat in the living room and sang it for John and Robby, "People are strange when you're a stranger/Women seem wicked when you're alone…"

The way John told this story made the whole band instantly real and human to me; I could actually hear Morrison's voice. John revealed to me that when Jim sang those lyrics he was as much in awe of him as any screaming fan. Those days in Paris with John were some of best I had working on this film.

Both John and Robby have expressed to me that they feel When You're Strange *is a real and honest depiction of The Doors as it happened. Robby in particular considers it his favourite visual document on The Doors. How does that feel to you, that the band regards the work so highly?*

All I wanted to do was tell their story as truthfully as I could and give each of them the respect I felt they deserved. For John, Robby and Ray to say to me, "You told our story", is rewarding on a level I can't begin to describe.

CHAPTER NINE

Down in Shadowland

'I had no idea what I was going to do with the shots ... But, I did know that something was compelling me to keep shooting.'
— Tom DiCillo

Within the five years it has taken to complete this book Tom DiCillo directed his eighth feature film, *Down in Shadowland*. As of writing, DiCillo is in negotiations with a distributor to release the film nationwide. Thus far the film has made numerous festival appearances in the US, and a preview screening in Ireland.

Down in Shadowland is a brooding vérité documentary about New York and New Yorkers. But its theme is perhaps DiCillo's grandest and most universal of all: an examination of basic human connection and interaction. DiCillo's observational camera captures life in motion while roaming the subterranean world of New York's underground mass transit system. The subway is a pounding underworld that heaves with the organic flow of the city's population around its pillars of concrete and grinding steel. DiCillo utilises this shadowed space as fertile ground to explore human nature under the microscope.

Down in Shadowland is an incandescent piece of maverick filmmaking. Inherent are the soulful qualities and human complexities of DiCillo's aesthetic that inspired me to write this book, the deft humanist approach adhered to in his observations of life and of people. The film takes the viewer on a journey through loneliness, despair and anger, yet there is an overarching sense of hope, humour, humanity and affection that shines through. The yearning for connection and recognition is compounded by a

Beauty on the platform

Bird of Passage: the surrealist realism of life in the underground

subtext that hauntingly ruminates upon the missing children of New York City and in reflection of some of the greatest tragedies of recent American society.

Down in Shadowland is an indelible tone poem, marrying expressive imagery to lyrical ambiance, contrasting with the fieriest political and social commentary of DiCillo's career. The film is as evocative and melancholic as it is alternately optimistic and apoplectic; a vivid and arresting work that touches the soul with stirring moments of humanity in isolation amongst the throng.

* * *

The following Q&A is the culmination of several years of discussions with DiCillo and his collaborators, of intensely analysing in detail what makes these films so unique and special to those artists, and to me, on a profoundly personal, professional, and aesthetic level.

Wayne Byrne: *When we started this book I asked you how you perceived a way forward with future films, to which you suggested perhaps going back to basics: two actors, one small apartment. Several years later, your next step forward was indeed a scaling back of sorts yet one of your biggest films in terms of themes and ideas. Instead of one small apartment* *we have New York City; instead of two actors, we have a cast of thousands of New Yorkers. Where did* Down in Shadowland *come from?*

Tom DiCillo: The answer to that question reveals a reality that is increasingly difficult for me to acknowledge; that it has been quite a long time since I have made a narrative feature film. So the most honest explanation is that part of me just couldn't stand not making a movie, no matter how small. I'd been carrying my video camera with me on the subway for several years, shooting people in moments of intimacy or human vulnerability that moved me. I had no idea what I was going to do with the shots. But I did know that something was compelling me to keep shooting.

I also knew I was tired of waiting for producers or financiers to tell me when I could make a film. I was tired of sending my scripts to actors and never hearing a word of response. I was tired of feeling that what my eye was seeing was useless and had no purpose. So I had begun taking this idea of documenting the underground world beneath NYC more seriously. It became like a private, personal quest for me to make a film based entirely on what I was seeing. Once I committed to it, it took over seven years to finish.

You made the film entirely by yourself. How did you find working by yourself on this in terms of shooting, editing, scoring, etc? What were the advantages or disadvantages of building this film without collaboration?

Well, the advantages were enormous. I could do whatever I wanted, whenever I wanted. Every director strives for the kind of success that enables them to have this freedom on every film. This privilege is rare and comes to only a very few and extremely fortunate people. In my heart I believe that having this freedom is the most natural way to make a film. Every time I've had to fight vehemently to get what I knew was crucial to the film, it always seemed bizarre and alien to me. Of course, compromise is a given in this business. But making the film the way you think it should be made also seemed like a given; as natural as breathing.

With *Down in Shadowland* I reduced the number of people interfering with me to zero. It felt fantastic. But it was a little disconcerting at first. It took me a while to get used to the complete freedom it offered, and the responsibility it required. It forced me to be very clear about what I wanted, and what I wanted to say.

In that sense it is the most personal film I've made. Every shot is mine; every shot is something that interested me and inspired me to film it the way I did. Every cut in the film, every dissolve, every sequence is there because it was something I wanted to do. I did not intentionally exclude collaborators. I found that reducing the filmmaking process to this kind of simplicity was the only way I could make the film.

Despite being shot guerrilla-style there is a commanding visual mode and cinematic grammar throughout the film. The framing and composition of shots come across as consciously considered. When you are shooting spontaneously like this how much consideration goes into the visual ideas as opposed to just content? I find it amazing that content is not attained at the expense of style, but both are achieved concurrently.

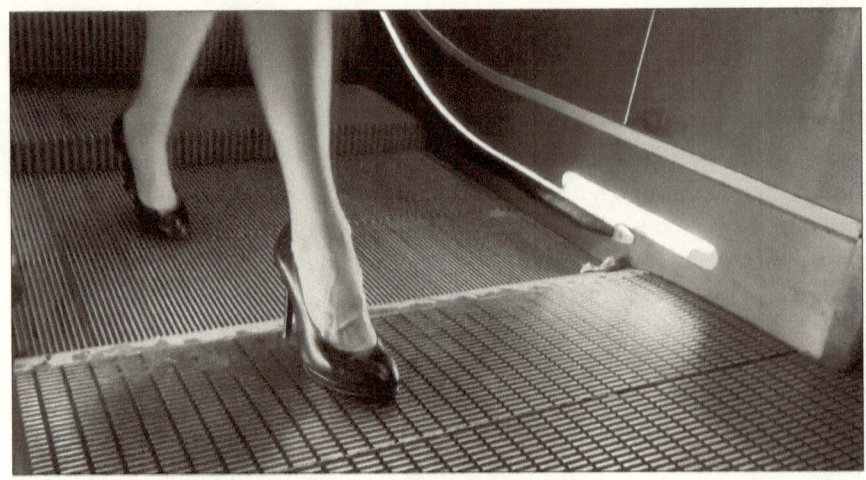

DiCillo's sharp sense of framing and mise-en-scene evident in the documentary, *Down In Shadowland*

I shot the whole film shot on a small Sony Handycam about as big as a pack of Marlboros. I did not intentionally try to hide the camera but definitely its small size made it very inconspicuous. I also shot everything without holding the camera up at eye level, especially when shooting people on the train. Usually, I would hold the camera in my lap and use the zoom to finese the framing. It took massive concentration. First of all, you never know when something unexpected is going to happen. I developed a intuitive sense in watching people that enabled me to start filming them just before they revealed something strange or beautiful. Much of what I shot was sheer luck. I do have an eye for composition and that is something that has been a tool in my arsenal since I started in this business. But mainly, every shot was treated as a completely separate entity. I just tried to use the camera to glean the purest essence of what I was seeing.

Once the idea of a structure became clearer to me I began shooting more specifically. I designed a camera mount consisting of a plastic ball head on the end of an extendable monopod. This enabled me to get shots with the lens just above ground level, and to raise it up high and use it as a crane. I hung between the cars on the express and extended the camera out past the body of the car, holding on to the monopod with one hand and the exterior rung of the train with the other. I could barely see the camera screen and I was terrified I'd stick it out too far and the camera would get smashed against the tunnel.

Did you start out with a structure in mind or did you discover this film as you shot your footage?

I had no structure in mind. I just kept shooting scenes or images that caught my eye. After several years I began to think about how I was going to put it all together. It took quite a while to find the central theme even though it was inherent in just about every

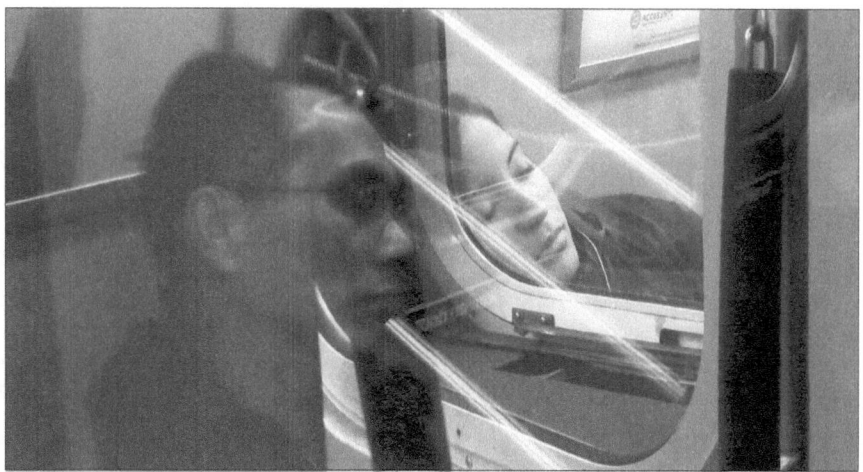

Tranquillity in transit

shot. There's a surreal quality to the film.; it's not strictly a documentary. It carries an emotional weight that shifts it into an entirely different realm. What I discovered is that the shots were all contemplating an aspect of humanity; something intimate and personal in this underground world of strangers.

There is a sense of anonymity that exists on trains that makes people think they are invisible. And it is precisely because of this that people actually allow themselves to be completely open and visible – the mass of humanity they are in gives them the feeling they're wearing a cloak of invisibility. And so their guard comes down and they revealed things to me without knowing it.

Images of Innocence: a touching moment which underscores the recurring motif of lost children and lost innocence present throughout the film

The whole film is about observing this intimate, personal world. My first clue at a structure came when it felt like this world underground was actually a mirror of the harsh, bright world above ground – as if it was a shadow world or a reflection that actually offered a deeper vision into what it was reflecting. That gave me the idea to structure the film as a kind of journey, moving deeper and deeper toward some kind of meaning and revelation. The structure took the form of moving through a series of levels; an idea which I admit stealing from Dante because it seemed to work for him.

Down in Shadowland contains your most pointedly political discourse thus far; as much as there is immense humanity and tenderness in the film there is a fierce sense of anger and distrust. There is a central repeating theme of a lost child and you present an entire sequence using footage of movie violence you shot off the monitors in the Times Square underground video stores. Socio-political commentary and religious iconoclasm have up to now been subtextual in your work, but here it is blatantly on display.

Three things prompted that. Over the course of the seven years I was filming a child went missing in the subway system and posters began appearing in all the stations seeking help in finding him. Audio announcements were made every ten minutes giving the details of the child's physical appearance. I started filming every place I saw the posters and heard the announcements.

Another thing that had intrigued me was the people stopping to watch the video monitors beneath Times Square. Most of the images that attracted people, primarily men, were of violence. And finally, around that time the slaughter of twenty pre-school children in a small New England town had ripped through the country's consciousness and became permanently etched in mine.

The alignment of these three events prompted me to delve deeper into something that has really been troubling me for years; the increased occurrence of gun violence against children. I devoted a whole section of the film to this idea; basically expressing my outrage and confusion as to why this country refuses to acknowledge its fixation on violence.

What are your hopes for the film?

Just that it get seen. This is proving harder than I imagined. The film has been rejected by just about every major US festival including Sundance, Seattle, San Francisco, Tribeca and the New York Film Festival. It did get accepted into the Woodstock Film Festival where it screened in the Main Documentary competition. But a member of the jury there revealed to me the film was dismissed for any award consideration because a key member of the jury thought the film was "not a documentary". This really puzzled me. Every frame of the film is real. So what does that make the film? I was particularly surprised that this came from a festival whose motto is "Fiercely Independent". How can you be fiercely independent and negate a film simply because it doesn't conform to a conventional format?

It does worry me. The film does not fit into most accepted ideas as to what a documentary is. But you don't have to go too far to find films about real things that also stretch the genre; like the films of Werner Herzog, Frederick Wiseman or Errol Morris.

There is a great history of films like this and my hope was that festivals like the New York Film Festival would see the film and understand it. I put seven years into this film. I think it turned out quite beautiful in an intensely real but strangely surreal way. It would be very hard for me to conceive that it could never be seen.

Just that concept itself is something that really troubles me. Why would I spend seven years making a film that no one would see? That is either an exercise in utter futility or a revelation of my complete and utter blindness as to what the fuck I am doing.

Writing this book has been an intense emotional journey for me. It started back in the early-1990s when I was a lonely teenage cineaste wandering the shelves of the local video store where I happened upon a strangely attractive neon video sleeve containing Johnny Suede, *a moment that would change my life. It led to collaborating with you and your actors in an attempt to put all your films in context, to look at the difference and impact these films made in your life and in those that worked on them. My love and respect for the films has grown with each repeat viewing, now knowing so intimately the blood, sweat and tears that went into their making. Having spent so much time looking back at your body of work with me for this book, what is the legacy of these films to you as their author, and where to next for you?*

I look at the films now and part of me is completely amazed that any of them ever got made. I'm serious. So much work went into them. So much luck was required. But looking back on these seven films is like looking back on someone else's lifetime. I can clearly see the changes that were going on in my life reflected in each film.

I see that part of me is just like Johnny Suede, Toby or Kid. I've always had a hard time understanding that hope and innocence are not the only answers. I keep trying to find my way in this business thinking this is all I need to see the path ahead.

But part of me is also Les Galantine. I feel the ache and sting of every single rebuke and disappointment. Some days my biggest struggle is to simply get through the day believing that it is still worth it. It happens to everyone at some point. I think much of this comes from the difficulty I've been experiencing over the past few years in trying to get another movie made. But in some ways I suppose you could say I am exactly where I want to be. If I wanted to be someplace different then I'd be trying to get there.

So, where do you want to be?

Like a million other directors I'd like to be in the position where I could keep making the films that interested me, only on a little more regular basis. I always believed that the honesty I was striving for, whether comedic or dramatic, was worth the commercial battles. I always believed that if given a chance, audiences would respond to the films. Not in gigantic numbers but enough to provide an echo for me; some kind of feedback that the themes and ideas that interested me were interesting to other people as well.

The whole sensibility of independent filmmaking has changed. The social and cultural environment that enabled you to make Johnny Suede *or* Living in Oblivion *simply does not exist anymore.*

That's true, but this business is 98% game. It always has been. Even the artiest of art films needs some kind of success in order to enable the filmmaker to make another film. You've got to work the room and you've got to love doing it. Although I have made serious efforts to play the game, the relentless flood of bullshit can make you feel like you're suffocating in it. I still believe that the best way to make a film is to write the script that most excites you, then cast the actors whom you feel are absolutely perfect for the parts no matter what their 'star meter' rating is. As soon as I feel I can't do either of these things I start to freak out. I think I've lost some of the patience that you need to keep from punching someone.

What about television? You've been directing for it over the past seven years. I don't agree with the sentiment but many people think TV is the new independent film.

Yes, I've directed some television. But if I were to be totally honest I'd have to say if I were directing a film every year and a half I'd never do TV. It pays the bills but there are too many bosses. The director is the lowest person on the creative power ladder. Anybody above you, from the hundreds of producers to the writers, studio execs and their limo drivers can tell you what to do. No matter how "edgy" the show, the ultimate goal is to get as many people to see it as possible.

TV as the new independent film? I'm not really convinced of that. There is some great stuff being done, no question about that. *True Detective* was great for the first three episodes. I love *Veep*, especially Julia Louis-Dreyfus.

But the independent films that inspired me were complete, specific expressions of an idea. Their beginning and end was part of their beauty – and their power. Even the most cutting-edge TV shows still feel to me that they're under the thumb of some consortium of suits. No matter how far out they are, they still don't push the limits with as much courage and abandon as a real independent film. No matter how bold we are told they are, they all still operate under a strict formula: grab the audience's attention in the first few minutes, hold them, and then end with a jolt that makes them want to come back next week. How is this different from any standard network TV show?

From what I gather, there seems to be a lot more freedom and willingness to explore difficult themes in some of the more respected cable shows.

That's true. But the fact that these shows are series makes them seem a little vacuous. Anything can happen, to any character, at any time. For me, this removes any real emotional commitment to the character or the show. If anything can happen then nothing means anything. Ultimately, all the straining of envelope pushing becomes routine. It all starts to feel the same.

The great independent films that inspire me make a conscious choice to commit to an idea. They take you someplace specific and leave you there. There is no next week. This is the kind of visual storytelling that motivates me.

So, how do you see yourself fitting into the contemporary film landscape?

Landscape is a good word. It implies something solid, something that actually exists. My biggest concern right now is that I don't know what exists. It all feels like smoke and quicksand. Even if I were lucky enough to accomplish the miracle of making another film I have no idea what would happen to it.

Whether it would get a theatrical release or not?

Not even that. More like, where are people watching films? Someone told me just yesterday that they watched *Jackie Brown* on their iPhone, propped up on their belly while they were trying to go to sleep.

But doesn't that prove there are many more release options for filmmakers?

Yes, but I'm more concerned with what it says about the film-watching experience. It's great to have the ability to watch a film on your belly but I think something is lost when images that used to come to life on a fifty-foot screen are minimized to an LCD sliver. It affects the kinds of movies being made. And it affects how they're being made.

More and more it seems it is mainly spectacle and big-budget action films that get theatrical releases.

The reason is understandable: they bring in audiences and money. I used to feel the fight was worth it because you knew your film was going to end up on a real screen somewhere. But having this creeping doubt about what dim Internet micro-corner the film is going to end up on really sucks out a lot of the motivation. I still want to make a film more than anything. I just dread the thought of releasing it into a vacuum.

But surely you must have some great sense of satisfaction in having made these iconic films so emblematic of the American independent film movement?

I do. And the thing I'm the most proud of is that to a large degree each film is the film I wanted to make. Some people get me; some people don't. It's been that way from the beginning. Sundance accepted every one of my films. And every one of my films was rejected by Cannes.

When I was in the sixth grade my school had a contest for this annual event called Sadie Hawkins Day. The idea was for kids to dress up in hillbilly clothes and act 'country'; a strange, rather demeaning concept to anyone who actually did live in the country. But something struck my twelve-year-old brain and I put a costume together. It came mainly from my Dad's closet. He was in Vietnam at the time. I borrowed a pair of combat boots he'd left behind that were so huge my legs looked like toothpicks sticking out of them. I took a big, red flannel shirt of his and wore some old cut-off jeans with a rope holding them up. To my amazement I was chosen to represent my class at the lunchtime competition.

It was held in the gym. All the kids in costume were lined up on the basketball court. The rest of the school was jammed into the bleachers and the judging was based on their applause. The school principal walked behind each of us and held his hand over our heads one by one. It was the first time I'd ever been in a public competition. I was excited to see what would happen when the principal held his hand over my head.

About three kids applauded, very briefly. The crush of that silence was so sudden and unexpected I was barely aware that the principal was already two kids past me. He'd stopped behind Donnie Dane. Donnie had twinkling blue eyes, a warm, sleepy smile and a face as smooth and perfect as a cartoon. He was one of the most popular kids in the school. On this day he was dressed exactly how he dressed every other day of the year, in light blue Levi corduroys, suede ankle boots and a soft blue flannel shirt hanging out of his jeans. His only effort at a costume was the faintest smudge of a moustache he'd rubbed on with a burnt cork.

When the principal held his hand over Donnie's head the audience erupted into a gigantic roar. The principal raised Donnie's arm in triumph even though there were three kids still waiting to be judged. I looked over at Donnie and he was just kind of smiling, his eyes twinkling. And all I could think of was in that light you couldn't even see his moustache.

I think there was no event in my life that prepared me for the film business as much as this sixth-grade Sadie Hawkins Day.

DiCillo at the San Sebastian Film Festival with *Delirious*, 2006

NOTES

1 http://www.rogerebert.com/rogers-journal/an-indie-director-asks-is-the-whole-thing-a-kafkaesque-nightmare
2 hhttp://thephoenix.com/boston/movies/99519-interview-ray-manzarek-of-the-doors/#ixzz3HipZC5vE
3 http://movieline.com/2010/04/08/moment-of-truth-doors-keyboardist-ray-manzarek-on-new-doc-and-oliver-stones-folly/
4 http://collider.com/ray-manzarek-and-robby-krieger-interview-when-youre-strange/#ZMokqfu14seXGoxT.99
5 http://www.tomdicillo.com/64-from-mr-d/
6 http://movieline.com/2010/04/08/moment-of-truth-doors-keyboardist-ray-manzarek-on-new-doc-and-oliver-stones-folly/
7 http://www.youtube.com/watch?v=SK25lV0gfII (The Doors Documentary to debut at Sundance Festival, Artisan News Service)
8 http://www.youtube.com/watch?v=vyLUEI5Fl9A (When You're Strange, interviews, AMC News)
9 http://popcultureblog.dallasnews.com/2013/05/chris-vognars-2010-interview-with-the-late-doors-keyboard-player-ray-manzarek.html/

FILMOGRAPHY

WRITER AND DIRECTOR

God Save the King, 1977 (short film Written and Directed by Tom DiCillo

Johnny Suede, 1991. Written and Directed by Tom DiCillo

Living in Oblivion, 1995. Written and Directed by Tom DiCillo

Box of Moonlight, 1996. Written and Directed by Tom DiCillo

The Real Blonde, 1997. Written and Directed by Tom DiCillo

Double Whammy, 2001. Written and Directed by Tom DiCillo

Delirious, 2006. Written and Directed by Tom DiCillo

When You're Strange: A Film About the Doors, 2009. Feature documentary Written and Directed by Tom DiCillo

Down In Shadowland, 2016. Feature documentary. Written and Directed by Tom DiCillo

CINEMATOGRAPHER

Underground U.S.A., 1980. Written and Directed by Eric Mitchell

Permanent Vacation, 1980. Written and Directed by Jim Jarmusch

Burroughs: The Movie, 1983. Feature documentary by Howard Brookner

Variety, 1983. Written and directed by Bette Gordon

Stranger Than Paradise, 1984. Written and directed by Jim Jarmusch

Coffee and Cigarettes, 1986 (short film). Written and directed by Jim Jarmusch

Robert Wilson and the Civil Wars, 1987. Feature documentary by Howard Brookner

End of the Night, 1990. Written and Directed by Keith McNally

TELEVISION

Flaked, 2016, Netflix. Starring Will Arnett. Two episodes: Season One Director: Tom DiCillo

BIBLIOGRAPHY

Berardinelli, James (2005) *Reel Views 2: The Ultimate Guide to the Best 1,000 Modern Movies on DVD and Video*. Boston, MA: Charles Justin.
Caughie, John (ed.) (1981) *Theories of Authorship*. London: Routledge.
Cox, Alex (2016) *Alex Cox's Introduction to Film: A Director's Perspective*. London: Kamera.
Ebert, Roger (1998) 'The Real Blonde' [film review], *Chicago Sun-Times*, 27 February.
____ (2007) November 29, http://www.rogerebert.com/rogers-journal/an-indie-director-asks-is-the-whole-thing-a-kafkaesque-nightmare
Falsetto, Mario (1999) *Personal Visions: Conversations with Independent Filmmakers*, London: Constable, 90.
Holmlund, Chris (ed.) (2004) *Contemporary Independent Film: From the Margins to the Mainstream*. London: Routledge.
King, Geoff (2005) 'Merging with the Mainstream, or Staying Indie?' in *American Independent Cinema*. London: IB Tauris, 261–3.
LaSalle, Mick (1998) 'The Real Blonde' [film review], *San Francisco Chronicle*, 13 March.
Levy, Emanuel (1999) *Cinema of Outsiders: The Rise of American Independent Film*, New York: New York University Press, 202–5.
Maslin, Janet (1997) 'Made for Each Other, Truly and Obviously' [*Box of Moonlight* film review], *The New York Times*, 25 July.
Newman, Michael Z. (2011) 'Introduction' in *Indie: An American Film Culture*. New York: Columbia University Press, 1–18.
Siskel, Gene (1998), 'The Real Blonde' [film review], *Siskel & Ebert*, tx 28 February.
Soter, Tom (2002) *Investigating Couples: A Critical Analysis of The Thin Man, The Avengers, and The X-Files*, Jefferson, NC: McFarland, 28.

Turan, Kenneth (2004) *Never Coming to a Theater Near You*. New York: PublicAffairs.
Welch, Barnaby (2001) 'Tom DiCillo' in Yoram Allon, Del Cullen and Hannah Patterson (eds) *Contemporary North American Film Directors: A Wallflower Critical Guide*. London and New York: Wallflower Press, 138–9.
Westbrook, Caroline (1998) 'The Real Blonde', *Empire*, May.
Weston, Judith (1999) *Directing Actors: Creating Memorable Performances for Screen and Television*. Studio City, CA: Michael Weise Productions.

INDEX

8BC ix
9/11 131

absurdity 27, 29, 55, 56, 59, 60, 70, 93, 102, 114, 122, 123, 129, 146, 177
　humour, 7, 8, 29, 46, 49, 72, 81, 100, 106, 118, 119, 148, 149, 180
Adams, Amy 129
Afghanistan 167
Aguilera, Christina 139
Aldredge, Tom 143, 144
Allen, Woody 21, 30, 99
Alphaville (film) 115, 123
Altman, Robert 44, 100, 115, 146
Argo, Vic 127, 128
Ashby, Hal 100
Asphalt Jungle, The (film) 112
Austin Powers (film) 127
auteur filmmaking 2–6, 33, 100, 101, 103, 148, 149

Bach, Johann, Sebastian 185
Band, The (band) 131
Baumbach, Noah 6
Beatles, The (band) 175
Belack, Doris 143
Benedek, Laszlo 12
Berkley, Elizabeth 97

Berlin 41
Blake, William 168
Blanchett, Cate 129
Blount, Lisa 72, 79, 81, 88
Boardwalk Empire (film) 151
Bonnie and Clyde (film) 100
Boone, Mark, ix 47
Box of Moonlight (film) 2, 5, 69–91, 80, 81, 104, 124, 130
　financing 46, 58, 68, 74
　independence 101
　music 78, 86, 89
　reception 128, 133
　script 45, 82
Brando, Marlon 12
Bridges, Jeff 77
Britain 124
Brooklyn 137
　Williamsburg 23, 33, 37, 41
Brookner, Howard 2
Buñuel, Luis 116
Burton, Tim 44, 138
Buscemi, Steve ix–x, 3, 6, 16, 17
　Delirious 135–62
　Double Whammy 113–32
　Living in Oblivion 46–68
　Real Blonde 100
Busey, Gary 77

INCLUDE ME OUT   203

Cage, Nicolas 41, 138
California 172
Canada 98–9
Cannes 14, 90, 197
Cassavetes, John 46, 56, 57
Caughie, John 2
Caulfield, Maxwell 93–8, 100, 107
Cave, Nick 23, 25, 41, 86
Chantays 86
Chapelle Dave 100, 106
chemistry 26, 57, 58, 75, 101, 113, 115, 117
Chicago 70
Cimino, Michael 77, 100
cinematography 30, 60, 65, 78, 87, 157
  DiCillo ix, 1, 2, 13, 18, 74, 99, 147
Collective for Living Cinema ix
Coltrane, John 185
Compte, Maurice 125
Confessions of a Dangerous Mind (film) 81
conformity, 70, 72, 121, 122, 148, 194
Corrigan, Kevin 53–4, 58, 60, 146, 147
Costello, Elvis 145, 149
Crawford, Joan 50
Crockett, Davy 70, 77, 83
Curtis, Jackie 14

Dante (Alighieri) 194
Davis, Bette 50
Day for Night (film) 15, 44
Dean, James 31
Death of a Salesman (play) 110
Deauville Film Festival 1, 69, 101
delinquency 15, 82, 156, 184
Delirious (film) x, 3, 4, 5, 61, 99, 105, 123, 133–62, 198
  financing 139, 150–51, 159
  music 90, 147–8, 157–9
  sexuality 141, 142
  women 140–41
DeMarco, Frank 157
Densmore, John 163–88
Depp, Johnny 169, 170, 171

Deprez, Therese 67, 78
Diana, Princess 135
Diaz, Melonie vii, 33, 113, 120, 127
Dickens, Charles 15
Dinklage, Peter vii, 33, 52–4, 57, 59–60, 134
director as actor 16, 17, 21, 31
documentary 3, 4, 5, 47, 105, 163–88, 189–98
Donen, Stanley 44, 56
Doors, The (band) 1, 163–88
Double Whammy (film) x, 2, 3, 5, 8, 16, 112–32, 133, 134, 141, 150, 157
  financing 115, 124, 125, 131
  sexuality 117, 118, 141
  violence 113, 114, 121, 124, 125, 126, 129
Downey Sr., Robert 46
Down in Shadowland (film) 3–4, 5, 189–98
DVD Premiere Awards 131

Ebert, Roger 160–61
Ebertfest 160
Edel, Uli 74
editing 2, 4, 19, 46, 51, 65, 68, 82, 101, 103, 107, 121, 144, 148, 157, 170, 172, 173, 174, 178, 181, 191
Ed Sullivan Show, The (TV) 168
ego 21, 22, 42, 44, 45, 49, 53, 92, 96, 136
Elektra Records 168
empathy 8, 55, 100, 136, 141, 183
Engel, Morris 46
Europe 180–81

Faison, Donald 113, 120, 125, 127
family 4, 5, 8, 70, 109, 114, 116, 122, 137, 138, 144–5, 169, 179, 180, 183
  familial dysfunction 54–5, 121, 142–3
Fargo (film) 136
Farmer, Jim 42, 55, 78, 89, 90, 157

fashion 9, 22, 42, 92, 93, 97, 100, 102, 104–5
fathers 8, 47, 54, 59, 113, 119, 120, 121, 143, 144, 150
  Box of Moonlight 70, 71, 83, 86
  DiCillo 9, 10, 11, 43, 70, 73, 74, 78, 84, 89, 145, 168, 179, 182, 197
  Morrison 168, 179, 180, 183
Fellini, Federico 9, 18, 20, 40, 55, 67, 122, 136
Ferrara, Paul 164
Filmmaker Magazine (magazine) 11
Florida 77
Forman, Milos 100
France 61, 187–9
Friedkin, William 139
Friends (TV) 110
Friske, Egon 89, 90, 105
Fuller, Sam 119

Game of Thrones (TV) 53
Gardner, Ashley 27
Gershon, Gina vii, 134, 139, 140, 161
Gil, Jane ix, 36, 37, 62, 137
  cousin 58–9, 68
Girls (TV) 141
Godard, Jean-Luc 12, 20, 33, 115
Gold Circle Films 115, 125, 131
Gordon, Bette 2
Graduate, The (film) 32, 100, 106
Grammy Award 1, 181
Grant, Cary 50
Guzman, Luis 113, 120, 127

Hannah, Daryl 94, 95, 106
Hartley, Hal 3, 77
Hawke Ethan 75
Hawn, Goldie 149
Hendrix, Jimi 175
Hedwig and the Angry Inch (film) 151
Henry, Buck 32, 100, 106
Herzog, Werner 181, 194
Hitchcock, Alfred 113

Hollywood 6, 14, 24, 44, 49, 53, 57, 59, 69, 74, 97, 111, 121, 163, 175
  New Hollywood, 1, 3, 20, 77, 100, 141
Holzman, Jac 168
homelessness 134
Hooks, Kevin 74
Hopkins, Anthony 106
Hopkins, Jerry 163
Hopper, Dennis 176
Hudson, Rock 50
Hurley, Elizabeth 113, 115, 124, 126, 127, 128
Huston, John 18, 112
Hutton, Timothy 32–3

Ice Age (film) 53
identity 4, 5, 56
  Delirious 143
  Double Whammy 114, 116, 118, 122
  Johnny Suede 22, 29, 38, 169
  music 89
  Real Blonde 92, 93, 104
  When You're Strange 169, 180
Illinois 160
improvisation 65, 136, 151, 161
independent film 1–6
Indians. *See* Native Americans
Indiewood 3
innocence 10, 165, 193, 195
  Buscemi 118
  Delirious 140
  Diaz 120, 121
  Johnny Suede 34, 35, 38
  Midnight Cowboy 77
Interview (magazine) 161
Iraq 167
Ireland 189
Italy 43

Jackie Brown (film) 197
Jankowski, Peter 164
Japan 10

Jarmusch, Jim ix, 2, 11, 12, 13, 18
   Permanent Vacation 2, 13, 148
   Stranger Than Paradise ix, 2, 13, 14, 18, 126, 148
Johnny Suede (film) x, 2, 5, 7, 20–43, 45, 46, 53, 64, 65, 75, 99, 106, 153, 169, 195
   costumes 40–41
   independence 101
   influences 9–10
   Locarno 90
   music 8, 22, 41–2, 55
   reception 133
   screenplay 15, 21, 22, 37, 61
   Sundance 68
Johnny Suede (stage persona) 2, 21, 31
Joplin, Janis 23
Joyce, James 9

Kafka, Franz 9
Kardashian, Kim 151
Keener, Catherine 6, 16, 134, 135
   Living in Oblivion 47–68, 130
   Johnny *Suede* 22–43
   Real Blonde 17, 92–111
Kelly, Gene 157
Kidman, Nicole 93
Kilmer, Val 164
Krieger, Robby 163–88
Kurosawa, Akira 18

Lakeshore Entertainment 90, 93, 97, 103, 105, 106, 107, 110, 129
La Mama ix
Lancaster, Burt 74
Lansing, Sherry 101
Last Detail, The (film) 141
La Strada (film) 9, 10, 20. See also Fellini, Federico
Law and Order (TV) 118, 164
Lawn Dogs (film) 81
Leary, Denis x, 96, 112–32
Led Zeppelin (band) 175

Lee, Spike 99
LeGros, James 49, 50, 58
Limbo Lounge ix
Lincoln Plaza Cinema 60
Lionsgate 122, 131
literature 9, 20, 36
Little Caesar (film) 126
Lively Ones, The (band) 165
Living in Oblivion (film) ix, x, 1–5, 16, 44–68, 81, 105, 114, 123, 124, 126, 130
   Deauville 69
   Densmore 167
   dreams 49, 52, 57, 62–3, 64, 67, 80
   dwarf 52–6, 63
   egos 49, 56, 66
   festivals 69, 133
   financing 58–9, 62, 63, 67
   golden apple 8
   handheld camera 52, 55, 61
   independence 101, 162, 195
   kissing 51, 52
   New Yorker, The 68, 80
   Pitt 34, 36, 64
   publicity 131
   Real Blonde 100, 106
   reception 111, 133
   relationships 66
   Rockwell 75
   score 55
   screenplay 61, 68
   Sundance 68, 69, 127
   Turturro 74
Lloyd, Christopher 100, 106
Locarno International Film Festival 1, 42, 43, 45, 90–91
Lohman, Alison, vii 134, 138, 148
Lord of the Rings (film) 138
Los Angeles 11, 24, 32, 36, 68, 77, 172, 174
Louis-Dreyfus, Julia 196
Louise, Tina 24
Lynch, David 44

Madonna 96, 97, 100, 102, 106, 109
magic 19, 23, 33, 40, 48, 61, 81, 83, 134, 164
Magritte, René 67, 116
Malick, Terrence 78
Mann, Thomas 9
Manzarek, Ray 163–88
　UCLA 179
Martens, Rica 47, 48, 65, 75
Marx Brothers 49, 56, 136
masculinity 4, 117, 141
Mastroianni, Marcello 30
Matchstick Men (film) 138
Mazursky, Paul 100
Miami 168, 177
Midnight Cowboy (film) 10, 20, 77, 99, 122, 141, 157. See also Schlesinger, John
Miramax 2, 43, 45, 79, 80
mise-en-scène 2, 192
Mitchell, Eric 2, 13, 14
Mitchell, John Cameron 151
Modine, Matthew 6, 92–111
Moir, Alison 22, 64
Moon (film) 81
Moore, Julianne 93
Morris, Errol 77, 182, 194
Morrison, Jim 4, 155, 163–88
　father 168, 179
　nephew 183
　Paris 164, 169, 170
　Pere Lachaise cemetery 175
　sister 183
　UCLA 168
Mulloch, Karl 159–60
Mulroney, Dermot 26, 36, 49, 58, 62, 72
Murphy, Peter 86

Nasoor, Chioke 161
Native Americans 85–6, 164
Nelson, Ricky 22, 38, 42
Netflix 29

New Hollywood 1, 3, 20, 77, 100, 141
New Jersey 60
New York City 8, 11, 20, 21, 23, 57, 68, 78, 83, 99, 114
　Down in Shadowland 189–98
　East Village ix
　energy 99, 104
　independent film scene 14, 15, 147, 167
　Lower East Side 21, 23, 119
　missing children 190–98
　No Wave 2
　Real Blonde 92–111
　setting 22, 57, 155
　subway 156, 189–98
　Times Square 107, 194
　unions 156
　Upper West Side 8
　World Trade Center 131
New Yorker, The (magazine) 68, 80
New York Film Festival 194, 195
New York Times, The (newspaper) 14, 46, 68, 81
Nichols, Mike 100
Nobbs, Keith 113, 120, 125, 127
North Carolina 15, 43
Noth, Chris vii, 6, 17, 115, 118, 119, 122, 127, 128, 164
NYU (New York University) 11, 12, 13, 20, 21, 22, 151

off-camera action 45, 63, 65, 105, 119
O'Neill, Eugene 21
Oregon 77
Oz, Frank 44

Paltrow, Gwyneth 36
Paltrow, Jake 6
Panavision 32
Paramount Pictures 97, 99, 101, 107, 110
Permanent Midnight (film) 127
Permanent Vacation (film) 2, 13, 148

Pitt, Brad 2, 7, 34, 36, 64, 134
   Johnny Suede 22, 23–43
   Thelma and Louise (film) 24, 36
Pitt, Michael 134–62
Point Break (film) 50
Priestly, Jason 75
Prinzi, Frank 65, 67, 107
Prochnicky, Jerry 163
Pulp Fiction (film) 114, 126

Quiz Show (film) 84

racism 83
Ray, Man 102
Real Blonde, The (film) 2, 3, 4, 5, 17, 32, 92–111, 124, 126–7, 130, 139
   ego 92
   financing 106
   Living in Oblivion 100, 106
   reception 128
   screenplay 98
   sex 92, 95, 108
   Sundance 17
Rebel Without a Cause (film) 9, 31
Redford, Robert 78
religion 19, 50, 76, 108, 194
Reservoir Dogs (film) 114
Riordan, James 163
Robertson, Robbie 131
Rocket Redglare's Taxi Cabaret ix
Rockwell, Sam 33, 70–91, 134, 138
Rolling Stones, The (band) 175
Rosenberg, Tom 90, 93, 105, 110
Rota, Nino 55. *See also* Fellini, Federico
Ryan, Paul 78

Salinger, J. D. 58
Salva, Victor 74
San Francisco Film Festival 194
Sanko, Anton 90, 157
San Sebastian Film Festival 159, 198
Santa Monica 124

Schlesinger, John 20, 44, 51, 99, 122
   Day of the Locust 44, 51
   Midnight Cowboy 10, 20, 77, 99, 122, 141, 157
Scorsese, Martin 11, 20, 21, 99
Scott, Ridley 138
Seagal, Steven 7, 130
Seattle Film Festival 194
Dr. Seuss 116
sex, lies and videotape (film) 126
Shakespeare, William 21
Sherwood, Bill 117
Short Cuts (film) 93
Shulman, Marcia 23
Singin' in the Rain (film) 44, 56, 157
Smith, Kevin 3
Sony Classics 68
Spears, Britney 138, 139
Stanley, Mike 70
Stone, Oliver 164, 166, 181, 184
Stranger Than Paradise (film) ix, 2, 13, 14, 18, 126, 148
Sundance Channel 11
Sundance Director's Lab 2, 31–2
Sundance Film Festival 1, 106, 197
   Box of Moonlight 80, 81
   Delirious 159, 160
   Double Whammy 122, 127, 131, 132
   Down in Shadowland 194
   Living in Oblivion 68, 69, 127
   Real Blonde 17, 99, 100
   When You're Strange 170, 176, 177, 186
Sundance Institute 32
surrealism ix, 5, 7, 22, 28, 29, 36, 39–40, 42, 64
   Box of Moonlight 88
   Double Whammy 114, 116, 119, 122, 123
   Down in Shadowland 190, 193, 195
   Living in Oblivion 54, 59
   music 55, 78, 185
   Real Blonde 98
   When You're Strange 173, 182, 185

Swayze, Patrick 50

Tarantino, Quentin 51, 77, 114
Taylor, Elizabeth 18
television 1, 9, 10–11, 18, 43, 58, 63, 83, 114, 160, 186, 196
  Access Hollywood 155
  colour 26
  detectives 118, 119
  directing 120, 164, 181–2, 196
  documentary 182
  Happy Days 34, 40
  reality 134
  satire 104–5
  soap operas 93, 94, 95, 102–3, 110
  women 141
Tennessee 77, 79, 82, 88
Texas 58
theatre 17, 21, 31, 54
Theater for the New City ix
Thomas, Marlo 100
Thunderbolt and Lightfoot (film) 141
Title, Stacy 3
Toronto 99, 156
Toronto Film Festival 45
Trees Lounge (film) x
Tribeca Film Festival 194
True Detective (TV) 195
Truffaut, François 15, 44
trust 10, 13, 19, 25, 35, 70, 76, 90, 97, 109, 117, 127, 136, 147, 150
Turner, Kathleen 100, 106
Turturro, John vii, 6, 69–91
Twain, Mark 9
Twilight Zone, The (TV) 131

Utah 99

Vanity Fair (magazine) 99
Van Sant, Gus 77
Variety (magazine) 186
Veep (TV) 195

Venice Film Festival 1, 90, 91
Verhoeven, Paul 139
Vietnam 10, 87, 164, 165, 167, 172, 197
violence 62, 72, 80, 113, 114, 121, 124, 125, 126, 129
  children, 194
Virginia 11
Voight, Jon 77
vulnerability 26, 34, 38, 51, 116, 126, 134, 139, 190

Wachowski Brothers 139
Waldburger, Ruth 33, 43, 45, 46
Wall of Voodoo 86
Waters, John 11
Weil, Kurt 185
Weinstein, Bob 79
Weinstein, Harvey 43, 45, 46, 79
Weston, Judith 154, 155
When You're Strange: A Film About The Doors (film) 3, 5, 105, 163–88
  Grammy Award 1, 181
  HWY: An American Pastoral 164–88
  narration 169–71, 177, 179, 186
  Paris 187–8
Whiskey-A-Go-Go 168
White Heat (film) 126
Who, The (band) 174, 175
Wilder, Billy 16, 44, 89
Williams, Tennessee 21
Wilson, Bridgette 94, 100
Winslet, Kate 129
Wiseman, Frederick 194
Wizard of Oz, The 80, 83
Wolf, Dick 164
Wolfe, Thomas 85
Woodstock Film Festival 194
Wray, Link 22, 42
Wright Robin

X-Men (film) 53

YouTube   161

Zerneck, Danielle von   49
Zwick, Edward   50

GPSR Authorized Representative: Easy Access System Europe, Mustamäe tee 50, 10621 Tallinn, Estonia, gpsr.requests@easproject.com